Preface

For some time there has been a need for a basic handbook of contract procedures in relation to the Standard Forms of Building Contract. The publication of JCT 80, with its new detailed procedures has prompted me to attempt to fulfill this need.

In the preparation of this book I have attempted a logical and, as far as possible, chronological sequence which should enable readers to quickly find any topic upon which they are seeking information and guidance. Unlike many writers on legal subjects, I have tried to explain the effect and operation of the various provisions of the contract by setting down in clear, simple, language the obligations and duties of the builder. In some cases, it has been necessary to draw attention to defects and inconsistencies in the Conditions. In such cases, I have given my personal understanding of the intention of the Joint Contracts Tribunal (JCT).

When considering the extent to which certain topics were to be dealt with, I have based my judgement on the position of a site manager or a site quantity surveyor concerned with day to day operations on site. I have tried to put myself in his shoes and have asked myself 'What does the contract require me to do if this, or if that, were to happen?'. The anser in more than sixty cases is that notice must be given to the Architect. For this reason there is a strong emphasis in my book on the requirement of the builder to give notice in order to protect his position.

The various matters that must in my opinion be included in any particular notice have been set down in a convenient tabular form in the text. The items listed must, of course, be 'rounded out' when drafting the actual text of the notice and this will give the builder the opportunity to emphasise one or other of those items. In addition, it is a good idea to include in any notice the actual words used in the text of any clause of the contract that is specified as the basis of the argument.

While the views I have expressed may evoke criticism in some cases, the consideration of them, whether the reader agrees with them or not, should contribute to a better understanding of the provisions of the Standard Form of Building Contract. If this greater understanding of contract procedures should help builders become more effective and professional at the business of constructing buildings, then this little book will have been worthwhile.

During the period of preparation of this book, many people within the Institute and within my employer's organisation have been consulted on various matters and I am grateful to them all for their assistance.

I.J. Dickason, FCIOB

Note:

Since this publication was issued a number of amendments to the contract have been made.

Readers of this guide are advised to refer to these amendments published by the Joint Contracts Tribunal when using the guide.

Contents

JCT 80 and the builder
an introduction

Ivan Dickason FCIOB

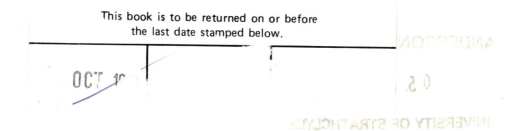
The Chartered Institute of Building
Englemere, Kings Ride, Ascot, Berkshire SL5 8BJ

Dedication

For my wife in coping manfully with the decorating and gardening while this book has been written.

I.J.D.

The Chartered Institute of Building
Englemere
Kings Ride
Ascot, Berkshire
SL5 8BJ

First published 1982
Reprinted with corrections 1985.

Dickason, Ivan
 JCT 80 and the builder : an introduction. –
Rev. ed.
 1. Joint Contracts Tribunal. Standard form of
building contract. 1980. 2. Building – Contracts
and specifications – Great Britain
 I. Title   II. Chartered Institute of Building
 692.8   TH425

ISBN 0-906600-77-4

The opinions expressed in this book are those of the author and not necessarily those of the Institute.

Preamble

The 1980 Edition of the Standard Form of Building Contract (JCT 80) is the latest in a series of standard forms prepared by the Joint Contracts Tribunal (JCT) and replaces the July 1977 Revision of the 1963 Edition . JCT 80 is nearly twice as long as the 1963 Edition (59 pages (excluding fluctuations) against 32 pages (excluding fluctuations)) and contains many new procedural requirements. The volume of the new contract, its language and the unfamiliar style and presentation all combine to make its content difficult to assimilate.

This book sets out to indentify the requirements of JCT 80, to identify the changes from the 1963 Edition, to consider the effect upon the builder of the new responsibilities he will assume under the contract, and perhaps most important of all, to examine the new complex procedural and administrative matters.

For convenience the several clauses dealing with each topic are considered together as a group. The clauses are, therefore, not dealt with in strict numerical order.

Unless expressly stated otherwise, the clause numbers quoted are those of the Local Authorities, With Quantities, Edition of JCT 80. The differences between that version and the Private, With Quantities, Edition of JCT 80 are identified in the text. References to the 1963 Edition are to the July 1977 Revision of that document.

HISTORICAL BACKGROUND

The principal reason for the publication of the new edition of the standard form (as opposed to a further revision of the 1963 Edition) was to introduce major changes in the treatment of nominated sub-contractors. The origins of the new Nominated Sub-Contract arrangements can be found in the Banwell report of 1964. The report recommended, among other things, that 'the organisations representing specialist sub-contractors should be granted full membership of the national consultative bodies which exist in the industry' and that 'the standardisation of sub- contract conditions should follow that of the main contract conditions'.

In 1966, the Federation of Associations of Specialists and Sub-Contractors (FASS) and the Committee of Associations of Specialist Engineering Contractors (CASEC) joined the Joint Contracts Tribunal which thereupon assumed 'responsibility for the production of the standard form or forms of sub-contract'. Consideration of the new Nominated Sub-Contract and its associated documents, with the consequent amendments to the main contract, have occupied the JCT more or less continuously ever since.

While there has been no revision of the 1963 Edition since 1977, the JCT have nevertheless agreed upon amendments concerning extension of time, liquidated damages, payments and fluctuations and these are incorporated into JCT 80.

STYLE AND PRESENTATION

The drafting style of the new edition is different but it is by no means certain that it makes an improvement. The complex detailed procedures, the incessant cross referencing and the legalistic language used, all combine to make a document that is difficult to read and understand. The 1963 Edition was once described as '...a farrago of obscurities...' and it may well be that JCT 80 will acquire a similar epithet in due course.

In contrast the changes in presentation are a major improvement since numerous signposts are provided throughout the contract. The principal changes are:

★ all clause numbers use the decimal numbering system; for example, clause 19 (2) (a) insurance becomes 21.2.1. This arrangement can however become cumbersome. For example, in clause 30 'Certificates and Payments, the right of the Employer to deduct monies from amounts due to the contractor in Interim Certificates is restricted by the provisions of clause 35.13.5.5.2. Five sub-divisions of the clause! A further consequence of the decimal numbering system is that sub-clauses, paragraphs and sub-paragraphs have disappeared − they are now all 'clauses'.

★ there is a new clause 1 'Interpretation, definitions etc.' which defines many of the words and expressions appearing within the contract. At first sight this can be disconcerting as in many cases there is no definition given. For example, for 'Contract Documents' the meaning given is 'see clause 2.1'. The principle adopted is that a definition is given in clause 1 where the word or phrase concerned appears repeatedly throughout the document, otherwise the user is merely directed to the clause in the Conditions containing the definition. The inclusion of this definitions clause is useful and will be of benefit to all users of the contract. The definitions are examined in more detail in the next section 'Interpretation, definitions etc.'

★ at the beginning of the contract there is a schedule of contents listing the clause titles and marginal notes relative to each clause.

★ the fluctuation clauses are published separately. The applicable fluctuation clause is incorporated into the contract by reference.

INTERPRETATION, DEFINITIONS, ETC.

An awareness of the principles of interpretation of the various parts of the printed documents and knowledge of the range and scope of the definitions are necessary to understand the first item in the printed document, the Articles of Agreement.

Clause 1.1

Clauses 1.1 and 1.2 are concerned with the interpretation of the various parts of JCT 80. Clause 1.1 provides that, unless otherwise stated, reference to a clause number in the Articles of Agreement (including the recitals and articles), the Conditions or the Appendix means that clause number in the Conditions.

Clause 1.2

In clause 1.2 it is made clear that the Articles of Agreement, the Conditions and Appendix are to be considered as being one document. Clause 1.2 reinforces this by stating that every article, clause in the Conditions, or Appendix entry must be read in conjunction with 'any relevant qualification or modification' in any one of the others.

Clause 1.3

The definitions given in clause 1.3 should be studied with great care, for some contain pitfalls of their own. For example, by its definition, the Appendix only becomes operative when all the relevant entries have been made and the Articles of Agreement have been executed by the parties. Up to that point the details of the Appendix given in the bills of quantities can only be considered as the proposed Appendix and, therefore, remain open for negotiation between the parties.

Comments on other definitions are set out below:-

'**person**' is defined as 'an individual, firm (partnership) or body corporate'. Thus, where the Conditions refer to a 'person', this could mean an individual, partnership, limited company, statutory and local authorities, nationalized industries etc. This is fine in most cases, for an Employer or Contractor could be any of these. In addition, an architectural practice would seem to qualify as a 'person', but

'Architect' is defined as a special type of 'person', namely one 'entitled to use the name 'Architect''. That entitlement arises from registration as an Architect by the Architects Registration Council. Since only individuals can be so registered, then the 'Architect' under the contract must therefore be an individual. (See also the discussion on Article 3 (page 6).

'Clause 22 Perils' are those items of loss or damage for which insurance may be required to be effected by the Contractor or the Employer under clause 22. The risks have assumed a grand title but are unchanged from the 1963 Edition.

'Date for Completion' only appears in the definitions and in the Appendix. It only has a status from the execution of the contract until the first award by the Architect of extension of time to the Contractor, since thereafter the 'Completion Date' is the only date that matters.

'Completion Date' is the expression used elsewhere in the Conditions. It is the 'Date for Completion' given in the Appendix or such later date as may be fixed by the Architect under clauses 25 (Extension of time) and 33 (War damage).

'Contract Bills' are those referred to in the first recital of the Articles of Agreement and which have been signed by the parties as one of the contract documents. Until that moment they remain merely bills of quantities. The form and content of the bills of quantities are more precisely set out in clause 2.2.2. The function of bills of quantities has changed and is not now limited to definition of quality and quantity of the work. This is considered in more detail in Section 3 - 'General obligations' (Page 15).

'Sub-Contract' when used in the Conditions refers only to the contractual rights and obligations of a Nominated Sub-Contractor.

'Domestic Sub-Contractor' is any sub-contractor permitted by the Architect to be employed by the Contractor upon the Works other than a sub-contractor nominated by the Architect. The definition specifically embraces a sub-contractor chosen by the Contractor under the procedure described in clause 19.3 (that is to say, the work is measured in the bills of quantities and a minimum of three named sub-contractors are given. The successful Contractor must appoint one of them).

'Quantity Surveyor' is named in the contract in recognition of the functions he is to carry out formally under the Conditions in regard to the Valuation of variations, the preparation of interim valuations and the final adjusted Contract Sum.

'Relevant Event' is one of the twelve items listed in clause 25 that may lead to an extension of time. In comparison with the 1963 Edition there are three new causes of delay for which extension of time may be granted. These are:-
   ★ default in the direct supply of materials by the Employer

   ★ Government interference

   ★ the failure of the Employer to provide access to the site.
These matters are considered in more detail in 'The time for the work' (Page 41).

'Valuation' (Uppercase 'V') is concerned with Valuation of variations (clause 13.4.1) and should not be confused with interim valuations (lowercase 'v') which are part of the interim payment procedure (clause 30.1.2).

Some terms that are not defined include:-

'consultants' are not recognised by the contract. If Employers or Architects wish to employ consultants in an active role on site (eg to supervise the specialist work), special provision for these matters will have to be made in the Contract Documents. Otherwise, such consultants will have no authority to approve or to condemn work, nor to issue a valid instruction to the Contractor.

the **'site'** is now an important feature in the contract, since the Employer is able to impose his own requirements on its use, (see clause 13.1.2). Where the bills of quantities contain obligations or restrictions of the Employer, the Contractor must, before executing the Contract Documents, ensure that the various parts of the site are positively identifiable from the bills of quantities or are clearly marked upon the Contract Drawings.

'this Contract' is frequently referred to in JCT 80; for example, articles 3A, 4, 5.1.1 and clauses 2.1, 2.2.2.2, etc. The expression even appears in the definitions themselves; for example, 'Contract Bills', 'Contract Drawings', etc. The expression is not defined even though the word 'Contract' has an initial capital letter meaning that one would expect to find a definition in clause 1.3.

Taking the lead from the definition of 'Sub-Contract' appearing in both JCT 80 and the Nominated Sub-Contract NSC/4, a suggested definition of ' contract' is:-

★ 'the contractual rights and obligations of the Employer and the Contractor are set out in the Contract Documents.'

These rights and obligations are revised upon the issue of each instruction of the Architect.

In this book, references to 'the Contract' will relate to the suggested definition given above. From time to time reference is made to 'the main contract' meaning the whole of the rights and obligations of the Employer and/or the Contractor as the case may be and the expression is used where it is appropriate to make a distinction between those rights and obligations and rights and obligations of the parties to any other contract, eg the Employer and any sub-contractor in a warranty agreement; the Contractor and a sub-contractor in a sub-contract, etc.

THE AGREEMENT

The document signed or sealed by the parties in order to give it complete legal effect is an agreement identifying the parties, giving a description of the work required, stating the price to be paid and naming the Architect and Quantity Surveyor for the purposes of the contract. It may also embody other documents. Any memorandum or deed of agreement could be used for this purpose provided it concludes an agreement on the several points mentioned. Some local authorities use their own form for this purpose, and in these cases builders are recommended to have such agreements examined by legal advisers before executing it.

The JCT has provided Articles of Agreement for use of the parties in JCT 80. The Articles of Agreement comprise:-

★ four recitals

★ five articles

★ space for attestation and for execution by the parties

★ an Appendix scheduling various important and detailed matters in connection with the Works.

4

The agreement incorporates or embodies by reference the 'Conditions' which set out the technicalities of the various procedures to be followed by the Employer, the Contractor and his sub-contractors, the Architect and the Quantity Surveyor in the execution of the Works.

The agreement becomes a binding 'contract' when executed by the parties and consideration will be given in this Section to the various matters that are covered by the agreement and the associated Appendix.

THE ARTICLES OF AGREEMENT, RECITALS AND ARTICLES

Articles of Agreement

Space is provided in the Articles of Agreement for insertion of the name of the Employer, the name and address of the Contractor and the date of the agreement. The date to be inserted will normally be the date of execution by the second of the parties executing the agreement.

Recitals

Recitals are preliminary or historical statements placing the agreement into the context of previous events and if necessary relating it to other agreements concerned with the same matters. They preface the operative part of that agreement.

The four recitals in JCT 80 are now numbered. Three of them are virtually unchanged from the 1963 Edition but the fourth is new. There is an introductory recital setting out the motive for the agreement, ie the Employer wishes to have a building built at a specified location and for which drawings and bills of quantities have been prepared by a named person. This is followed by three narrative recitals setting out certain facts upon which the agreement is based, ie the Contractor has provided fully priced Contract Bills; the Contract Drawings have been identified and signed and the Contract Bills have been signed; and reference to an Appendix entry setting out the status of the Employer under the statutory tax deduction scheme.

First recital   The first recital requires entries to be made to describe the proposed Works and give their location. The definition of the 'Works' given in clause 1.3 now includes the words 'shown and described in the Contract Drawings and in the Contract Bills'. The entry made in the recital for the location of the Works need, therefore, only be sufficient to ensure the uniqueness of the documents for identification purposes.'

The name of the person responsible for the Drawings and Bills of Quantities also has to be entered in the first recital. It would appear (because of the word 'said' in article 3 (Private Editions) or article 3A (Local Authorities Editions)) that the name to be entered in the recital must be the same as the entry for the 'Architect' in the articles.

Second recital   The second recital confirms that the Contractor has provided a fully priced Bill of Quantities to the Employer.

Third recital   The entry made in the third recital detailing the Contract Drawings must be carefully examined before the Contract Documents are executed by the Contractor. The drawings entered should be those available to the Contractor at the time of tender. In particular, those drawings **must** carry the same revision suffix as those available at the time of tender. The inclusion of revised drawings could lead to unnecessary argument between the Quantity Surveyor and the Contractor during the computation of the final adjusted Contract Sum (the final account).

Fourth recital The new fourth recital, together with the associated Appendix entry, ensures that the Contractor knows when tendering whether or not the Employer is a 'Contractor' under the Construction Industry Tax Deduction Scheme.

Articles

The articles are the terms of the actual agreement between the parties. They are the operative part of the agreement and express the main features of the contract, including the principal obligations of the parties. There are five articles in JCT 80. Articles 2, 3 and 4 are unchanged from the 1963 Edition, article 1 has been redrafted and article 5 is new.

Article 1 Redrafted article 1 sets down the principal obligation of the Contractor and requires him to carry out the work 'upon and subject to the Contract Documents' (the Contract Drawings, Contract Bills, Articles of Agreement, the Conditions and the completed Appendix). It appears to have broadened the basis of the Contractor's obligations under the contract, but this may be of no practical significance for it would seem to have also been the intention of the 1963 Edition.

Article 2 Article 2 contains the principal obligation of the Employer. The Employer undertakes to pay a lump sum (the 'Contract Sum') for the whole of the work. However, this undertaking is qualified where article 2 continues '...or such other sum as shall become payable...in the manner specified in the Conditions.'

Thus articles 1 and 2 have created what is commonly called a 'lump sum' contract, in that the actual contract (the Articles of Agreement) consists of a single promise by each party. The Contractor promises a building, the Employer promises one lump sum payment. The terms of JCT 80 modify the strict interpretation of a 'lump sum' since they contain certain distinguishing features. In particular, the Conditions contain provisions enabling the actual lump sum to be changed (Variations, fluctuations etc) and permit interim payments by the Employer to the Contractor. The distinction should be noted between this special type of 'lump sum' contract and other types of contract occurring in the industry such as:-

an 'entire' contract - applicable to perhaps minor works where no payment is due until absolute (ie entire) completion in every detail has been achieved.

a 'remeasurement' contract - applicable to civil engineering work under the ICE Conditions of Contract, or to routine maintenance work, where completed work is measured and valued against a schedule of rates.

a 'cost plus' contract - applicable to work under, for example, the JCT 'Fixed Fee Form of Prime Cost Contract', where a builder is entitled to reimbursement of the defined costs incurred in carrying out the work and to be paid a percentage addition for overheads and profit.

Article 3 The name of the Architect appointed for the purpose of the contract is to be recorded in article 3 (Private Editions) or article 3A (Local Authorities Editions). The name to be entered should be that of an individual, to be compatible with the definition of Architect in clause 1.3, that is to say, a person entitled to use the name 'Architect'. The name of an architectural practice would appear to be invalid. Perhaps the answer is to enter 'Mr. R.T. Crafty of Bloggs and Partners'.

Where the Local Authorities Edition is applicable and the work is to be carried out under the direction of a member of the staff of the Local Authority, then article 3B applies. Again, the name of an individual must be entered.

Article 4   The name of the Quantity Surveyor for the purpose of the contract is to be recorded in article 4. In this case there is no complicating factor regarding the use of the name Quantity Surveyor, so that the entry of the name of a Quantity Surveying practice would seem to be in order. It must be said that by the ordinary use of the printed words, an individual is expected to be named, perhaps followed by the name of his practice.

THE ARBITRATION AGREEMENT

Article 5   Article 5 is new and is the arbitration agreement which appeared as one of the Conditions in the 1963 Edition. The arbitration provisions are an important feature of the agreement between the parties and now they rightly appear within the agreement itself. Apart from the new articles 5.1.4, 5.1.5 and 5.1.6 dealing with the joining together of arbitrations, the text and intent of article 5 (although redrafted into tabular form) seems broadly to follow clause 35 of the 1963 Edition.

Scope of arbitration

Article 5.1   Article 5.1 provides that any dispute or difference between the Contractor and the Employer shall be referred to arbitration. It is made clear that disputes or differences between the Contractor and the Architect acting on behalf of the Employer are included in the arbitration agreement. The right to arbitration does not cease upon completion or abandonment of the Works but ends only upon the expiry of fourteen days after the issue of the Final Certificate.

It is worth observing that the arbitration provisions apply equally to each of the parties, and that the Employer therefore has the same rights to arbitration as the Contractor in the event of a dispute or difference.

The Arbitrator to whom any dispute or difference is referred is appointed by agreement between the Contractor and the Employer, or, where agreement cannot be reached, by the President or a Vice-President of the Royal Institute of British Architects (RIBA).

The range of matters that can be the subject of arbitration is set out in articles 5.1.1 and 5.1.2. Article 5.1.1 refers to the 'construction of this contract'. The word 'construction' as used here is an expression given to the legal processes by which meanings are given to the words in a written contract. Thus the interpretation of the printed document can be the subject of arbitration. By article 5.1.2 almost any matter arising from the operation of the contract during the execution of the Works would appear to be subject to arbitration. It is made clear that determination of the employment of the Contractor does not have any effect on the arbitration agreement for the rights of the parties after such determination can be referred to arbitration. Other matters specifically mentioned as being subject to arbitration are:-

★ the witholding of any certificate by the Architect. (Any certificate meaning any Interim Certificate; the Final Certificate; any notification by the Architect that Practical Completion has been achieved etc.)

★ any measurement or valuation included in the calculation of the final adjusted Contract Sum (the final account)

★ (new to JCT 80) the unreasonable witholding of any consent or agreement required to be given by the Contractor (eg for partial possession by the Employer - clause 18); or by the Employer or the Architect on his behalf (eg for sub-letting by the Contractor - clause 19).

The only matters specifically excluded from the arbitration agreement are set out in article 5.1.3. These are those arising under clauses 19A (Fair Wages) and 31 (Finance (No. 2) Act, 1975 - statutory tax deduction scheme) and clause 3 of the VAT Agreement. In each of these cases provision is made in the Conditions for disputes to be settled by persons whose powers have been established under statute; clause 19A - the Minister of Labour; clause 31 - the Commissioners of the Inland Revenue; and clause 3 of the VAT Agreement - the Value Added Tax tribunal.

Joinder of arbitrations

Articles 5.1.4, 5.1.5 and 5.1.6 are new and are included in recognition of the fact that disputes on a building contract will often arise between persons other than the Contractor and the Employer. The Conditions introduce the concept of 'joinder of parties', ie the joining together of two or more persons in a single cause of action. Where, for example, if separate actions are brought by each person against the other(s), there arises in each of the actions some common question of fact or law. Thus, in article 5.1.4, the parties to the main contract agree that where there are disputes between them **and** between either of them and a nominated sub-contractor or a nominated supplier on related matters, such disputes can be referred to a single Arbitrator for settlement.

Provisions for the joining together of arbitrations have always been included in the 'blue' and 'green' forms of sub-contract published by the NFBTE and others, but not in the Standard Form. Provisions enabling the joining together of arbitrations also appear in the Nominated Sub-Contracts NSC/4 and NSC/4a, the Employer/Nominated Sub-Contractor Agreement NSC/2 and the Form of Tender by Nominated Suppliers. The sub-contract arbitration agreement in the new Domestic Sub-Contract contains similar arrangements. Only direct suppliers to the Contractor will, therefore, be outside the arrangements for the joining together of arbitrations.

Having made sensible provisions for the economical arbitration of disputes on related matters, JCT 80 then sets out some procedures which complicate rather than simplify.

Firstly, the joint arbitration arrangements are made optional by an Appendix entry that would have the effect of deleting articles 5.1.4 and 5.1.5 from the arbitration agreement. Thus the Employer (for he would normally decide these matters) could ensure that there were separate arbitrations even if the issues were identical. Presumably, it would then be possible for an Arbitrator under the main contract and an Arbitrator under a sub-contract or contract of sale to arrive at different conclusions on essentially the same facts.

Secondly, article 5.1.5 provides for either the Employer or the Contractor to reject the appointment of a joint Arbitrator if each consider that the Arbitrator initially appointed under, say, a sub-contract, is not properly qualified to settle the dispute under, say, the main contract. This may require the matter to be referred to another Arbitrator to be appointed under the arbitration agreement. This could mean that the qualifications of the original arbitrator become another point of dispute or difference that can only be settled by a preliminary arbitration.

Thirdly, the Arbitrator under the main contract is to be appointed by the President or a Vice-President of the RIBA whereas under the Nominated Sub-Contract and Domestic Sub-Contract the party requesting the appointment of an Arbitrator can request that the appointment be made in addition by the President or a Vice- President of the Royal Institution of Chartered Surveyors(RICS). This means that upon receipt of notice from a sub-contractor to concur in the appointment of an Arbitrator, the Contractor must decide whether the dispute or difference is such that the joining of the parties under the main contract arbitration agreement is desirable and, if so, must endeavour to ensure that the RIBA is approached for the appointment of the Arbitrator.

Timing of arbitration

Article 5.2
There has been no change to the general position existing in the 1963 Edition; namely, that an arbitration may not commence until after completion or termination of the Works. This limitation also applies to any dispute or difference under a sub-contract or a contract of sale where the parties may wish to invoke the joinder provision of article 5.1.4.

The parties to the main contract may agree between themselves in writing that an arbitration may commence immediately on any matter.

The arbitration agreement itself permits immediate commencement of the arbitration proceedings on a number of matters, principally where the dispute or difference is critical to the performance or otherwise of the Contractor in carrying out the Works. These matters may be summarised as follows:-

articles 3 & 4 - the appointment of a replacement Architect or Quantity Surveyor by the Employer.

clause 4.2 - the validity of an instruction of the Architect issued under clause 4.

various clauses - the wrongful withholding of a certificate by the Architect. (For a schedule of the fourteen types of certificate that may be issued by the Architect, see the discussion on clause 5.8 (pages 30 and 31).

various clauses - the correctness of any certificate issued by the Architect.

clause 4.1 - the validity of an objection by the Contractor to an instruction of the Architect issued under clause 13.1.2 (changes in the obligations or restrictions imposed by the Employer).

clause 25 - (new in JCT 80) - any dispute or difference concerning extension of time.

clauses 32 and 33 - any dispute or difference concerning 'Outbreak of hostilities' or 'War damage'.

Powers of the Arbitrator

Article 5.3
The powers of the Arbitrator are set out in article 5.3. Except for three specific items, the powers granted to an Arbitrator seem to be virtually unlimited. All decisions, valuations, certificates, opinions or notices made or given by the Employer, the Contractor, the Architect and the Quantity Surveyor and any sub-contractor appear to be subject to review by the Arbitrator.

The exceptions are:-

clause 4.2 - where the Architect has, in response to a request by the Contractor concerning the authority of an instruction, has given the clause ('provision of the Conditions') empowering the issue of that instruction to the Contractor, then the validity of that instruction can no longer be the subject of arbitration after the contractor has commenced to comply with it.

clause 30.9 - where the Final Certificate has been issued and notice of arbitration has not been given by either party within fourteen days of its issue, then an arbitration cannot subsequently be commenced on any of the matters for which the Final Certificate is to be final and conclusive. (See also the discussion on clauses 2.1 (page 15) and 30.9 (page 115)).

clauses 38.4.3, 39.5.3 and 40.5 - where the Contractor and Quantity Surveyor agree a lump sum under the relevant fluctuations clause to cover all, or any particular, fluctuations, then the matters dealt with in that agreement cannot be referred to arbitration.

Law of arbitration

Article 5.4   Article 5.4 states that the award of the Arbitrator is final and binding on the parties. This is not strictly correct, since the Arbitration Acts, 1950 to 1979 both contain machinery for the award of an Arbitrator to be itself subject to review by the High Court in certain circumstances. For example, the High Court could order the removal of the Arbitrator if he does not proceed to hear the arbitration with reasonable despatch, or if he misconducts himself or the arbitration proceedings. There are other possible courses of action available to the High Court. The Arbitrator can be ordered to reconsider his award where, for example, it is uncertain or ambiguous, or is inconsistant with a term of the contract; the Arbitrator can himself ask for the award to be passed back to him where, for example, the Arbitrator admits to a mistake in the award, or some new, material, evidence has been obtained; the award can be set aside where there is an error of fact or law within the award.

Article 5.5   Two entirely separate topics are dealt with in article 5.5 and it is strange that there are not two separate articles to cover them.

Firstly, article 5.5 makes it clear that the Law of England applies to all matters covered by the contract, irrespective of the location of the Works or the nationalities of the parties. Where the 'Building Contract and Scottish Supplement to the Standard Form of Building Contract issued by the Joint Contracts Tribunal' published by the Scottish Building Contract Committee is used, the amendments necessary to bring the contract into line with Scots law are automatically incorporated.

Secondly, article 5.5 requires that the Arbitration Acts 1950 to 1979 shall apply to any arbitration held under the contract (including any arising by the operation of the joinder provisions) irrespective of the location of the arbitration hearing, the Works and the nationality or location of the parties.

One of the effects of this clause is that the basic rules of procedure for conducting arbitrations set out in the Arbitration Act, 1950 are automatically included within the arbitration agreement. This accounts for the absence of any procedural matters from the arbitration agreement of JCT 80.

Appointment of the Arbitrator

The arbitration agreement does not contain any detailed procedure for the appointment of an Arbitrator. The minimum requirements are straight forward and a simple notice from the Contractor sent by recorded delivery or registered post to the Employer (with a copy to the Architect) would suffice. Such a notice should:-

★ inform the Employer that a dispute or difference has arisen between the Contractor and the Architect acting on behalf of the Employer

★ give a brief (one paragraph) statement of the matter in dispute, including reference to the correspondence containing the Contractor's 'final' plea on the matter in dispute and the Architect's 'final' decision

★ request that the dispute be referred to an Arbitrator for a final decision under article 5 of the Articles of Agreement

★ request that the parties seek to agree an Arbitrator

★ invite the Employer to propose the names of three Arbitrators acceptable to him

★ inform the Employer that if agreement on the appointment of an Arbitrator is not reached within fourteen days, then the President or a Vice-President of the RIBA (or the RICS in the case of a dispute involving a sub-contractor) will be requested to appoint an Arbitrator

★ (if necessary) request the written agreement of the Employer to the immediate commencement of the arbitration proceedings.

Requests by one party to the other for the appointment of an Arbitrator may be made at any time up to 14 days after the issue of the Final Certificate. Otherwise, there is no requirement for notice of arbitration to be given within a specified time after the event (or non-event, where, perhaps, the Architect has failed to issue a certificate) causing the dispute. The general position is that an arbitration may not commence until after Practical Completion of the Works but this should not prevent the early appointment of an Arbitrator. In the event of a dispute or difference, it is desirable for the parties to act quickly in seeking the appointment of an Arbitrator, for there is a considerable amount of preliminary work to be dealt with before the actual hearing of an arbitration commences.

Only when there has been positive non-agreement on the selection of an Arbitrator by the Contractor and Employer should the Contractor approach the RIBA (or in the case of a dispute involving a sub-contractor, the RICS) with a view to the appointment of an Arbitrator.

A Contractor who wishes the President of either the Royal Institute of British Architects or the Royal Institution of Chartered Surveyors to appoint an arbitrator for any particular dispute should note that the application must be made on prescribed forms which are obtainable from the respective institutions. Typically, the applicant will be required to pay a fee, to name the parties to the dispute and to give a short (one paragraph) statement of the nature of the dispute. The description of the dispute ought preferably be agreed between the parties and should be framed so as to enable the President to select an arbitrator experienced in the particular topic.

ATTESTATION

The final page of the Articles of Agreement in all Editions of JCT 80 provide space for execution of the actual agreement.

In the Local Authorities Editions a blank page headed 'Attestation' is included and a footnote invites execution by the parties after insertion of the appropriate attestation clauses. No further explanation is given. Two separate actions are required for the agreement to be properly executed. It is to be signed or sealed by (or on behalf of each) party in a manner which gives it a legally valid form. And secondly it is to be signed by a witness who attests (or confirms the authenticity of) such signature or seal. There seem to be no detailed requirements prescribed by the law for this purpose. However, each local or statutory authority using the Local Authorities Edition of the contract will have specific requirements that are enshrined in its 'Standing Orders' and the blank page is provided so as to allow for the many varied procedures that could be encountered. Similarly, of course, the Contractor will have his own specific requirements. If a limited company, these are contained in the Memorandum of Agreement and Articles of Association. It would be possible for either of the parties to ask the other for proof that the signatories of the agreement are properly authorised to do so by the constitution of the organisation concerned.

In the Private Editions of JCT 80, three pairs of optional attestation clauses are given that cover the usual circumstances. Where the contract is to be executed under seal, alternative attestations are given that are applicable when the party concerned is an individual or partnership and not having a legal seal, or, when the party concerned is a limited company or some other corporate body and having a legal seal.

The date of execution by the second of the parties executing the agreement must be entered in order to complete the formalities. Where the agreement has been executed under seal, a stamp duty (or tax) is payable. The Employer, who holds the original document, will be responsible for payment of the stamp duty.

APPENDIX

The purpose of the Appendix is to set out in one convenient schedule certain detailed matters that are particular to the individual contract. Clause B.4.3 of the Standard Method of Measurement, 6th Edition (SMM 6) requires that the proposed insertions for the Appendix to the Conditions should be stated in the bills of quantities.

The Appendix in JCT 80 is essentially reproduced from the 1963 Edition. Two new entries are required:-

★ the status of the Employer under the statutory tax deduction scheme

★ the optional joinder of arbitrations

All the entries proposed in the bills of quantities and subsequently inserted in the Appendix require careful consideration before any contract is signed. Entries **must** be made for some items, **may** have to be made in one case, and **need not necessarily** be made in other instances.

Entries **must** be made in the following cases for the relevant Conditions to be given their full meaning and for them to become operative under the contract. These are shown in Table I below:-

Table I Clause	Description of entry required
Recital 4 & Clause 31.2	The Employer's status under the statutory tax deduction scheme, ie the Employer is or is not a 'Contractor'.
1.3	The 'Date for Completion' at the date of execution of the contract, **not** the 'Completion Date'.
21.1.1	The minimum amount of insurance cover to be provided in respect of 'Third Party' claims.
23.1	The Date for Possession at the date of execution of the contract.
24.2	The amount of liquidated and ascertained damages and the period to which that amount applies.

(Table I continues overleaf)

(Table I continued)

28.1.3.2	The period of delay to the Works due to loss or damage by Clause 22 Perils, after which the Contractor may determine his own employment.
28.1.3.1 & 28.1.3.3 to 28.1.3.7	The period of delay to the Works by reason of any other circumstances, after which the Contractor may determine his own employment.
38.7 or 39.8	The percentage addition to the amounts payable under the traditional fluctuations clauses.
40.1.1.1	The date or other identification of the Formula Rules applicable to the formula fluctuations clause.
Formula Rule 3	The base month for the purpose of calculating the amounts payable under the formula fluctuations clause.
Formula Rules 10 and 30	The method by which work will be allocated (ie Work Categories or Work Groups) for the purpose of calculating the amounts payable under the formula fluctuations clause.

In the case of the Retention Percentage (clause 30.1.3) an entry **may** be required, but only if the agreed percentage is to be less than 5%. The JCT recommend that where at the tender stage the Contract Sum is expected to exceed £500,000 the Retention Percentage shall be not more than 3%.

Entries **need not necessarily** be made in the following cases (see Table II) for the text provides a recommendation and if the parties agree to the recommendation it is automatically applicable where no entry is made:-

Table II Clause	Description and applicable item	Possible alternatives
Article 5.1	Joinder of arbitrations will apply.	Joinder of arbitrations will not apply.
17.2	Defects Liability Period -Six months.	a. Twelve months b. Some trades, twelve months.
22A	Percentage addition to Clause 22 Perils insurance to allow for professional fees in reconstruction - No percentage addition.	Percentage addition required.
30.1.3	Period of Interim Certificates - One month.	Fortnightly.
30.6.1.2	Period of Final Measurement (after presentation of final account documents) - Six months.	a. One month b. Three months c. Twelve months.
30.8	Period for issue of Final Certificate (after completion of making good defects, or from presentation of final account documents) - Three months.	a. One month b. Two months.

(Table II continues overleaf)

(Table II continued)

35.2	Nominated Sub-Contract Work for which the Contractor wishes to tender - None.	Any work normally carried out by the Contractor and which is the subject of a PC Sum.
37	Fluctuations arrangements - clause 38, Contribution, levy or tax fluctuations will apply.	a. Clause 39, Labour and materials cost and tax fluctuations will apply b. Clause 40, Use of price adjustment formulae will apply.
Local Authorities Editions Only		
Formula Rule 3	Non-adjustable element - Nil %.	a. 5% b. 10%.

The recommendations that have been made by the JCT can be taken as representing good practice and builders should beware of signing contracts that contain substantial deviations from these recommendations.

14

General Obligations

In this section the general responsibilities of the Contractor in relation to the Employer and his Architect, the role and functions of the Architect, and the extent of his authority, are discussed within the framework laid down in the Contract Documents. In JCT 80 these matters appear in clause 2 (Contractor's obligations), clause 4 (Architect's/Supervising Officer's instructions) and clause 5 (Contract Documents - other documents - issue of certificates).

CONTRACTOR'S OBLIGATIONS

Definition of Contract Documents

Clause 2.1

The definition of the Contract Documents will be found in clause 2.1. The Contract Documents are:-

★ the Contract Drawings, as listed in the Articles of Agreement and signed by the parties

★ the Contract Bills, signed by the parties

★ the Articles of Agreement (including the recitals and the articles), executed by the parties

★ the Conditions (including the applicable fluctuations clause and the supplemental VAT Agreement)

★ the completed Appendix

AND NO OTHER DOCUMENTS.

The only change from the 1963 Edition is that the documents embraced by the definition now includes the completed Appendix.

Materials and workmanship

Clause 2.1

The remainder of clause 2.1 contains the basic obligation of the Contractor to carry out and to complete the Works according to the Contract Documents using the materials and workmanship described in those documents. The text is virtually identical to the 1963 Edition. The quality of materials and standard of workmanship in the execution of the work is subject to the approval or reasonable satisfaction of the Architect only where so specified in the Contract Documents. The Contract Documents (normally the Contract Bills) must, therefore, expressly state those matters that the Architect is required to approve. When such work or materials are available for inspection or approval the Contractor should given written notice to the Architect. Such notice should:-

For approval of materials:

★ identify the materials by reference to the Contract Bills

where bulk materials are concerned:

★ state the anticipated date of delivery of a sample

★ invite the Architect to inspect and approve the materials prior to final ordering by the Contractor.

in other cases:

★ state the name of the proposed manufacturer and catalogue number

★ request the Architect to approve the materials prior to ordering by the Contractor.

For approval of workmanship:

★ identify the work by reference to the Contract Bills and its location in the project

★ (if appropriate) state the date the work is expected to be covered up

★ invite the Architect to inspect the work and approve the workmanship.

Any approval given by the Architect at this stage must be construed as a provisional approval, since only the issue of the Final Certificate can be considered as conclusive.

If the Architect declares that he is not reasonably satisfied then the Contractor could, if practicable or reasonable to do so, obtain samples from alternative suppliers or execute further work with better workmanship. In the event of absolute conflict on these matters then it would be possible to have the matter arbitrated upon, but not until the Contractor has commenced to fix the materials or has continued to carry out the work and only after the Architect, by an instruction under clause 8.4 has ordered its removal and the Contractor declines to do so. The matter then becomes subject to immediate arbitration on the question whether or not the instruction is valid. The instruction would not be valid if an arbitrator were to find that the materials or workmanship **were** in accordance with the Contract Documents.

The Contractor must beware of producing materials and workmanship of a standard higher than that required by the Contract Documents and allowed for in his tender without an instruction of the Architect to cover any additional costs.

Where materials and workmanship are not expressly stated in the Contract Documents to be subject to the approval of the Architect, then it would seem that the Contractor is not required to seek or obtain the approval of the Architect at any time. The obligation of the Contractor is simply to carry out the Works according to the Contract Documents and to be able to satisfy the Employer that he has done so. This aspect of the role of the Architect in the duty of the Contractor to the Employer is also relevant to the Final Certificate. (See the discussion on clause 30.9 commencing on page 115).

However, if the Architect is of the opinion that materials or workmanship do **not** conform to the Contract Documents, then he has powers under clause 8 to order tests, inspections, etc and the removal of such non conforming materials or workmanship from the site. (See page 36).

The Contract Bills

Clause 2.2   The status of the Contract Bills is set out in clause 2.2 ('bills of quantities' are used at tender stage. They only become 'Contract Bills' when incorporated into the Contract Documents and signed by the parties). Clause 2.2 contains some of the matters dealt with in clause 12 of the 1963 Edition; namely, nothing in the Contract Bills can override the articles, the Conditions and the Appendix; that the bills of quantities have been prepared by reference to a (specified) method of measurement, and where the Contract Bills do not accurately represent the work shown on the Contract Drawings, then any errors in description or quantities, or any accidental omission of items of work are to be corrected as if they were Variations and valued under the Valuation rules of clause 13.

A specific change from the 1963 Edition concerning bills of quantities and measurement appears in clause 2.2.2.1. The bills of quantities must have been prepared in accordance with the **actual rules** of SMM 6 except for those items for which the bills of quantities expressly state otherwise. In the 1963 Edition they were deemed to have been prepared according to the **principles** of SMM 5. As a corollary of this more rigid regulation of the method of measurement, clause 2.2.2.2 provides that the correction of any error in the method of measurement becomes a Variation and is valued under the Valuation rules of clause 13.

Function of Contract Bills

In the 1963 Edition, the Contract Bills were restrained to 'the quantity and quality of the work'. In JCT 80 these words have not been transferred to clause 2 with the remainder of the items referred to above, but now appear in clause 14 where the reference is apparently in connection with the arithmetical calculation of the Contract Sum. The implication is that the Contract Bills are intended to cover a wider range of matters.

An obvious example of the extension of the function of Contract Bills is to be seen in SMM 6 where clause B.8 requires that any obligations and restrictions to be imposed by the Employer upon the Contractor in the execution of the Works are to be set out in the Preliminaries section of the bills of quantities. The obligations and restrictions can include:-

★ limitation of working hours

★ specific requirements as to the order in which the work is to be executed or completed

★ any other obligation or restriction.

Such obligations and restrictions set out in the bills of quantities cannot override the Conditions. For example, the bills of quantities alone cannot impose effective contractual obligations for part of the Works to be completed in advance of the Date for Completion entered in the Appendix. The Conditions themselves must be amended, perhaps by introducing the Sectional Completion Supplement.

By an Architects instruction, the obligations and restrictions imposed by the Employer may be changed during the execution of the work, and provision is specifically made in clause 13.1.2 for such changes to be dealt with as a Variation and valued under the Valuation rules of clause 13.

Procedure for correction of errors

Except where the error or omission is also a discrepency or divergence (in which case the provisions of clause 2.3 apply), there is no requirement for the Contractor to inform the Architect or the Quantity Surveyor of the discovery of any error or omission in the Contract Bills, whether this be in the method of measurement, or in the description or quantity of the work described therein. However, it would seem to be desirable for the Contractor to give written notice to the Architect and the Quantity Surveyor that such an error or omission has been discovered. Such notice should be sent to the Architect (copy to the Quantity Surveyor) and should:-

★ specify the item in the Contract Bills claimed to contain the error

★ state whether the error is in the method of measurement, or is one of description or quantity.

Since there is no requirement for the Architect to issue an instruction to correct the error or omission, there is no necessity to request one in the notice and the Contractor may proceed to carry on with the work shown on the Contract Drawings. Where possible, it is desirable that such notice be given in sufficient time to enable the Architect to issue other instructions if necessary.

Discrepancies and divergencies

Clause 2.3

Clause 2.3 contains the provisions for dealing with discrepancies in or divergencies between the Contract Drawings, the Contract Bills, Architect's instructions, drawings or documents issued under clause 5.3.1.1 ('descriptive schedules or other like document...for use in carrying out the Works'), clause 5.4 ('further drawings or details...to explain and amplify the Contract Drawings'), and clause 7 ('accurately dimensioned drawings...(to)...enable the Contractor to set out the Works').

A **discrepancy** is a disagreement or difference occuring **within** any one of the aforementioned documents (eg partitions described on a drawing as 100 mm thick but drawn 80 mm thick).

A **divergence** is a difference **between** any two of the aforementioned documents, (eg floor screeds measured in the Contract Bills as 50 mm thick, but shown on the drawings as 60 mm thick). This clause does not contemplate a divergence between the Conditions and the Contract Bills for clause 2.2.1 makes it clear that the Contract Bills shall not override the Conditions.

The first word in clause 2.3 ('If') is important, for it highlights the fact that the Contractor has no positive obligation under the Conditions to search for discrepancies or divergencies. The Contractor only has an express duty to inform the Architect of a discrepancy or divergence on each occasion one is found. The Conditions remain silent on what happens if the Contractor does not find each and every instance. While there is no general penalty for not finding any particular one, difficulties could be anticipated should discrepancies or divergencies occur between the Contract Documents, 'any descriptive schedules or other like documents' (clause 5.3.1.1, see page 26), and 'further drawings or details...' (clause 5.4, see page 27) and they are not spotted. The result could be delay to the completion of the Works and loss and/or expense could be caused for the Employer. If a court were to decide that in not finding an obvious error, the Contractor was in breach of an implied term or duty to the Employer to use proper skill in carrying out the Works or in administering the contract then the Contractor could find himself responsible for the loss and expense incurred by the Employer.

Upon discovering a discrepancy or divergence, the Contractor must immediately give notice by recorded delivery or registered post to the Architect. Such notice should:-

★ inform the Architect of the discovery of an apparent discrepancy in, or divergence between the (specified) documents

★ give a brief (one sentence) description of the discovery

★ request that the Architect issue his instructions to clarify or resolve the discrepancy or divergence

★ (if appropriate) inform the Architect of the date by which his instruction must be received in order to avoid an effect on the regular progress of the Works or delay in the completion of the Works.

The last point in the notice is necessary in order to introduce the general question of delay and extension of time. The late issue of an instruction in regard to apparent discrepancies or divergencies could have an effect on the progress of the Works and cause delay in the completion of the Works, thus becoming a 'Relevant Event' under clause 25 leading to an extension of time and could become a 'matter' under clause 26 giving rise to a claim for reimbursement of loss and expense. The notice referred to in the preceding paragraph should not be regarded as the only notice with which to raise the question of a late instruction. The proper disciplines of contract management and the more formal notice requirements of clause 25 and 26 must always be applied.

ARCHITECT'S INSTRUCTIONS

Authority of the Architect to issue instructions

Clause 4

There are numerous references in the Conditions to the instructions issued by the Architect and clause 4 sets out the obligation of the Contractor to comply with such instructions. Except for instructions of the Architect relating to obligations and restrictions of the Employer, there are no major changes from the 1963 Edition.

Clause 4 permits the Architect (the person named in the articles) to issue instructions. There is no authority for an instruction to be issued by an assistant to the Architect or any other person. It would appear that any such document is invalid and could be disregarded by the Contractor with impunity. Where the Architect is part of an architectural practice, the Employer and the Architect could agree with the Contractor that some person or persons other than the 'Architect' be authorised to act for him for certain specified matters. Such an agreement should be made at the commencement of the Works so as to avoid embarrassment in the administration of the contract.

There is no definition of an instruction of the Architect and the Conditions do not require an instruction to be in any prescribed form. Any document would appear to suffice providing it uses clear words to give a definite order to the Contractor and is signed by the Architect. It is believed that the issue of a drawing by the Architect is not, in itself, sufficient for this purpose. In order not to prejudice his rights to the valuation of instructions (including recovery of loss and expense) the Contractor should arrange that all drawings issued by the Architect be accompanied by an instruction. Otherwise, it would appear that the Contractor is obliged to identify those matters in all new or revised drawings which he considers to be variations and to give notice to the Architect requesting that an instruction be issued for each and every matter he has identified.

Many new and revised drawings issued to the Contractor will involve additional expenditure by the Contractor in one form or another and there must be no doubt that he will be able to recover that expenditure in due course.

It would be good practice for the Architect to use the standard form of instruction published by the RIBA and the Contractor should enquire, prior to commencement of work on site, as to the format that will be used by the Architect.

Type and purpose of instructions

The Conditions under which the Architect is expressly empowered to issue instructions and brief descriptions of the purposes of such instructions are set out in Table III.

Table III Clause	Purpose of instruction
2.3	To resolve discrepancies and divergencies.
4.3	To confirm verbal instructions.
6.1.3	To order a Variation because of Statutory Requirements.
7	To specify levels and setting out.
8.3	To require opening up, inspection, or testing.
8.4	To order removal of defective work.
8.5	To require exclusion of persons.
12	To confirm directions of the Clerk of Works.
13.2	To order Variations.
13.3.1	To authorise expenditure of provisional sums in the Contract Bills.
13.3.2	To authorise expenditure of provisional sums in any nominated sub-contract documents
17.2	To order making good defects specified in the schedule of defects.
17.3	To order making good defects during Defects Liability Period.
21.2	To order insurances on property other than the Works.
22C.2.3.2	To order removal of debris after damage.
23.2	To require postponement of work.
32.2	To order protective work during hostilities.
33.1.2	To order work after war damage.
34.2	To order special work after discovery of antiquities.
Nominated Sub-Contractors	
35.5.2	To change method of nomination.
BASIC METHOD OF NOMINATION	
35.7.1	To issue preliminary notice of nomination.
35.8	To assist after failure of Contractor and Nominated Sub-Contractor to agree.

(Table III continued overleaf)

(Table III continued)

35.9	To give instructions after withdrawal by Nominated Sub-Contractor.
35.10.2	To issue nomination instruction.
	ALTERNATIVE METHOD OF NOMINATION
35.11.2	To issue nomination instruction.
35.18.1.1	To nominate substitute sub-contractor after failure of Nominated Sub-Contractor to remedy defects.
35.23	To give instructions after failure of Contractor and Nominated Sub-Contractor to agree.
35.24.4.1	To authorise preliminary notice of determination by Contractor.
35.24.4.2	To authorise notice of determination by Contractor.
35.24.4.3	To nominate another sub-contractor after detemination by Contractor.
35.24.5	To nominate another sub-contractor after bankruptcy, etc of Nominated Sub-Contractor.
35.24.6	To nominate another sub-contractor after determination by Nominated Sub-Contractor.
35.25	To instruct determination of Nominated Sub-Contractor.
	Nominated Suppliers
36.2	To issue nomination instruction.

The Architect has no express powers to issue instructions to:-

★ vary or waive the terms of the contract

★ vary the nature of the Works

★ omit work so that it may be carried out by any other Contractor or the Employer

★ nominate a sub-contractor or supplier unless a prime cost sum has been entered in the Contract Bills, or unless a prime cost sum has been created within an instruction of the Architect as to the expenditure of a provisional sum.

Compliance with Architect's instructions

Clause 4.1.1   The Contractor is required by clause 4.1.1 to comply 'forthwith' with any instructions issued by the Architect for which the Conditions grant him express powers. One definition of forthwith is 'immediately, at once, without delay or interval'. Therefore, the Contractor must at least commence to comply with the instruction immediately upon receipt of it.

The general position that can arise as a consequence of the failure of the Contractor to comply with an instruction of the Architect is dealt with in clause 4.1.2.

Instructions in regard to the Employer's obligations and restrictions

A specific proviso has been introduced into clause 4.1.1 dealing with an instruction of the Architect requiring a Variation, where that instruction is in connection with the obligations or restrictions imposed by the Employer. In this case the Contractor need not comply with the instruction but **only** to the extent that

★ the objection is in writing

★ the objection is reasonable.

This new protection for the Contractor arises from the introduction of changes in the obligations and restrictions imposed by the Employer into the definition of 'Variations'. (See also the notes on clause 13.1.2, page 72). It is probably only intended to apply in the comparatively rare instances where the instruction, although permitted by the Conditions, is of such major consequence that it upsets the basis of the tender of the Contractor.

Any such notice of objection should be sent to the Architect and should:-

★ identify the instruction

★ inform the Architect that the Contractor does not intend to comply with the instruction

★ give a brief (one sentence) explanation of the nature of the objection.

The Architect may then either agree that the Contractor need not comply and withdraw the instruction; revise the instruction so that the Contractor will no longer object to it; or reject the plea of the Contractor and require him to comply with the instruction. If the Contractor still objects to the instruction, his only recourse is to proceed to arbitration. A dispute on this point is one upon which immediate arbitration is permitted; article 5.2.3 - 'any dispute or difference under clause 4.1 in regard to a reasonable objection by the Contractor...'.

All is well where an arbitrator agrees that the objection by the Contractor was reasonable, for the Contractor is not then required to comply with the instruction. A major difficulty arises should an arbitrator not endorse the objection of the Contractor, meaning that the Contractor must comply with the instruction of the Architect. Presumably, in these circumstances the instruction of the Architect is deemed to have come into effect at the date of its original issue, for the Conditions only suspend the requirement to comply with the instruction where the objection of the Contractor is reasonable. It follows, therefore, that the Contractor becomes responsible for any effect on progress of the Works or delay in completion of the Works by reason of non-compliance with the instruction upon its first issue and the Contractor must take account of this possibility before initiating arbitration.

Failure to comply with instructions of the Architect

Clause 4.1.2   The consequences of failure by the Contractor to comply with valid instructions of the Architect (other than one requiring a change in the obligations or restrictions of the Employer) are set out in clause 4.1.2. The Architect may by written notice require the Contractor to comply with an instruction. Such a notice should be sent by registered post or recorded delivery to the Contractor and need only:-

★ identify the instruction

★ request the Contractor to comply with the instruction within seven days after receipt of the notice

★ remind the Contractor that if he does not comply with the request, then the Employer may, without further notice, arrange for the work to be carried out by himself or by others, and that the costs so incurred will be recovered from the Contractor.

Upon receipt of such a notice, the Contractor must ask:-

★ whether the (specified) instruction has been validly issued by the Architect. (If no; see 'Validity of instruction of the Architect', page 24).

★ whether he indeed has not complied with the (specified) instruction without valid reason. (He may not have complied with some other instruction, but this does not matter for the present purpose.)

There could be many reasons why the Contractor has not complied with the instruction (eg awaiting delivery of materials), and where appropriate the Contractor must respond to the notice of the Architect with an explanation of his apparent failure to comply with the instruction.

Where the failure of the Contractor to comply with the instruction continues for seven days after receipt of the notice of the Architect, then the Employer may carry out the work himself, or may arrange for the work to be carried out by others on his behalf, and recover the cost of such work from the Contractor.

There is no apparent need for the Employer to inform the Contractor either that he is making his own arrangements to have the work carried out or when it is to be carried out. Where the Contractor fails to comply with an instruction of the Architect there is a breach of contract. Presumably, the JCT has considered that the Contractor has therefore foregone his right to the exclusive use of the site and that the seven days notice given by the Architect is sufficient in the circumstances to waive the provisions of clause 23.1 giving the Contractor exclusive possession of the site, and to grant persons employed or engaged by the Employer the right of temporary access.

More importantly, the present clause does **not** state that persons employed or engaged by the Employer carrying out work not executed by the Contractor are persons for whom the Employer is responsible. This leaves open the important matters of indemnities to be given by the Contractor and insurances. The general rule where Employer or persons employed or engaged by him carry out the work on site is that the Contractor is given relief from certain matters for which he normally indemnifies the Employer, or for which he effects insurance; namely:-

clauses 20.1 and 21.1.1.1. − no indemnity to Employer and no liability to insure where personal injury, etc. occurs as a result of act or neglect of the Employer or persons employed or engaged by him.

clauses 20.2 and 21.1.1.1 − indemnity to Employer and liability to insure **only** against damage to property, etc. occurring as a result of negligence, etc., of the Contractor, his servants or agents; but **not** damage to property, etc. occurring as a result of negligence, etc. of the Employer or persons employed or engaged by him.

It is odd that the Conditions do not tie up the obvious loose ends and grant relief to the Contractor from these liabilities.

Where the Employer does advise the Contractor that he proposes to carry out work on the site in accordance with the rights granted to him under clause 4.1.2, then the Contractor must ensure that notice is given to the Employer (copy to the Architect) that will protect his position. Such notice should:-

★ refer to the advice from the Employer

★ inform the Employer that the Contractor will consider that any person employed or engaged by him (the Employer) entering upon the site will be considered to be a person for whom he (the Employer) is responsible.

The Conditions do not specify who is to ascertain the costs incurred by the Employer in carrying out the work, nor is there any requirement for agreement between the Contractor and the Employer as to the amount of such costs. The Employer is entitled to deduct his costs from monies due to the Contractor in Interim Certificates or the Final Certificate, or action may be taken through the courts to recover the costs. It would appear that the value of the work contained in the original instruction of the Architect would be taken into account in computing the final adjusted Contract Sum under clause 30.6.2, and that the Employer deducts his costs under the provisions of clause 30.1.1.2.

Validity of an instruction of the Architect

Clause 4.2   The power of the Architect to issue instructions is limited to the express powers granted to him in the Conditions. If, upon receipt of an instruction of the Architect, the Contractor is of the opinion that it may not be within the scope of these powers, then the Contractor may request the Architect to specify the Condition under which he claims to be authorised to issue the instruction. Such a request is a notice to the Architect and should:-

★ identify the instruction

★ inform the Architect that in the opinion of the Contractor, the instruction is not authorised by the Conditions

★ request that the Architect state under which Condition he has issued the instruction.

Where the response by the Architect is to specify a Condition that is still not acceptable to the Contractor, then the only recourse open to the Contractor is to proceed with arbitration and again the Contractor is entitled to immediate arbitration; (article 5.2.2 - 'Whether or not...an instruction is empowered by the Conditions'). Any notice of arbitration must be given before compliance with any part of the instruction of the Architect concerned, otherwise the Contractor would seem to lose his right to have the authority of the Architect to issue the instruction arbitrated upon.

In the case of a request by the Contractor for arbitration on the question of the power of the Architect to issue any particular instruction, there seems to be no provision suspending the obligation of the Contractor to comply with the instruction. It appears that the Contractor must comply with the instruction and the Architect may issue notices under clause 4.1.2 requiring compliance by the Contractor, even though the validity of the instruction of the Architect is being challenged by the Contractor.

A major difficulty arises where an Arbitrator finds that the Architect did **not** have the power to issue the instruction, meaning that the instruction is invalid and that the Contractor need not comply. Any work carried out in accordance with the 'instruction'

24

obviously cannot be valued as a Variation under the Valuation rules of clause 13, for that clause only deals with valid instructions of the Architect.

It is believed that, since the Contractor has complied with the 'instruction' in accordance with the Conditions, the Employer has an obligation to pay the Contractor for any work carried out before the 'instruction' was found to be invalid. Any such payment would, of course, have to be outside the financial arrangements of the contract and no doubt the Employer would look to the Architect for redress for any such payments made to the Contractor.

Instructions to be in writing

Clause 4.3.1   The obligation for the Architect to issue his instructions in writing has been reinforced by giving it a clause to itself.

Instructions not in writing

Clause 4.3.2   The possibility of oral instructions of the Architect is contemplated and the elaborate provisions of the 1963 Edition remain essentially unchanged. The Contractor is to confirm such oral instruction by notice in writing within seven days of its issue and if not dissented from by the Architect within a further seven days, the instruction becomes valid. Such notice should:-

★ state when the instruction was issued and by whom

★ give the nature of the instruction

★ request confirmation in writing from the Architect.

There is a final backstop provision (clause 4.3.2.2) that enables the Contractor to advise the Architect that he has acted upon a oral instruction but that he has omitted to confirm it in writing within seven days of issue. In these circumstances the confirmation to the Architect should also include the date on which the work was carried out. The Contractor should not place absolute reliance on this clause, since it is discretionary on the part of the Architect. He **may** confirm the instruction in writing, so as to permit Valuation under the Valuation rules of clause 13.

This provision may be useful where, for example, the Architect has given an oral instruction requiring work to be carried out as a matter of urgency and there is insufficient time to permit the normal confirmation procedure to be implemented.

Postscript to clause 4

The Contractor is not required under the present clause to request the Architect to issue instructions at any time. It is a different matter when the issue of instructions is being considered in relation to both the award of extension of time and the reimbursement of loss and expense, since timely applications requesting their issue are conditions precedent to such award and such reimbursement. (See also the discussion on clauses 25.4.6 (page 50) and 26.2.1 (page 84).

The major difficulty here is that for many matters - Variations, for example - the Contractor does not know he needs an instruction, so it may not be possible for a written application to be made. On the other hand, in order to reject a plea by the Contractor for the award of extension of time by reason of late instructions the Architect would have to show that the Contractor could reasonably have known that an instruction was required.

Where it is known that an Architect's instruction is required, then such instructions should be requested by giving written notice to the Architect. Such notice should:-

★ identify the work concerned by reference to the Contract Bills and/or Contract Drawings

★ give a brief (one sentence) explanation of the instruction that appears to be required.

★ request that the Architect issue his instruction to clarify or resolve the problems

★ (if appropriate) inform the Architect of the date by which his instruction must be received in order to avoid an effect on the regular progress of the Works or delay in the completion of the Works.

The last point in the notice is necessary to introduce the general question of delay and extension of time and is necessary in order to satisfy the requirements of clauses 25 and 26.

CONTRACT DOCUMENTS AND ISSUE OF CERTIFICATES

Various practical matters in regard to the Contract Documents are substantially the same as in the 1963 Edition and are set out in clause 5. The requirement for a master programme (clause 5.3.1.2) is new and there is a significant change in the destination of all certificates issued by the Architect (clause 5.8).

Contract Documents

Clause 5.1   Clause 5.1 provides that the 'original' of the Contract Drawings and the Contract Bills be held by the Employer (Local Authorities Editions), or the Architect or Quantity Surveyor (Private Editions).

Clause 5.2   The Contractor is entitled to a certified copy of the complete Contract Documents. The 'original' Contract Documents are held by the Employer. For the purpose of carrying out the Works the Contractor is entitled to receive two further copies of the Contract Drawings and the blank bills of quantities. All are to be issued immediately after the execution of the Contract Documents. The Conditions do not state who is to issue the copy of the Contract Documents to the Contractor. Taken literally, this provision would effectively prohibit commencement of the Works on site until **after** execution of the Contract Documents, which is, of course, quite unrealistic in many cases.

Further drawings and details

The Conditions recognise in clauses 5.3.1.1 and 5.4 (when read in conjunction with the 'Relevant Events' leading to extensions of time (clause 25.4.6) and the 'matters' giving rise to claims for reimbursement of loss and expense (clause 26.2.1)) that the Contract Documents do not themselves provide sufficient information to enable the Works to be completed.

Clause 5.3   The Architect is required (clause 5.3.1.1) to issue descriptive schedules or other like documents (perhaps reinforcement schedules, finishing schedules, etc) showing the location of the various components and necessary to facilitate the execution of the Works. Such descriptive schedules, etc. are to be issued as soon as possible after execution of the Contract Documents. It is made clear in clause 5.3.2 that any descriptive schedules, etc. shall not impose any additional obligations upon the Contractor.

Should any descriptive schedules, etc. issued by the Architect show any changes from the materials and workmanship contained in the Contract Documents then an instruction of the Architect must also be issued before the Contractor is required to carry out the varied work. An instruction of the Architect will often accompany the descriptive schedules, etc. when these are issued. If an instruction of the Architect has not been received, then the varied work indicated on the descriptive schedules, etc. becomes a discrepancy or divergence and the procedure detailed in clause 2.3 must be followed in order to obtain the requisite instruction of the Architect.

Clause 5.4   The Contract Drawings are normally drawn to a small scale and only show the general arrangement of the Works in sufficient detail for the purpose of obtaining tenders. Clause 5.4 requires that the Architect provide the Contractor with additional and/or further drawings, details, etc. necessary to enable him to carry out the Works. Such drawings and other details will be drawn to larger scales and will be the working drawings.

The Architect is to provide such additional drawings, etc. '...to enable the Contractor to carry out and complete the Works in accordance with the Conditions'. That is to say, to enable the Contractor to complete by the Completion Date (ie the Date for Completion plus any extension of time then awarded) irrespective of any date that the Architect may consider to be the probable date of practical completion. In other words the Architect may not delay issuing the further drawings and other details merely because the Contractor does not appear to the Architect to be capable of achieving Practical Completion by the Completion Date.

Where any additional and/or further drawings or other details issued by the Architect show any change from the materials and workmanship contained in the Contract Documents, then an instruction of the Architect must also be issued before the Contractor is required to carry out the varied work. An instruction of the Architect will often accompany the drawings or details when these are issued. If an instruction of the Architect has not been received, then the varied work shown on the additional drawings and details becomes a discrepancy or divergence and the procedure under clause 2.3 must be followed in order to obtain the requisite instruction of the Architect.

Should the Contractor proceed with varied work shown upon any descriptive schedules, etc. or upon any additional drawings or details without obtaining an instruction of the Architect, then the Contractor can expect difficulties from the Quantity Surveyor when endeavouring to secure payment.

TO THIS EXTENT, THEREFORE, THERE **ARE** PENALTIES IN NOT SPOTTING DISCREPANCIES OR DIVERGENCIES AND PROCEEDINGS TO OBTAIN INSTRUCTIONS UNDER CLAUSE 2.3.

The Contractor should agree with the Architect at the commencement of the contract that all descriptive schedules, etc., and additional drawings and details should be issued under the authority of an instruction of the Architect.

The Contractor is not required under the present clause to request issue by the Architect of descriptive schedules etc., and/or additional drawings and details at any time. However, it is a different matter when the issue of descriptive schedules, etc., and/or additional drawings and details is being considered in relation to both the award of extension of time and the reimbursement of loss and expense, since timely applications requesting their issue are conditions precedent to such award and such reimbursement. See also the discussion on clauses 25.4.6 (page 50) and 26.2.1 (page 84).

Since the descriptive schedules, etc., and/or additional drawings and details are explanations or amplifications of the Contract Documents it will be obvious that there are few, if any, occasions when the Contractor cannot make the timely written applications required by clauses 25.4.6 and 26.2.1.

In practice, therefore, the Contractor must consider that written requests for the issue of descriptive schedules, etc., and/or additional drawings and details by the Architect are contractual requirements. Where descriptive schedules, etc., and/or additional drawings and details are required by the Contractor, then these must be requested by giving written notice to the Architect. Such notice should:-

★ identify the work concerned by reference to the Contract Bills and/or Contract Drawings

★ give a brief (one sentence) explanation of the nature of the additional or more detailed information required

★ request that the Architect issue the descriptive schedules, etc., and/or additional drawings and details necessary to explain or amplify the Contract Documents

★ (if appropriate) inform the architect of the date by which the descriptive schedules, etc., and/or additional drawings and details must be received in order to avoid an effect on the regular progress of the Works or delay in the completion of the Works.

The last point in the notice is necessary in order to introduce the general question of delay and extension of time and is necessary in order to satisfy the requirements of clauses 25 and 26.

Master programme

**Clause
5.3.1.2**

The provision of a 'master programme' by the Contractor is an entirely new requirement introduced into JCT 80, although it should be noted at once that the clause is optional. Where clause 5.3.1.2 applies the Contractor is to provide the Architect with duplicate copies of his 'master programme' for the Works. The Contractor is to provide the programme as soon as possible after the execution of the Contract Documents and is to update it from time to time to take account of each decision of the Architect to fix a new Completion Date. Since clause 5.3.1.2 is optional, the tender bills of quantities must therefore state whether a master programme will be required by the Architect. The bills of quantities should also state whether the master programme is to be in any specified format and whether the Employer or the Architect will require any particular operations to be detailed especially.

It is interesting to observe that the master programme is not mentioned elsewhere in the Conditions. There is no mention, for example, that in considering requests for extension of time by reason of late information, the Architect is to have regard to any dates given in the master programme for the commencement of the work concerned. Nor, in regard to Nominated Sub-Contractors, that the preliminary notice of nomination by the Architect or the final nomination instruction are to be issued having regard to the dates set out in the master programme for the commencement of the Nominated Sub-Contract Works. Nor, in considering any request by the Contractor for reimbursement of loss and expense caused by disturbance of the regular progress of the Works, that such disturbance will be ascertained by reference to the master programme.

Regarding the timetable for the presentation of the master programme, it is clear that it can be little more than the programme produced by the Contractor during the preparation of his tender. Such a master programme will set out in brief overall terms the intentions of the Contractor regarding the execution of the Works. For the various parts of the Works it will show the dates for the receipt of information, their proposed durations, their intended sequence and regular progression, and provide a reference from which the Architect will be able to judge the progress of the Works and to be able to report authoritatively to the Employer on progress. The Contractor is entitled to prepare the master programme in any way he wishes to suit his own particular proposals for carrying out the Works, and therefore the dates given for receipt of information, periods for the duration of the works of Nominated Sub- Contractors, etc., are entirely at the discretion of the Contractor. The right of the Contractor to programme the Works includes the privilege of building into it a 'float' or contingency for his own protection. While one could envisage difficulties if the amount of float included was extensive, there can be little doubt that a modest allowance would be perfectly acceptable. The complications would occur if the question of extension of time because of late receipt of information from the Architect should arise, for any extension would be awarded in relation to the date for receipt of that information established by reference to the Completion Date. That date would clearly not be the same as the date established by reference to the master programme if it contained a substantial allowance for 'float'.

The master programme will enable the Architect to develop a timetable for co- ordinating the preparation and issue of drawings and other information necesssary for the execution of the Works. The methods and intentions of the Contractor, upon whiich the tender sum was established, are shown on the programme. The effect on these programmed intentions of late receipt of instructions or information and the effect of the nature and timing of variations ought to be readily apparent to both the Architect and the Employer. It should be remembered that any shortcomings of the Contractor in executing the Works will be equally apparent to the Architect and the Employer.

While the Contractor is required to provide the master programme as soon as practicable after the execution of the Contract Documents, it would be in the best interests of the Contractor to submit it immediately after acceptance of his tender. The Contractor should not await the execution of the Contract Documents, for these are sometimes not executed promptly. The Conditions do not seem to require approval by the Architect of the master programme so that all that is required is a simple notice to the Architect. Such notice should:-

★ refer to clause 5.3.1.2 of the Conditions and inform the Architect that the (specified) master programme is enclosed

★ request that the Architect acknowledge its receipt

★ invite the Architect to comment.

Neither the Architect or the Employer are required to approve or appraise the master programme. The reason for this is the historical concept that neither the Employer nor the Architect is entitled to interfere with the freedom of the Contractor to choose his own methods of working. The only exception to this would be where the Sectional Completion Supplement is incorporated into the Contract. There would seem to be no reason why the Architect should not be invited to comment if he wishes. It would be unreasonable if the Architect were to merely acknowledge receipt of a master programme if upon proper examination, he could see obvious errors, say in regard to Nominated Sub-Contractors, where the Architect may already know the periods proposed by Nominated Sub-Contractors for the Nominated Sub-Contract Works and the period of notice required before commencement.

On the other hand, the programme is not a Contract Document and does not change the basic contractual responsibility of the Contractor to achieve practical completion by the Date for Completion, so that there is a limit to the extent of discussion that is possible. Clause 5.3.2 reinforces this by making it clear that the master programme cannot impose any additional obligations upon the Contractor. Thus if the master programme should show a 'float' at the end of the contract period, the Contractor cannot be penalised for not completing by the target date on the master programme, nor can the Contractor be penalised for not complying with the master programme.

It is not surprising that the master programme has not been made a Contract Document. The many arguments that this would create will have been rehearsed 'ad nauseam' by the prospective protagonists within the JCT; Architects wanting Contractors to be bound to every single item shown on the master programme, but without reference to the production of working drawings, etc. by themselves; Contractors wanting Architects to be obligated to produce every snippet of information according to the master programme, but not wanting to be themselves tied to the master programme; Quantity Surveyors sitting on the fence, envisaging problems for themselves however the matter is settled.

The requirements of the contract in regard to notification of delay and the timing of awards of extensions of time are much more stringent than under the 1963 Edition (see clause 25, commencing on page 43). Clearly, the master programme is an important document for both the Contractor and the Architect in considering delays, extensions of time, and disruption in the execution of the Works.

The provision of a master programme means that the requirements of the Contractor regarding information, instructions, etc., are more clearly set out at the outset in a document recognised in the Conditions, even though it is not given a formal status. This should provide the Contractor with a better base from which to initiate his applications for extensions of time.

There are two points to be stressed. Firstly, in regard to extensions of time it would be easy for the Contractor to fall foul of the complex procedural matters detailed in clause 25. Secondly, the presence of any particular activity on the master programme **does not seem to satisfy** the obligation to give the particular notices required upon the occurrence of a 'Relevant Event' under clause 25 or a 'matter' under clause 26.

Clause 5.6 Under the provisions of clause 5.6, all drawings, etc. issued by the Architect may have to be returned to him after the Contractor has received the final payment. There is no reason why the Contractor should do this free of charge. The Contractor should ascertain, prior to the issue of the Final Certificate, whether the drawings, etc., are to be returned to the Architect or destroyed and then request the issue of an instruction of the Architect. This should ensure that a sum is included in the final adjusted Contract Sum to cover the cost.

Certificates of the Architect

Clause 5.8 The Conditions required that the Architect (the person named in the Articles) shall issue certificates for many different purposes. Clause 5.8 provides that, unless otherwise stated in the Condition concerned, certificates of the Architect will be issued to the Employer with a copy to the Contractor. The following schedule Table IV shows the purposes for which the Architect could be required to issue certificates:-

Table IV Clause	Purpose of Certificate
17.1	To name the date of Practical Completion of the Works.
17.4	To certify completion of Making Good Defects.
18.1.1	To establish the approximate value of each part, following partial possession.
18.1.3	To certify completion of Making Good Defects in each part, following partial completion.
22A.4.2	To authorise payment for restoration after damage by Clause 22 Perils.
24.1	To certify the failure of the Contractor to complete by the Completion Date.
27.4.4	To certify loss and expense of the Employer after determination.
30.1.1.1	To authorise interim payments to the Contractor.
30.7	To authorise the penultimate payment (the final payment to Nominated Sub-Contractors).
30.8	The Final Certificate.
35.15.3.2	To certify the failure of the Contractor to pay Nominated Sub-Contractor(s).
35.15.1★	To certify the failure of a Nominated Sub-Contractor to complete by the sub-contract completion date.
35.16	To name the date of Practical Completion of Works by Nominated Sub-Contractors.
35.17	To authorise final payment to Nominated Sub-Contractor(s).

★ the certificate under clause 35.15.1 is sent to the Contractor with a copy to the Nominated Sub-Contractor concerned. Otherwise all the certificates referred to above are sent to the Employer with a copy to the Contractor.

While certain of the certificates are included in the 'Definitions' of clause 1.3, the Conditions do not require certificates to be in any prescribed form and any document would appear to suffice, providing it comprises a clear, authoritative statement of the occurrence. To avoid disputes it is clearly good practice for the Architect to use standard forms such as those published by the RIBA.

The certificates issued directly to the Employer include certificates for payment issued under clause 30 in both Private and Local Authority Editions of the Contract. This means that the Contractor is not required to present Interim Certificates issued by the Architect to the Employer prior to payment. This small change in procedure should improve the cash flow of the Contractor since the fourteen day honouring period begins from the date of issue of the certificate and not from the date of presentation, as was the case in the Private Editions of the 1963 Edition.

Executing the Work

The preceding Section discussed those documents the Contractor receives showing **what** he is to build. In this Section certain restraints on **how** he is to build will be examined. Such restraints can be statutory (clause 6 -Statutory obligations, notices, fees and charges), physical (clause 7 - Levels and setting out of the Works), contractual (clause 8 - Materials, goods and workmanship to conform to description; clause 9 - Royalties), personal (clause 10 - Person-in-charge; clause 11 - Access for Architect; clause 12 - Clerk of works), or - Local Authorities Editions only - industrial (clause 19A - Fair Wages).

STATUTORY REQUIREMENTS

Clause 6 has been substantially reproduced from the 1963 Edition and introduces the 'Statutory Requirements'.

Compliance with Statutory Requirements

Clause 6.1 The Contractor is required to comply with Acts of Parliament, byelaws of local authorities, and regulations of statutory undertakers in so far as they have any jurisdiction over any part of the Works.

Where the Contractor finds a divergence between the Statutory Requirements and any of the Contract Documents or any instructions of the Architect, clause 6.1.2 requires the Contractor to give notice to the Architect. Such notice should:-

★ draw attention to the apparent divergence between the document concerned and the Statutory Requirement

★ give a brief note of the problem including reference to the authority for the Statutory Requirement (eg refer to the Building Regulation concerned)

★ request that the Architect issue instructions to resolve the conflict

★ (if appropriate) inform the Architect of the date by which his instruction must be received in order to avoid an effect on the regular process of the Works or delay in the completion of the Works.

The last point in the notice is necessary in order to introduce the general question of delay and extension of time. The late issue of an instruction in regard to such divergencies could have an effect on the progress of the Works and cause delay in the completion of the Works, becoming a 'Relevant Event' under clause 25 leading to an extension of time, and could become a 'matter' under clause 26 giving rise to a claim for reimbursement of loss and expense. The notice referred to in the preceding paragraph should not be regarded as the only notice with which to raise the question of a late instruction. The proper disciplines of contract management and the more formal notice requirements of clauses 25 and 26 must always be applied.

Under clause 6.1.3 the Architect is required to issue his instructions in response to the notice by the Contractor within seven days of receipt of the notice. The Conditions remain silent on the procedure to be followed by the Contractor if the Architect does not issue such instructions within the prescribed seven days. There is no requirement for the Contractor to await an instruction, but there is no obvious authority for the Contractor to proceed on his own initiative with the Works in accordance with, either, the (incorrect) Contract Documents, or, the Statutory Requirements. Much will depend upon the nature of the divergence and the consequences of the failure of the Contractor to carry out the work under consideration. It is considered that the Statutory Requirements should be complied with in order to best protect the interests of the Employer. In addition, since the failure to comply with any Statutory Requirements (eg Building Regulations) would, prima facie, be a breach of contract by the Contractor, it is more than likely that the Employer would be able to recover from the Contractor all costs of remedial work necessary to make the building comply with the Statutory Requirements. In appropriate cases, the Contractor must then give the notices required under clauses 25 and 26 to ensure that his position is protected. A prudent Contractor would endeavour to secure an instruction of the Architect before changing the design or modifying any work, for the Architect may have his own ideas for resolving the divergence.

The first word in clause 6.1.2 is once again 'If...'; highlighting that the Contractor has no positive obligation under the Conditions to search for divergencies, but leaving the Contractor at risk in certain circumstances should he not find every divergence. The comments on page 18 in connection with clause 2.3 apply equally to the present clause.

Under clause 6.1.5, the Contractor seems to be indemnified against any liability to the Employer resulting from the execution of work that is not in compliance with the Statutory Requirements but, nevertheless, built exactly in accordance with the Contract Documents or instructions of the Architect. The indemnity given by clause 6.1.5 is restricted, however, to those matters for which notices have been given under clause 6.1.2, or where the Contractor has not spotted the divergence.

For some further comments on the duty of the Contractor to comply with Statutory Requirements, see the postscript to clause 6.1 on page 40.

Emergency Work

Clause 6.1.4   It is possible for an emergency to arise on the site that relates to a divergence between the Contract Documents and the Statutory Requirements. In such situations the Contractor may under the provisions of clause 6.1.4.1 carry out the minimum amount of work necessary to ensure compliance with the Statutory Requirements.

Where such work is carried out clause 6.1.4.2 requires the Contractor to inform the Architect 'forthwith' of the events occurring on the site and this should be considered as a notice to the Architect. Such notice should:-

- ★ inform the Architect of the nature of the emergency including (presumably − the Conditions do not say so) the authority informing the Contractor of the divergence

- ★ give a short (one sentence) description of the action taken by the Contractor in response to the emergency

- ★ (if appropriate) request instructions from the Architect in regard to any consequential matters not covered by the 'emergency' work.

Readers should note the word 'is' which appears in clause 6.1.4.2, thus underlining the obligations of the Contractor to give the notice upon **commencement** of the emergency work. The Contractor may not wait until after the emergency work has been completed.

Work done in such an emergency is deemed to be a 'Variation' required by the Architect and is to be valued under the Valuation rules of clause 13.

Fees or charges

Clause 6.2   The amount of fees or charges payable under Acts of Parliament (including Regulations, etc. made thereunder) and regulations or byelaws of local authorities or statutory undertakings are, by clause 6.2, to be paid by the Contractor. The expression 'fees or charges' includes rates on the temporary buildings of the Contractor and 'taxes'. It is not clear which tax is meant since value added tax is specifically excluded here and is dealt with in clause 15 and the VAT Agreement. The only apparent qualification of 'fees or charges' is that they must be 'in respect of the Works'. They cannot, for example, include any new or increased tax on the employment of labour, for that is specifically dealt with in the fluctuations clauses.

Clause B.7 of SMM 6 'Local Authorities fees and charges' provides that, unless the conditions of contract expressly state otherwise, such fees or charges (including rates on the temporary buildings of the Contractor) shall be given as provisional sums. As a consequence the amount of any fees or charges properly paid by the Contractor will normally be refunded to him by including the amounts concerned in the final adjusted Contract Sum, clauses 30.6.2.2 and 30.6.2.10.

There seem to be two express provisions in the Conditions that qualify the general rule given in the previous paragraph. These are where the fees or charges arise as a result of work carried out, or goods supplied, by a statutory undertaker employed by the Contractor as a nominated sub-contractor or nominated supplier, in which case the fees or charges will presumably be included in the adjustment of the PC Sum. This is also the case where the Contractor has priced an item in the bills of quantities described as inclusive of such fees or charges. In relation to the latter, reference to SMM 6 shows that the only items required to be described in the bills of quantities as inclusive of fees to local authorities and statutory undertakers and to be priced by the Contractor, are in relation to those matters covered by clause B.13 'General facilities and obligations, items for convenience in pricing'. Examples of items that are required to be priced by the Contractor as inclusive of such fees and charges are:-

★ fees for scaffolding licences

★ charges for the installation of temporary water, electricity and telephone installations

★ charges for the installation of crossovers and the like

★ fees for hoarding or gantry licences etc.

Work by public bodies

Clause 6.3   Clause B.11 of SMM 6 requires that work by public bodies be given in the bills of quantities as a provisional sum. Clause 6.3 provides that where local authorities or statutory undertakers carry out work that must be carried out by them under their statutory obligations, then such local authorities or statutory undertakers are **not** sub-contractors under the contract. The reason for this is quite simple. When carrying out work under their statutory obligations, such bodies will only trade upon their own terms and conditions. Neither the Employer, nor the Architect, nor the Contractor can do anything about this.

Since the work is covered by a provisional sum, the Contractor will only need to arrange for work to be carried out when instructed by the Architect to do so. The amount of any charges made by the local authority or statutory undertaker will be refunded to the Contractor by including the amounts concerned in the final adjusted Contract Sum, clauses 30.6.2.2 and 30.6.2.12.

There is nothing to preclude the employment of a local authority or statutory undertaker as a sub-contractor to carry out ordinary contract work (eg an electricity board carrying out the electrical installation for a building) and it would be obliged to enter into a sub-contract agreement for the purpose. The local authority or statutory undertaker could even be employed as a Nominated Sub-Contractor, provided of course that the Nominated Sub-Contract procedures of JCT 80 have been followed.

LEVELS AND SETTING OUT

Clause 7   The text of clause 7 dealing with levels and setting out of the Works is unchanged from the 1963 Edition. The Architect is responsible for determining any levels required for the execution of the Works. The exact extent of his responsibilities in this are not made clear, but it is presumed to mean that the Architect will identify for the Contractor a point on or adjacent to the site and will give its level. The Contractor appears to be responsible for the subsequent transfer of the given level to other points on the site.

The Architect is required to provide the Contractor with drawings containing sufficient information to enable the Work to be set out at ground level. The late provision of such drawings could become a 'Relevant Event' leading to an extension of time under clause 25 and a 'matter' giving rise to a claim for reimbursement of loss and expense under clause 26. The Architect does not specifically have to approve the setting out, the Contractor takes total responsibility.

MATERIALS AND WORKMANSHIP
Compliance with Contract Documents

The quality of materials, goods and workmanship to be provided by the Contractor in the execution of the Works is referred to in clauses 8.1 to 8.4. The text is the same as the 1963 Edition. By clause 2.1 the Contractor has undertaken to carry out the Works using materials and workmanship described in the Contract Documents.

Clause 8.1   In clause 8.1 that obligation is qualified to the extent that the materials, goods and workmanship need only be 'so far as procurable' as described in the Contract Bills. Two particular points arise from this clause. Firstly, the word 'reasonable' does not appear, thereby reinforcing the absolute responsibility of the Contractor to provide the specified material. For example, merely long or longer delivery of a specified material does not absolve the Contractor from his responsibility under the Contract. Secondly, there is no express provision within this clause for the Contractor to take action in the event that materials or goods are, or become, unprocurable. However, when the absence of such materials or goods will cause delay to the contract, the Architect will be made aware of the problem faced by the Contractor when he receives from him the notice required under clause 25. The inability of the Contractor to procure materials is a 'Relevant Event' for which an extension of time may be granted.

It seems to be wrong for the progress of the Works to be potentially in delay before the Architect is made aware of any problem that the Contractor may have in meeting the requirements of the Contract Documents. The Contractor should not, therefore, wait until progress is likely to be delayed before giving notice to the Architect. He should give notice to the Architect immediately upon discovering any difficulty in regard to the supply of materials or goods. Such notice should:-

★ identify the item concerned

★ give a brief (one sentence) explanation of the problem

★ request the Architect to issue his instructions to resolve the difficulty

★ (if appropriate) give the notice required by clause 25 that there is or is likely to be an effect on the progress of the Works, or that there is or is likely to be delay in the completion of the Works.

Upon receipt of such notice the Architect could issue an instruction changing the item concerned to something that is more readily procurable and such an instruction becomes a variation to be valued under the Valuation rules of clause 13. Alternatively, the Architect could do nothing, thereby accepting that there could be an effect on the progress of the Works, or delay in completion of the Works, by the use of the specified materials or goods.

It is not recommended that the Contractor offer alternative products or suppliers until or unless asked to do so by the Architect. For any alternative products or suppliers chosen by the Architect, there **must** be an instruction of the Architect authorising the change. Should there be no instruction of the Architect the Contractor could become involved in some liability for the performance of the items concerned should they fail to meet **all** the requirements of the Architect and the Employer.

Proof of compliance

Clause 8.2   The Architect is empowered under clause 8.2 to request the Contractor to prove that materials and goods are as described in the Contract Bills. That is to say, to demonstrate the quality of materials and goods by presentation of authoritative statements or certificates from the supplier (eg concrete test cube results).

Tests and inspections

Clause 8.3   Under clause 8.3 the Architect may issue instructions to the Contractor requiring an inspection or test on any materials and goods. The Contractor must ensure that the instruction of the Architect is in writing and that it is absolutely clear what material the Architect wants tested and how it is to be tested. The instructions of the Architect can be in respect of completed work or materials and goods already installed in the Works and the Contractor is required to expose or uncover such work or materials if necessary.

The Conditions envisage that the costs of these inspections or tests will be refunded to the Contractor except where the results of the inspection or test shows that the workmanship or materials and goods are not as described in the Contract Documents. Such refunds of the cost of testing could be made directly by inclusion of the amounts concerned in Interim Certificates and the final adjusted Contract Sum, clause 30.6.2.10 or, indirectly where the specification of the material requires regular routine testing (eg concrete), and the Contract Bills provide an item (either in the preliminaries section or in the appropriate measured work section) within which the Contractor is able to allow for such testing.

The consequences of complying with instructions of the Architect issued under clause 8.3 may have an effect on the progress of the Works and cause delay in completion of the Works and become a 'Relevant Event' under clause 25.4.5.2 leading to an extension of time and become a 'matter' under clause 26.2.2 giving rise to a claim for reimbursement of loss and expense.

Any instruction of the Architect issued under clause 8.3 requiring opening up or testing must, therefore, receive particular consideration in order that the formal notices, particulars and estimates are given at the proper time to satisfy the requirements of clauses 25 and 26. Of course, no extension of time will be granted or loss and expense reimbursed if the inspection or test shows that the workmanship, materials and goods did **not** comply with the Contract Documents.

Removal of materials, etc.

Clause 8.4   The Architect may by an instruction under clause 8.4 require that any materials and goods or workmanship be removed from the site if such materials and goods or workmanship do not comply with the description or specification appearing in the Contract Documents, as amended by the subsequent issue of any instructions of the Architect. The latter point must be implied into this clause, otherwise the Architect would not appear to have the right to order the removal of materials and goods or workmanship properly ordered by an instruction of the Architect, and this is illogical. Needless to say, the costs of removing defective materials and goods or workmanship are not reimbursed to the Contractor.

Although it may appear logical, the failure of an inspection or test ordered under clause 8.3 is not a pre-requisite to the issue of instructions for removal. There does not seem to be any restriction on the timing of the issue of such instructions by the Architect. It would appear that only the issue of the Final Certificate could prevent the Architect from issuing instructions for removal of materials and goods or workmanship.

In the event of a dispute as to whether or not the materials and goods or workmanship are in accordance with the Contract Documents, the only recourse open to the Contractor would seem to be arbitration. This point is not one upon which there is immediate arbitration. The Contractor must comply with the instructions of the Architect and preserve the evidence for eventual examination by an Arbitrator.

The failure of the Contractor to remove defective work or improper materials after an instruction of the Architect to do so and after the requisite notice in writing under clause 4.2 could lead to determination of the employment of the Contractor by the Employer under clause 27.

Removal of persons

Clause 8.5   Clause 8.5 empowers the Architect to instruct the exclusion of any person employed upon the Works. The definition of 'person' in clause 1.3 should be ignored for the purpose of this clause since it is believed that the exclusion forming the opening words of clause 1.3 ('unless the context otherwise requires...') is to be implied here. If this is the case, the clause would then only refer to people employed upon the Works which would seem to be the intention.

The Architect may instruct that any person be excluded from the Works. This means that the Contractor may continue to employ the person, but not upon the Works.

The present clause does not specify any reasons that would provoke the Architect into issuing instructions requiring exclusion of persons. Presumably it is to ensure that the Contractor only employs upon the Works competent workpeople capable of producing the standard of workmanship required by the Architect and to give the Architect some remedy if the Contractor does not do so.

There does not appear to be any provision in the Conditions enabling the Contractor to dispute the instructions of the Architect other than the tedious procedure prescribed under clause 4.2 and the arbitration agreement.

The right of the Architect to require the exclusion of workpeople from the Works is not apparently limited to those employed by the Contractor. Where the instruction of the Architect is in regard to a person employed by a Nominated Sub- Contractor, such an instruction is passed on to the sub-contractor under the provisions of clause 4.2 of Sub-Contract NSC/4. The Nominated Sub-Contractor is required to comply with the instruction under clause 4.3 of Sub-Contract NSC/4 which incorporates the similar disputes procedures available to the Contractor under the main contract.

ROYALTIES AND PATENT RIGHTS

Clause 9
There are two distinct methods of dealing with royalties and patent rights and these are set out in clause 9, where the text is identical to the 1963 Edition.

Firstly, where the sums are payable in respect of royalties and the like that occur as a result of the pricing of items in the bills of quantities (eg patented scaffolding systems), the Contractor is to allow for them in his tender. The Contractor is further required to indemnify the Employer against any claims that may be made against him.

Secondly, where sums become payable in respect of royalties and the like as a consequence of instructions of the Architect such charges are to be refunded to the Contractor by including the amounts concerned in the final adjusted Contract Sum, clause 30.6.2.10. The Conditions assume that the Architect will know when royalties and patent rights are involved since there is no requirement for the Contractor to inform either the Architect or Employer that such a situation exists.

PERSON-IN-CHARGE

Clause 10
The Contractor is required by clause 10 to keep a person-in-charge constantly upon the Works. Apart from the change in name to the neutral 'person-in-charge', the text is similar to the 1963 Edition. His sole function under the Conditions is to receive instructions of the Architect and directions of the clerk of works. Strangely, there is no requirement for the person to be named by notice to the Architect, although it would be courteous for the Contractor to do so upon the commencement of the Works on site. This clause means that instructions given by the Architect when he is on the site and directions given by the clerk of works can **only** be given to the person-in-charge. The Architect is not prevented from sending his instructions to the head office of the Contractor.

ACCESS FOR ARCHITECT

Clause 11
The rights of the Architect to enter upon the site and the Works are described in clause 11. This provision is necessary because the Contractor has been given exclusive possession of the site. The text is essentially the same as the 1963 Edition.

The Architect may also have access to the premises of both Nominated and Domestic Sub-Contractors but, strangely, not the premises of suppliers. No reference is made to any right of the Employer to enter upon the site.

CLERK OF WORKS

Clause 12 The right of the Employer to appoint a clerk of works is established by clause 12. The text is the same as the 1963 Edition and this regretfully fails to deal with the reality of the situation found upon building sites.

The sole duty of the clerk of works under the Conditions is to act as an inspector of the Works executed by the Contractor. In carrying out this function, the clerk of works is responsible to the Employer but acts under the direction of the Architect. He is **not** a representative of the Architect. The clerk of works may give directions to the Contractor, but these are of no effect until they have been confirmed in writing by the Architect, whereupon they become instructions of the Architect. Unconfirmed directions of the clerk of works may be disregarded by the Contractor with impunity.

The Conditions require that confirmation by the Architect of a direction of the clerk of works must be issued within two days of the direction being given. The direction of the clerk of works becomes an instruction of the Architect upon the date of issue by the confirmation by the Architect. The Contractor does not know that date until he receives the confirmation. The Conditions do not state what is to happen if the confirmation is given more than two days after the issue of the direction. Presumably the Architect could issue his own instruction in the same terms at any time and all would be well, except that in this case the operative date is receipt of the instruction by the Contractor.

The JCT has not made provision in JCT 80 for any powers of the Architect to be delegated to the clerk of works. There seems to be no obvious difficulty in allowing the clerk of works to issue instructions for certain matters, and to carry out some of the functions of the Architect in supervising the Works that presently are state to be the exclusive authority of the Architect.

If any delegation of the authority of the Architect to the clerk of works is required by the contracting parties then some amendment to the Conditions would be required, for which the relevant clauses of Form GC/Works/1 or the ICE General Conditions could be the starting point.

FAIR WAGES

The only reference in JCT 80 to the question of industrial relations appears in clause 19A of the Local Authorities Editions. The basis of clause 19A is the 'Fair Wages Resolution' passed by the House of Commons on 14th October, 1946 and much of that resolution is reproduced verbatim in clause 19A.

Clause 19A The Contractor is required – in effect – to pay rates of wages not less than those prescribed in the National Working Rule Agreement (NWRA) of the National Joint Council for the Building Industry (NJCBI), to recognise that his employees may be members of trade unions, and to display copies of clause 19A upon the Works and other places. The Contractor is made responsible (clause 19A.6) for ensuring that clause 19A is also observed by his sub-contractors. Many sub-contractors will not be concerned with the NWRA of NJBCI. They will have their own wage fixing agreements that would satisfy the requirements of clause 19A.

Clause 19A.7 and 19A.8 require the Contractor to keep records of wages paid to his employees and make them available to the Employer if required to prove the wages paid and to demonstrate the conditions of employment of his employees.

No remedy is given in clause 19A should the employer find that the Contractor is not complying. However, the Employer is given the right to determine the employment of the Contractor under clause 27 subject to the proper notice requirements of that clause.

Postscript to clause 6.1 – compliance with Statutory Requirements

Where the contractor has complied with clauses 6.1.2 and 6.1.3 – that is to say, he has identified a divergence between the Statutory Requirements and the Contract Documents or an instruction of the Architect; has given notice to the Architect; and has executed the work in accordance with those instructions – the Contractor may not be responsible to the Employer for work not in compliance with the Statutory Requirements.

BUT THE CONTRACTOR MAY HAVE A LIABILITY TO OTHERS.

In the case between *Anns and London Borough of Merton*, it was suggested in the House of Lords that the builder had a duty to comply with Building Regulations and that, quite apart from any question of negligence, a claim could be made against the builder for breach of that statutory duty. That proposition has been followed in the more recent case between *Eames London Estates Limited and Others and North Hertfordshire District Council and Others* concerning defective foundations to some warehouse buildings. A specialist contractor responsible for the design and construction of the concrete frame (including the foundations) was found liable for damages in consequence of his breach of statutory duty to comply with bye-laws and in negligence for the breach of his duty of care to the then owners of the buildings and their tenants. The specialist contractor was not wholly liable; on the facts of that particular case the original developer, the Architect, and the local authority shared liability. An important point to stress is neither of these cases involved the original client or Employer; in each case the contractor was found to be liable to a subsequent purchaser.

The two cases referred to in the preceding paragraph do not seem to have been concerned with contracts in the terms of the Standard Form of Building Contract but it is thought that the principles would be followed were a Standard Form case to arise on similar facts since in these consumer conscious times the courts are looking for a stricter standard of liability to owners and tenants than has hitherto been the case. In view of this development in the law it is questionable whether the apparent indemnity given to the Contractor by clause 6.1.5 is of great value. Under Common Law one cannot by the terms of a contract 'contract out' of compliance with a statutory duty and this may be a factor in guiding the courts to these conclusions.

The Contractor must therefore ensure that his management systems are able to identify proposed work that will **not** comply with Statutory Requirements. Failure to do so will remove any protection given by clause 6.1.5 and may leave the Contractor exposed to the risks of claims from the Employer alleging negligence for failure to identify a divergence from the Statutory Requirements and from subsequent purchasers and other alleging breach of statutory duty and duty of care.

The time for the Work

Under the Conditions, the Contractor undertakes to carry out the Works to an agreed timetable. In this Section the nature of that undertaking will be examined. The basic obligation to commence and complete the Works is set out in clause 23 (Date of Possession, completion and postponement); the consequence of failure to complete is in clause 24 (Damages for non-completion); the procedure for extending the Completion Date (thus relieving the Contractor from the liability to pay damages to the Employer) is set out in clause 25 (Extension of time) and the obligation to complete the whole of the Works may be mitigated by the operation of clause 18 (Partial possession by the Employer). The actual event of completion of the Works and the consequences of that event is dealt with in clause 17 (Practical Completion and Defects Liability).

POSSESSION AND COMPLETION

The dates for possession and completion

Clause 23
The agreed contractual timetable comprising the dates for possession and completion is introduced in clause 23 and the text is essentially the same as in the 1963 Edition. The Date of Possession entered into the Appendix is the date upon which the contract period commences, whether or not the Contractor actually commences on that date. The Contractor should beware of falling into the trap of agreeing a Date of Possession that does not allow sufficient time for proper preplanning of the work so that he is unable to make an effective start upon the Date of Possession. The Date of Possession must be settled so that there is sufficient time for planning, for the appointment of sub-contractors, for the procurement of materials and plant, for the recruitment or reallocation of labour and for the mobilisation of these resources onto the site.

Clause 23.1
Clause 23.1 provides for the Contractor to begin the work on the Date of Possession and then to 'regularly and diligently proceed' with the Works, achieving Practical Completion not later than the Completion date. There is no prohibition on finishing the work early. It is believed that the Architect may certify Practical Completion even if it is earlier than the Completion Date. Similarly, it would seem that the Employer may take responsibility for the Works at that time, although presumably the Architect could issue instructions requiring the Contractor to continue to provide security services and other facilities such as insurances against Clause 22 Perils.

The definition of Completion Date includes any extension of time granted under clause 25 and there is, therefore, no necessity to repeat that fact in the present clause. The failure of the Contractor to proceed with the Works regularly and diligently could lead ultimately to determination of the employment of the Contractor by the Employer, see clause 27.1. The consequences of the failure of the Contractor to complete by the Completion Date are dealt with in clause 24.

Postponement of any part of the Works

Clause 23.2
By clause 23.2 the Architect is empowered to issue instructions requiring the Contractor to postpone the carrying out of any part of the Works. Such a postponement could become both a 'Relevant Event' (clause 25.4.5.1), so qualifying for the award of an extension of time; and a 'matter' (clause 26.2.5) which may lead to a claim by the Contractor for reimbursement of loss and expense. The extent to which the Architect is entitled to issue instructions to postpone is not limited in the Conditions; presumably the Architect

would be entitled to postpone the whole of the Works.

Should the whole of the Works be postponed, or should a large enough part of the Works be postponed so that execution of the remainder of the Works becomes impracticable, then the Contractor may become entitled under clause 28.1.3.4 to determine his own employment under the Contract. The right of the Contractor to determine his own employment comes into effect when the period during which he is unable to work exceeds the period of delay (recommended to be one month) entered in the Appendix against the item 28.1.3.4. (See notes on clause 28, page 140).

Failure of the Employer to give possession

The Conditions do not seem to deal clearly with the situation where the Employer does not give the Contractor possession of the site on the Date of Possession.

Where the Architect issues an instruction postponing the whole of the Works, all would seem to be well. If the postponement is of short duration, then clauses 25 and 26 seem to deal with the situation adequately. If the postponement is of longer duration and the Contractor has determined under clause 28, then the Contractor need not commence the Works if he does not so wish. The Employer could agree to reimburse the Contractor for the loss and expense incurred and arising from the delayed start, but new Contract Documents would be required to be executed between the parties in this situation incorporating the new Contract Sum and the revised Date of Possession and Completion Date.

Where the Employer does not give the Contractor possession of the site and there is no instruction of the Architect, then the Contractor must give written notice to the Employer sent recorded delivery or registered post with a copy to the Architect. Such notice should:-

★ confirm that on the Date of Possession the Contractor was not given possession of the site

★ request that the Employer grant possession of the site to the Contractor forthwith

★ inform the Employer that if such possession is not granted then the Contractor will consider the contract to have been rescinded by the Employer and reserve the right to claim damages.

The proceedings to be taken by the Contractor are for breach of contract by the Employer and will probably be pursued through the High Court.

EXTENSION OF TIME

Clause 25 Extension of time to complete the Works is granted to the Contractor by the Architect when a new Completion Date is fixed under the provisions of clause 25. This clause has been completely rewritten by comparison with the 1963 Edition.

Clause 25 may well be more favourable to builders than the similar provisions in the 1963 Edition, but this has only been achieved by the inclusion of detailed procedures of some complexity. The Contractor must take care not to lose his right to an extension of time by reason of any failure to administer those procedures precisely.

The introduction of JCT 80 provides the opportunity for all builders to initiate a review of their management techniques and disciplines for the identification of all incidents that are or may become Relevant Events. The review should include a critical examination of the administrative procedures required under JCT80 so as to ensure that no stage is overlooked.

The ability to promptly and accurately analyse any incident and allocate it to a particular Relevant Event is important for the Conditions seem to require the Contractor to specify in notices to the Architect a ground that appears in clause 25.4. It does not seem to be sufficient to merely describe the delay as a 'Relevant Event' under clause 25 using a blanket approach. As will be seen in the discussion on clause 25.2.3 (page 44), the Contractor is obliged to revise all notices and there would seem to be no reason why such a revision notice should not include a correction to the identification of the Relevant Event specified in an earlier notice.

Generally

Clause 25.1 It is made plain in clause 25.1 that there is no limit to the number of occasions that delays, notices and awards of extension of time can occur.

The obligation to give notice

Clause 25.2.1 The Contractor is to give notice to the Architect upon the happening of any incident that is delaying or is likely to delay the progress of the Works. Note that the word used here is **'progress'** of the Works; not **completion** of the Works. Such notice is to be given to the Architect 'forthwith' and must contain '...the material circumstances including the cause or causes of the delay...' and, if the incident is a Relevant Event, the notice must specify the same. There is no explanation of the word 'forthwith' but failure of the Architect to award an extension of time could in due course come before an Arbitrator where the question of the timing of the issue of the notice by the Contractor would be heard. The Architect does not seem to be required to inform the Contractor that he does not intend to recognise and act upon the notice by the Contractor.

Under the Conditions the Contractor is required to give notice to the Architect of any incident that is or is likely to affect the progress of the Works. It matters not whether the incident is a Relevant Event. The purpose of this requirement is to ensure that the Architect can keep the Employer informed of the progress of the Works and the likely date of practical completion.

Where the incident concerns a Nominated Sub-Contractor, the Contractor is to send a copy of the notice to the Nominated Sub-Contractor.

Particulars and estimates

Clause 25.2.2   Where the notice is in respect of an incident that is a Relevant Event, the Contractor is required to submit to the Architect certain additional information. The additional information may be either in the notice concerned or must be given '...as soon as possible...' thereafter. The Contractor is required to submit '...particulars of the expected effects...' of the Relevant Event on the progress of the Works and to '...estimate the extent, if any, of the expected delay in the completion of the Works beyond the (then) Completion Date...'. This latter point is qualified to the extent that the information must be given in relation to each incident that is a Relevant Event, without regard to a concurrent Relevant Event. The effect of this qualification is presumed to be that in regard to each notice particulars and estimate, such particulars and estimate must be in relation to the then Completion Date. This means that upon the Award of each and every extention of time, the estimates (of delay in the completion of the Works) for all other Relevant Events currently in the hands of the Architect must be revised, since the Completion Date upon which each estimate was based will have changed. Where in the opinion of the Architect, the effect of any particular Relevant Event does not warrant the fixing of a new Completion Date since it is concurrent with another Relevant Event, some adjustment of other estimates of delay currently being considered by the Architect may also be required.

Where any particulars and estimate concern a Nominated Sub-Contractor then the Contractor is required to send a copy of those particulars and estimate to the Nominated Sub-Contractor.

The requirement for the Contractor to estimate the extent of the delay in the completion of the Works is new. This should not cause any difficulty to an experienced Contractor for he will be used to assessing these periods for his own management purposes. Even if the Contractor does get it wrong, clause 25.2.3 comes to his aid.

Revising notices, particulars and estimates

Clause 25.2.3   The Contractor is required by clause 25.2.3 to revise his notices, particulars and estimates in respect of each Relevant Event '...as may be reasonably necessary...' by the submission of such further written notices as are necessary to keep the Architect informed of the up to date position. Obviously, the Contractor will want to revise his notices, particulars and estimates in any case when there has been any material change in the information already given. There would seem to be no reason why a correction of information previously given should not be included in the further written notices.

The Architect is entitled to specify any other requirements of himself or of the Employer for the submission of further written notices. For example, the Architect could require the Contractor to submit notices monthly in regard to each Relevant Event, giving any revised information or confirming that there has been no change since submission of the original notice.

Notices

There appears to be at least three types of notice that the Contractor is required to give the Architect where progress of the Works or completion of the works is being or is likely to be delayed:-

(a) Where there is a delay, but it is not a Relevant Event (ie in the comparatively rare instances where the Contractor admits to being in error). Such notice should be sent to the Architect and should:-

★ state that progress of the Works is being or is likely to be delayed

★ give an explanation of the circumstances or causes of the delay, with, if appropriate, a note of the steps being taken to eliminate or mitigate the causes

★ confirm that the Contractor is using, and will continue to use, his best endeavours to prevent or avoid delay to the completion of the Works.

(b) Where there is a delay in progress of the Works or completion of the Works and the cause is a Relevant Event. Such notice should be sent to the Architect and should:-

★ state that progress of the Works is being or is likely to be delayed

★ give an explanation (one paragraph) of the circumstances or causes of the delay

★ state that in the opinion of the Contractor such matters are a Relevant Event and will cause delay in the completion of the Works

★ specify the Relevant Event

★ (if possible) give particulars of the effects on the progress of the Works, or

★ inform the Architect that particulars of the effects will be given as soon as possible

★ (if possible) give an estimate of the extent of the delay in completion of the Works, or

★ inform the Architect that the estimate of the delay in the completion of the Works will be given as soon as possible

★ (where the particulars and estimate have been given) request that the Architect confirm that the particulars and estimate are sufficient for him to form an opinion on the matter

★ (where the particulars and estimate have been given) request that the Architect grant an extension of time by fixing a later Completion Date

★ confirm that the Contractor is using, and will continue to use, his best endeavours to mitigate the potential delay to the completion of the Works

★ (if appropriate) give a brief explanation of the steps being taken to mitigate the delay.

Where there is any doubt as to the ability of the Contractor to provide either or both the particulars of the effects and the estimate of the delay, then the Contractor **must** give the notice without the associated particulars and estimate. This is because the notice is required to be given 'forthwith', whereas the particulars and estimate may be given later. Not much later – '...as soon as possible...' are the words used in clause 25.2.2.

(c) Where the Contractor chooses or is required to inform the Architect of the up-to-date position in regard to a previously presented notice, particulars and estimate. Such notice should be sent to the Architect and should:-

★ refer to the previously submitted notice, particulars and estimate

★ (if appropriate) give a brief note of any changes in the circumstances or causes previously given

★ (where there has been a change in the circumstances or causes) give a revised estimate of the delay in the completion of the Works

★ confirm to the Architect that there has been no change in the circumstances or causes and that, therefore, the previously submitted estimate of the delay in the completion of the Works remains unchanged.

Duty of Architect to consider notices

Clause 25.3   The Architect is obliged by clause 25.3 to consider the notices, particulars and estimates given by the Contractor and to award a proper extension of time. Where the Architect is satisfied with the sufficiency of each notice, and with the associated particulars of the effects and estimate of the delay, he must give his opinion and fix a new Completion Date or not (as the case may be) within 12 weeks of receipt of each notice, particulars and estimate. The requirement for the Architect to award an extension of time to a predetermined timetable is one of the major improvements for the Contractor in JCT 80.

The twelve week period only begins when the Architect is satisfied that he has sufficient information to enable him to form an opinion as to the merits of the request of the Contractor. Builders must be alive to the possibility that the Architect may seek to disrupt the programme of events by pleading that he has insufficient information. Hence the need, when submitting any particulars of the effects and estimate of delay, to request the Architect to confirm that the details given are sufficient. Where no such confirmation is given and the Architect does not request any further information, it would be difficult for the Architect to argue that the time during which he has to form an opinion had not begun on the date of receipt of the particulars and estimate.

Before the Architect can award any extension of time, he must be satisfied that each notice, particulars of effects and estimate of delay is in regard to an event that **is a Relevant Event** and that **completion** of the Works is likely to be delayed beyond the then Completion Date. The Conditions are silent as to what happens when, after considering the information given to him by the Contractor, the Architect decides that the event is not a Relevant Event or that there will be no delay in completion of the Works. There is no requirement for the Architect to inform the Contractor of his opinion in these circumstances. For the Contractor to wait twelve weeks and then discover by default that the Architect has rejected the plea of the Contractor is most unsatisfactory.

The introduction of a timetable for the award has various consequences. For example, the Architect may well be required to award an extension of time to the Contractor before the actual delay has occurred. Since the Architect in his final review of extension of time cannot reduce the award already granted (see clause 25.3.3 page 47) it is clear that the Architect will tend to be naturally cautious in making his initial award. While the effect of an over-cautious extension of time can be corrected withhout serious difficulty, the same is not true where a parallel claim for reimbursement of loss and expense is being pursued and the Contractor must be aware of the possibility that recovery of loss and expense could be curtailed because of the caution of the Architect. Again, the industry is used historically to receiving awards of extension of time that equate to the difference between the original Date of Completion entered in the Contract Documents and the actual date of Practical Completion. The introduction of a timetable for the award of extension of time means that the extensions must be awarded on the merits of each case as entitlements of the Contractor under the Conditions, not related solely to the time required to relieve the Contractor of his liability to pay damages to the Employer, thus making it perfectly possible for the Contractor to complete the Works prior to the (extended) Completion Date.

Award of extension of time

The award of extension of time by the Architect must be given in writing and should contain details of the Relevant Events taken into account when making the award. This is important because the ability of the Contractor to make a claim for reimbursement of loss and expense in respect of the 'matters' listed in clause 26 seems in certain circumstances to be dependent upon the award of extension of time. Particulars must also be given in the award where there has been a reduction of the extension of time that would otherwise have been awarded because of any omission from the Works.

The obligation of the Architect to give his opinion within twelve weeks of receipt of the notice etc. by the Contractor, does not apply where the notice of the Contractor is received by the Architect within twelve weeks of the then Completion Date. In such a case the Architect must give his opinion and must make his award not later than the Completion Date. This qualification is necessary because, where Practical Completion is not achieved by the Completion Date, the Contractor is automatically in default under clause 24 and may be liable to pay or allow damages to the Employer. The effect is to ensure that the Architect is prevented from issuing a certificate of non-completion under clause 24 until he has considered and given his award on all the notices, etc., submitted by the Contractor.

Effect of omissions

Clause 25.3.2 Under clause 25.3.2 the Architect may fix an **earlier** Completion Date than that previously notified to the Contractor where, in the opinion of the Architect, it is reasonable to do so because of instructions of the Architect requiring omissions of any work causing an effect on the progress of the Works. The Architect can only fix an earlier Completion Date if the instructions requiring the omissions have been issued after the most recent award of extension of time. The Architect cannot take into account instructions requiring omissions of work issued before the most recent award of extension of time.

In other words, on each occasion the Architect makes an award of extension of time to the Contractor, that award **must** take into account all instructions requiring omissions of work issued by the Architect since he last made an award of extension of time.

Clause 25.3.6 prevents the Architect from fixing a Completion Date that is earlier than the Completion Date entered in the Appendix.

The Architect does not seem to be required to notify the Contractor **in writing** that an earlier Completion Date has been fixed under this clause. Presumably this is a drafting error that will be corrected in the next revision of JCT 80.

Final review of extensions awarded

Clause 25.3.3 All extensions of time awarded are subject to a final review by the Architect under the powers given to him in clause 25.3.3. The review must be completed within twelve weeks after Practical Completion of the Works and the decisions of the Architect are required to be given to the Contractor in writing. The review is conducted by the Architect without any further representations by the Contractor and he is permitted to make various decisions.

Firstly, the Architect may fix a later Completion Date if in his opinion it is reasonable to do so. In formulating his opinion he is required to review his previous decisions relating to awards of extension of time for Relevant Events. This could presumably mean that where the actual delay for any particular Relevant Event is greater than the Contractor and Architect anticipated it would be, then some further extension of time can be awarded. The Architect is **not** entitled to fix an earlier Completion Date even if the actual delay is less than that previously anticipated by the Contractor and the Architect. Strangely, clause 25.3.3 also gives the Architect the right, not only to review his previous awards, but also to award extension of time for other Relevant Events where no extension of time has previously been awarded, whether or not the Contractor has notified the Architect under the procedures already described. The Contractor should not place too much reliance on this provision!

Secondly, the Architect may fix an earlier Completion Date where, since he last made an award of extension of time, there have been omissions of work that reasonably justify an earlier Completion Date. However, clause 25.3.6 prevents the Architect from fixing a new Completion Date that is earlier than the Date for Completion set out in the Appendix.

Finally, the Architect may decide that there are no grounds for changing the Completion Date previously fixed. In this case the Architect is required to confirm to the Contractor the Completion Date previously fixed.

Contractor to prevent or avoid delay

Clause 25.3.4   Clause 25.3.4 contains two important provisos to the whole question of delays and extensions of time. Firstly, the Contractor must constantly use '...his best endeavours...' to prevent delay in both progress of the Works and completion of the Works and, secondly, the Contractor must, to the satisfaction of the Architect, '...do all that may reasonably be required...' to proceed with the Works.

Where delays in progress or completion are due to failures by the Contractor, then the extent, and therefore the cost, of 'best endeavours' and 'all that may reasonably be required' to expedite progress and to ensure completion by the Completion Date must be balanced against the amount of liquidated and ascertained damages that may become due to the Employer and the preliminary costs that will be incurred by the Contractor in the event of his failure to complete by the Completion Date.

Where delays are due to Relevant Events and extensions of time are anticipated or have been awarded, then different considerations apply and the question of what constitutes 'best endeavours' and 'all that may reasonably be required' become a matter of concern to the Employer and the Architect as well as the Contractor. The point here is that where the Architect is of the opinion that the Contractor is not doing his best to avoid or mitigate the delay, then the Architect will be inclined to limit his initial award of extension of time and would be disinclined to be more generous to the Contractor in his review after Practical Completion. Presumably, the Contractor could ask the Architect what is expected of him in any particular situation. In either case, minor adjustments to the labour resources employed upon the Works and, perhaps, reprogramming would be expected. What is not in order is any significant expenditure on, say, overtime or additional plant resources unless, of course, the Architect and/or the Employer make some firm agreement with the Contractor that the additional costs are to be reimbursed. An instruction of the Architect is not good enough in these circumstances, since an instruction to accelerate the execution of the Works does not seem to fall within the powers of the Architect under the Conditions. Neither do clauses 13 (Variations and provisional sums) and 30 (Certificates and payments) appear to permit such additional costs to be taken into Valuations and the final adjusted Contract Sum.

Nominated Sub-Contractors

Clause 25.3.5　　The Architect is required by clause 25.3.5 to inform **every** Nominated Sub- Contractor of **every** decision he makes where a new Completion Date is fixed. No discretion is given, even in the case of a piling sub-contractor finished in the first month and no longer interested in the original Date for Completion, let alone any later Completion Date.

Disputing the award of the Architect

In the event of disagreement between the Contractor and the Architect in regard to delays and extension of time the arbitration agreement permits immediate arbitration on a number of matters, including those covered by clause 25. The text of the arbitration agreement is drafted so widely that **any** dispute or difference falling within the matters covered by clause 25 may be the subject of immediate arbitration. Such disputes can include (but obviously are not limited to) many of the points raised earlier, for example:-

★ has the notice been given at the right time?

★ is the incident a Relevant Event?

★ has the Relevant Event caused (will it cause?) delay in the completion of the Works?

★ have the particulars of the effects and estimates of delay been given in good time?

★ are they sufficient to enable the Architect to award an extension of time?

★ is the award reasonable?

★ is the final review of the Architect reasonable?

Relevant Events

Clause 25.4　　The Relevant Events are set out in detail in clause 25.4. There are three new Relevant Events, otherwise they are the same in principle as those of the 1963 Edition.

Table V gives a brief description of each Relevant Event and some explanatory notes applicable to the new and changed items.

Table V Clause	Brief description and comments
25.4.1	'force majeure'.
25.4.2	'exceptionally adverse weather conditions'. Revised to make it clear that any weather preventing the execution of work qualifies for extension of time.

(Table V continues overleaf)

49

(Table V continued)

25.4.3	'loss or damage...by...Clause 22 Perils'.
	Loss or damage caused by fire, etc., irrespective of whether the Contractor or the Employer carries the risk of such damage.
25.4.4	'...strike(s)...affecting...the trades employed upon the Works...or...engaged in the ...manufacture...of...materials...for the Works'.
	The scope of this clause would appear to incorporate labour employed or engaged by sub-contractors and suppliers.
25.4.5.1 and 25.4.5.2	'compliance with...Architects instruction...' etc.
	The opening words 'compliance with' are new and presumably have been included to make it clear that the Contractor has to carry out the instructions before becoming entitled to an extension of time.
	The Conditions listed in clause 25.4.5.1 specifying the instructions of the Architect for which an extension of time may be awarded has lengthened by including, particularly, instructions issued in regard to Nominated Sub-Contractors, Nominated Suppliers and antiquities.
25.4.6	'the Contractor not having received in due time...instructions, drawings, details or levels...for which he specifically applied in writing...' etc.
	In order to qualify under this clause for extension of time, it would appear that requests must specifically have been made for each snippet of information in each particular case. To have shown the dates by which information is required upon the 'master programme' or upon an 'information required schedule' is not sufficient to satisfy the requirements of this clause. Written application must be made in each case.
	When discussing the master programme earlier in this paper (clause 5.3.2, page 30) reference was made to the effect of incorporating 'float' within the master programme of the Contractor. Since the lateness or otherwise of receipt of the information correctly requested from the Architect is measured against the Completion Date (that is to say, the Date for Completion given in the Appendix or such later date as may be fixed by the Architect under clause 25), it will be obvious that any extended period of float within the master programme could seriously distort the effect of the late receipt of information etc. This would clearly be to the disadvantage of the Contractor in that the Architect would be prejudicing the possibility of early completion by the Contractor. On the other hand, once the Architect has taken advantage of any float within the programme of Contractor, the intrinsic benefit of that float to both the Contractor and the Architect has disappeared.
25.4.7	'delay on the part of Nominated Sub-Contractors or Nominated Suppliers...' etc
	This clause entitles the Contractor to an extension of time for any delay resulting from the operations of Nominated Sub-Contractors irrespective of the reason for that delay. The only apparent qualification is that the Contractor must have '...taken all practicable steps to avoid or reduce...' the delay. In the case of Nominated Sub-Contractors this presumably means the Contractor must have administered the nominated sub-contract properly, monitored progress and identified any delays, made representations to the sub-contractor to improve the situation, etc. The Contractor may endeavour to re-programme the Works to accommodate an errant sub-contractor, but is not required to incur any additional expense by, say, the loan of labour or plant, unless, of course, the sub-contractor has undertaken to meet the cost of these additional resources.

(Table V continues overleaf)

(Table V continued)

25.4.8.1	**'the execution of work...by the Employer...' etc.** Revised to make it clear the **work** to be carried out determines whether it comes under clause 29 and the present clause; not **who** actually executes the work. Extension of time may be awarded where the employees and contractors of the Employer carrying out that work cause delay in the remainder of the Works.
25.4.8.2	**'the supply by the Employer of materials...' etc.** A new provision applicable where in the Contract Documents the Employer has agreed to supply some or all of the materials for the Works and such supply causes delay in the remainder of the Works.
25.4.9	**'the exercise after the Date of Tender by the...government of any statutory power...' etc.** An entirely new provision anticipating imposition by government of some new draconian power that will affect the carrying out of the Works. Extensions of time may be awarded where such powers have affected the '...availability or use of labour...' (eg a wage freeze) or the supply of materials, goods, fuels or energy.
25.4.10.1	**'the Contractor's inability...to secure...labour...' etc.**
25.4.10.2	**'the Contractor's inability...to secure...goods or materials...' etc.** Unchanged from the 1963 Edition, but no longer optional clauses. The important qualifications remain; the reasons must be beyond the control of the Contractor and unforeseeable. Extensions of time awarded under this clause do not appear to entitle the Contractor to additional payment under any other Condition. Care should therefore be exercised before using this clause, for it may be that, for example, a change from direct labour to a sub-contractor, or a change of supplier, is less expensive in the long run.
25.4.11	**'the carrying out by a local authority or statutory undertaker of work in pursuance of its statutory obligations...' etc.** This clause does not apply where a local authority or statutory undertaker is properly employed as a Nominated Sub-Contractor. While there is no qualification requiring the Contractor to take steps to avoid or reduce the delay, a prudent Contractor would proceed for this purpose as though the local authority or statutory undertaker were a Nominated Sub-Contractor, see clause 25.4.7.
25.4.12	**'failure of the Employer to give...ingress or to egress from the site...' etc.** An entirely new provision dealing with the obligations or requirements of the Employer to which several references have already been made. The words used here are 'ingress' (meaning capacity or right of entrance) and 'egress' (meaning the right or liberty of going out); thus making it clear that this clause is nothing to do with possession of the site but is concerned with land or buildings adjoining the site which are under the control of or are owned by the Employer. Naturally, the question of extensions of time will only arise where a new restriction on access occurs or where a restriction specified in the Contract Bills and presumably accepted by the Contractor is not met by the Employer.

FAILURE TO COMPLETE

Clause 24   Where, notwithstanding the provisions in the Conditions that entitle the Contractor to extensions of time, the Contractor nevertheless fails to complete and hand over the Works to the Employer by the Completion Date, then the Contractor may be called upon to pay or allow liquidated and ascertained damages (damages) to the Employer, in accordance with clause 24. The principles are the same as the 1963 Edition.

Certificate of non-completion

Clause 24.1   Upon the failure of the Contractor to complete by the Completion Date, the Architect must issue a certificate to that effect. The certificate will be issued to the Employer with a copy going to the Contractor. Because of the provisions already described for the award of extensions of time, the Contractor will not be in a position to dispute that certificate since the Architect will already have given his opinion on all the notices, particulars and estimates submitted by the Contractor. Any dispute would, therefore, be on the individual award of extension of time by the Architect, **not** on the certificate of non-completion issued by the Architect.

Right of Employer to damages

Clause 24.2   The right of the Employer to damages is contained in clause 24.2.1. Although issue by the Architect of a certificate of non-completion is a condition precedent to deduction of damages, the Employer may at any time up to the issue of the Final Certificate waive his right to claim damages. Whether the Employer wishes to exercise his right to claim damages, or to waive that right, he is required to inform the Contractor in writing of his intentions. The Conditions do not appear to prohibit the Employer from changing his mind about exercising his right to claim damages. If the Employer is to deduct an amount for damages from the amount due in an Interim Certificate or the Final Certificate, then presumably, (the Conditions do not say), the written statement of his intention so to do must be given by the Employer and received by the Contractor before the date on which payment is due under that certificate.

Where a deduction for damages has been made by the Employer, then he is required by the provisions of clause 30.1.1.3 to '...inform the Contractor in writing of the reason for that deduction...'. No timetable is given for the issue of that explanation; for example, that it should accompany the payment by the Employer.

Where there is extended delay, it is assumed that the Architect would issue a series of certificates of non-completion at the time each Interim Certificate is issued, so that the Employer is able to deduct damages progressively if he so wishes. Should it happen that, following the final review of his awards of extension of time after Practical Completion, the Architect fixes a later Completion Date with the result that there would be an over-deduction of damages by the Employer, then clause 24.2.2 provides for repayment to the Contractor of such over-deduction by the Employer.

If the amount of damages due to the Employer exceeds the amount certified to the Contractor in Interim Certificates or the Final Certificate, then such difference becomes a debt due to the Employer. This means the Employer may obtain a summary judgement in the High Court for the recovery of monies due to him.

Where the Employer makes a deduction from the amount due in an Interim Certificate and part of that amount represents retentions, then the Employer may not make a deduction from that portion of the retention that represents retention payable to any Nominated Sub-Contractor, see clause 35.13.5.4.2. Thus, the retentions of Nominated Sub-Contractors remain sacrosanct.

PRACTICAL COMPLETION AND DEFECTS

Clause 17   The important event of Practical Completion, together with the immediate consequences of that event, including the obligation of the Contractor to remedy defects in the Works, is to be found in clause 17. The text is practically identical to the 1963 Edition, the only change meriting comment is that the schedule of defects to be issued by the Architect is to be given to the Contractor as an instruction of the Architect. This means that should the schedule of defects contain contentious matters (for example, defects or faults that in the opinion of the Contractor are not the result of defective workmanship or the use of improper materials) the Contractor is now able to challenge the Architect to demonstrate his authority to issue the instruction (clause 4.2) and to cause such authority to become the subject of arbitration under the arbitration agreement. Since the dispute or difference occurs after Practical Completion, the Contractor would be entitled to immediate arbitration on the point.

Practical Completion

Clause 17.1   Practical Completion is an important event for it marks the end of a number of obligations of the Contractor and the commencement of the timetable for the final adjustment of the Contract Sum (the final account). Table VI attempts to set down some of the matters that are effected by the issue of the certificate of Practical Completion by the Architect.

Table VI Clause	Effect
Article 3	The opening of arbitration proceedings on those disputes not subject to immediate arbitration.
13.2	The end of the obligation of the Contractor to carry out instructions of the Architect except in regard to defects.
17.2 and 17.3	The commencement of the Defects Liability Period.
20, 17.2 and 17.3	The end of the responsibility of the Contractor for loss or damage to the Works except for frost damage occurring before Practical Completion.
22A	The end of the obligation of the Contractor to insure the Works.
24	The end of the liability of Contractor for liquidated and ascertained damages in the event of non-completion by the Completion Date.
30.4	The Retention Percentage applicable in the next Interim Certificate is reduced by one half.
30.6	The commencement of the Period of Final Measurement and the commencement of the period for production by the Contractor of the documents necessary for the final adjustment of the Contract Sum (the final account).

It should be noted at once that although clause 1.3 (definitions) refers users to clause 17.1 for a definition of Practical Completion, no such definition is given there. It is obvious that 'practically complete' must mean something less than wholly complete in every particular; but how much less? Builders could consider the Works to be practically complete when the building owner could, if he so wished, take possession of the building and use it for the purpose for which it is intended. Unfortunately, clause 17.1 does not provide for the Contractor to offer an opinion. The Architect is required to decide when, in his opinion, '...Practical Completion of the Works is achieved...' and then to issue a certificate naming the day upon which Practical Completion was achieved. No special certificate is prescribed for this purpose and any document signed by the Architect and using clear words to state that Practical Completion had been achieved on a specified date would suffice.

It is worth noting that Practical Completion relates to the progress of the Works and is not necessarily linked in any way to the Completion Date. As the certificate of Practical Completion is not related to the Completion Date, its significance concerns the progress of the Works, not the time scale of the programme.

If, in the opinion of the Contractor, the Works have progressed to the point where they are practically complete, or are about to become practically complete, it would be in order for the Contractor to give notice to the Architect to that effect. Such a notice is not a contractual requirement and, if sent, should:-

   ★ state that in the opinion of the Contractor the Works are practically complete, or

   ★ inform the Architect that by a (specified) date the Works will have progressed to the point where they are practically complete

   ★ invite the Architect to inspect the Works should he wish to do so

   ★ request the Architect to issue his certificate naming the date of Practical Completion.

If the Architect does not name the date of Practical Completion and the Contractor is firmly of the opinion that practical completion has been achieved, the only recourse open to the Contractor is to proceed to arbitration. A dispute on this point is one upon which immediate arbitration is permitted, that is to say, Article 5.2.2, a certificate improperly withheld.

Defects Liability Period

The Defects Liability Period commences at the date of Practical Completion. Clause 17.2 contains the obligations of the Contractor to make good defects, etc. in the Works that arise because the quality of materials and standard of workmanship in the Works are not as described in the Contract Documents, or because of the effect of frost occurring before Practical Completion.

The schedule of defects

Clause 17.2   After expiry of the Defects Liability Period the Architect has fourteen days in which to inspect the Works and prepare a schedule of defects. Under the Conditions, the Contractor must **receive** the schedule before the expiry of fourteen days after the end of the Defects Liability Period. Strictly speaking, a schedule of defects received more than fourteen days after the end of the Defects Liability Period is invalid and the Contractor is not required to act upon it.

It is proper for the Contractor to dispute items on the schedule if he feels that they are not the result of defective workmanship or the use of improper materials, eg cracks in plaster at the angle of wall and ceiling, defects arising as the result of improper use of the building, defects due to the effect of frost occurring **after** Practical Completion, etc. In such cases prompt written notice to the Architect must be given. Such notice should:-

★ acknowledge receipt of the schedule of defects

★ request that the Architect agree that certain of the items are not the result of defective workmanship or the use of improper materials

★ schedule the items concerned and give a brief (one sentence) explanation of why they are not, in the opinion of the Contractor, defects requiring rectification under the Conditions

★ (if desired) offer to carry out the necessary remedial work on, for example, a cost reimbursement basis.

It is important to stress that since such defects are not the responsibility of the Contractor, he is not liable under the Conditions to carry out the Work and the Architect cannot issue valid instructions requiring the Contractor to carry out the necessary remedial work.

The Contractor may choose to carry out the work required by the Employer if he so wishes, and it may make good sense for him to do so, depending on the extent of the work required and the relationship between the Contractor and Employer. Where the Contractor does agree to carry out certain additional work required by the Employer, it is important that the financial arrangements for such work be properly agreed with the Employer as an entirely separate transaction not related to the Conditions. This must be so, since the work is outside the scope of the contract. In any event, the Valuation rules of clause 13 would not be an equitable basis upon which to establish the worth of such work.

The Architect is only entitled to issue one schedule of defects. Any second or supplementary lists are not valid documents or instructions under the Conditions and the Contractor is not required contractually to remedy defects contained in any such list.

Making good by the Contractor

The Contractor is required, '...within a reasonable time...' after receipt of the schedule of defects, to make good the items listed in it. What is a reasonable time is left to the Architect. The consequences of failure of the Contractor to make good the defects properly notified to him suggests a further reason why the issue of the schedule has been made an instruction of the Architect. By the powers granted to him in clause 4.1.2, the Architect may give the Contractor a notice requiring that he comply with that instruction. The failure of the Contractor to react to the seven day notice could lead to the Architect or Employer making arrangements for the work to be done by others and, and in such a case, the cost would be deducted by the Employer from any further payments due to the Contractor.

When, in the opinion of the Contractor, the defects have been made good, it would be in order for the Contractor to give notice to the Architect to that effect. Such a notice is not a contractual requirement and, if sent, should:-

★ state that in the opinion of the Contractor the defects listed in the specified schedule issued by the Architect have been made good, or

★ inform the Architect that by a specified date the making good will have been completed

★ invite the Architect to inspect the Works should he wish to do so

★ request that the Architect issue his 'Certificate of Completion of Making Good Defects'.

Defects during Defects Liability Period

Clause 17.3   A further procedure requiring the Contractor to make good defects appears in clause 17.3. In this case, the Contractor is required to make good defects at any time before the end of the Defects Liability Period upon the issue of an appropriate instruction by the Architect. The obligations of the Contractor to comply with the instruction and make good the defects are identical to those outlined in regard to clause 17.2. The provisions described in clause 17.2 that enable the validity of the instruction to be challenged and the content to be disputed apply equally to the present procedure.

There would appear to be no restriction on the timing or frequency of instructions of the Architect issued under this clause, except that none may be issued after delivery of the schedule of defects referred to in clause 17.2, or later than fourteen days after the expiry of the Defects Liability Period.

'Certificate of Completion of Making Good Defects'

Clause 17.4   The Architect is required by clause 17.4 to decide when, in his opinion, the Contractor has completed making good the defects in the schedule of defects (clause 17.2) or in the instructions of the Architect (clause 17.3) and then to issue a 'Certificate of Completion of Making Good Defects'.

The issue of this certificate is important for several reasons concerned with financial matters and the timetable for the final adjustment of the Contract Sum (the final account), is as shown in Table VII.

Table VII Clause	Effect
30.4	The issue of a further Interim Certificate in which the Retention Percentage applicable is 'NIL'
30.6	The end of the period during which the Contractor must produce the documents necessary for the final adjustment of the Contract Sum (the final account)
30.8	The commencement of the Period for issue of the Final Certificate.

It is odd that in clause 17.4 the 'Certificate of Completion of Making Good Defects' is expressly referred to as a formal document and that it is accorded a definition in clause 1.3; whereas in clause 17.1 the certificate of Practical Completion is granted no such formal status and is not given a definition.

Damage by frost

Clause 17.5   In clause 17.5 it is made clear that the Contractor has no responsibility to make good defects caused by the effect of frost occurring after Practical Completion, although he remains responsible for frost damage occurring before Practical Completion.

PARTIAL POSSESSION BY THE EMPLOYER

Clause 18   Partial possession by the Employer is anticipated in clause 18. The text is practically the same as the 1963 Edition, the only significant difference being that the provisions for adjustment and payment of retention now feature in clause 30.

It is strange that this clause should have remained unaltered since it was the subject of criticism in the case between *English Industrial Estates Corporation and George Wimpey and Company Limited.* The House of Lords criticised, in particular, the lack of precision with which the important matter of the actual dates of partial possession are to be established and the absence of any obligation for the Architect to issue a certificate that would authoritatively delineate the part concerned. That criticism was apparently unheeded by the JCT.

Consent by the Contractor

Clause 18.1   Where the Employer expresses a wish to take possession of part of the Works, the Contractor should bear in mind that such a request should only arise where the Contract Documents have been drawn up on the basis of a single completion date. Any pre-arranged partial possessions should properly have been dealt with by using the JCT Sectional Completion Supplement. Accordingly, clause 18.1 provides that partial possession can only occur where the Contractor has given his consent. There would seem to be nothing the Employer can do if the Contractor does not consent. Should it happen that the proposed partial possession would have an effect on the execution of the remainder of the Works, or disturb established access routes (whether or not these were the subject of obligations or restrictions imposed by the Employer in the Contract Bills), then **now** is the time to raise these matters. In any event, it would appear that the Contractor can, to his advantage, give his consent in writing. The consent constitutes a notice and must be sent to the Employer, with a copy to the Architect. Such notice should:-

★ acknowledge the request of the Employer for partial possession

★ express consent in principle to the request of the Employer

★ (if applicable) set out any conditions to which that consent is subject

★ specify precisely the area(s) proposed to be the subject of the partial possession (perhaps by use of a marked up drawing)

★ request that the Employer or Architect give the Contractor a formal receipt for example, for the keys of the part to be taken over and a signed document stating that he has taken over that part of the Works

★ (where applicable) remind the Employer that from the date of partial possession the insurances held by the Contractor against the Clause 22 Perils on the part taken over will cease

★ request that the Employer remind the Architect that he is to issue, within seven days of the date of partial possession, a certificate stating the approximate total value of the part taken over

★ remind the Employer that Interim Certificates issued after the date of partial possession should include a reduced sum for Retention because of the partial possession.

There is no guarantee that a notice to the Employer containing all the above mentioned points will, even if they are all acted upon in good faith, ensure that there will be no problems arising out of a partial possession by the Employer.

Issue of Certificate by the Architect

Clause 18.1.1   The Architect is required by clause 18.1.1 to issue a certificate within seven days of the date of partial possession. The certificate is, strangely, not used to settle authoritatively the date of partial possession, hence the requirement in the notice of consent by the Contractor for a signed document from the Employer giving the date of partial possession. There is no other authority. In fact, the certificate seems only to be required to state the amount of an estimate by the Architect of '...the approximate total value of the relevant part...'. The amount of the estimate is used in due course to calculate the new, lower, amount of Retention held by the Employer in the next Interim Certificate. It is obvious that the approximate total value can only be computed by reference to the amounts included in the interim valuations of the Quantity Surveyor.

Effect of Partial Possession

Clause 18.1.2   By the provisions of clauses 18.1.2 and 18.1.3 the date of any partial possession by
and 18.1.3   the Employer is deemed to be 'Practical Completion' of the relevant part. This enables the procedures on Practical Completion, Defects Liability Period and making good defects detailed in clause 17 and the provisions for reductions of Retention under clause 30 to be applied. However there is no requirement in this clause for the issue of a formal 'Certificate of partial Practical Completion'.

Clause 18.1.4   Where the Contractor has effected insurances under clause 22A and following a partial possession by the Employer, the Contractor is required to reduce the value of the Works covered by such insurances. The amount of the reduction is stated to be '...the full value of the relevant part...' that has been the subject of partial possession. Reference to clause 22A shows that this is the full reinstatement value plus professional fees (if applicable) and the amount concerned is therefore considerably greater than the approximate total value that clause 18 has previously been concerned with. The Contractor would be well advised to consult his insurance broker or his insurer before being committed to any such reduced value.

It is only the insurances under clause 22A that are to be reduced, any other insurances the Contractor may have in effect must remain unaltered. Upon partial possession by the Employer, insurance against Clause 22 Perils on the part taken over is the entire responsibility of the Employer.

Clause 18.1.5   In the event that the Contractor is subsequently in default in handing over a later part or the remainder of the Works, the calculation of the amount of damages that the Contractor may be required to pay or allow to the Employer will be affected by the value of the part handed over.

However, in order to ascertain the new, reduced, amount of damages that would apply, a third calculation of the value of the relevant part has to be made. This time, the amount to be determined is the total value of the relevant part in the original Contract Sum, and the amount of the reduction in damages is in the same proportion as the value of the relevant part is to the Contract Sum.

Indemnities and Insurances

The Contractor is normally liable for the consequences of injury or death to persons and damage to property and is required:

(a) to indemnify the Employer against claims arising from such injury or damage (clause 20)

(b) to effect insurances in respect of certain of the matters for which he has indemnified the Employer (clause 21).

Either the Contractor or the Employer is required to effect insurances against damage to the Works by fire, etc. (clause 22). The text of these clauses has been redrafted by comparison with the 1963 Edition, but there are no significant changes in principle.

The indemnities given by the Contractor and the insurances to be effected are subject to various limitations, the more important of which are now discussed.

INDEMNITIES

Injury to persons

Clause 20.1
By clause 20.1 the Contractor is made totally liable for the consequences of injury, including death, to any person arising out of the execution of the Works and he indemnifies the Employer against any claim arising from such injury. Neither the liability assumed by the Contractor nor the indemnity given to the Employer include injury to persons caused by any act or neglect of the Employer himself, or of '...any person for whom the Employer is responsible...'. Thus, in particular, the Contractor is not responsible for injury to persons caused by act of neglect of '...persons employed or engaged by the Employer...'. In the 1963 Edition such persons were known as artists and tradesmen. The text would seem to be wide enough to exclude injury to persons caused by act or neglect of the Architect, the Clerk of Works and any other consultants employed by the Employer.

Damage to property

Clause 20.2
Similarly, by clause 20.2, the Contractor is made totally liable for the consequences of injury or damage to '...any property real or personal...' belonging to any third party and arising out of the execution of the Works and he indemnifies the Employer against any claims arising from such injury or damage. Neither the liability assumed by the Contractor, nor the indemnity given to the Employer include injury or damage to property that is at the risk of the Employer under clauses 22B or 22C.

A major qualification to the liability of the Contractor (and, therefore, to the indemnity given to the Employer) is that the injury or damage must be due to negligence by the Contractor, his employees, or his sub-contractors. Therefore, injury or damage **not** caused by the negligence of the Contractor is excluded both from the liability of the Contractor and the indemnity given to the Employer. The major areas of risk that would arise in this case (damage to adjoining buildings) may be dealt with by insurance under clause 21.2. There remains, however, an area of potential risk where a claim from a third party may have to be met by the Employer where he has been unable to prove negligence by the Contractor.

The position of the Employer in this case should be contrasted with his position where there has been injury to persons and where, under clause 20.1, the liability remains with the Contractor unless it is proved to be with the Employer.

INSURANCES

Injury to persons; damage to property

Clause 21.1   The Contractor is required by clause 21.1 to effect insurances against specified risks and to assume an obligation to ensure that his sub-contractors are also insured against the same risks. Although the words used in the present clause to describe the insurances required to be effected by the Contractor are the same as the words used in clause 20 to describe the liability assumed by the Contractor and indemnity given to the Employer, the extent to which the risks are to be covered is qualified in clause 21.1.1.2. The principal restriction is monetary, in that (except in the case of injury or death to employees of the Contractor or any sub-contractor) the extent of the indemnity to be given by the insurer is limited to the amount that has been entered in the Appendix.

The purpose of the opening words of clause 21.1.1 'Without prejudice to his liability to indemnify the Employer...' is now apparent. In the case of a very large claim it could be that the insurances, because they are so limited, would not meet the whole loss and the third party or the Employer would then be entitled to claim the balance from the Contractor under the indemnity given in clause 20. This would have to be met by the Contractor from his own resources.

In the event of injury or death to an employee of the Contractor or any sub-contractor, the insured risks must comply with the Employer's Liability (Compulsory Insurance) Act, 1969. That Act clearly lays down that there is no monetary limit on the amount of any claim.

The Conditions anticipate that the specified insurances may in practice be effected by the normal Contractor's All Risks policy held by the Contractor. Such a policy may contain cover for a significantly wider range of risks than are required by the Conditions and may contain a limit of indemnity in excess of that stated in the Appendix. In the event of an insurance claim arising under such a policy, the Employer would receive the benefit of the wider cover and higher indemnity limit.

Proof of insurances

Clause 21.1.2   Either the Employer (Local Authorities Editions) or the Architect (Private Editions) is entitled by clause 21.1.2 to request the Contractor to demonstrate that the insurances required by the Conditions have been effected. Apart from current premium receipt(s), the Conditions do not specify the documents required to confirm that the insurances exist and that the terms are as required by the Conditions. Although the contractual right to request proof of insurances is with the Employer or the Architect, it would seem to be prudent for the Contractor to take the initiative on this point following the acceptance of any tender. A simple notice to the Employer (copy to the Architect) or to the Architect (copy to the Employer) as the case may be would suffice. Such a notice should:-

★ inform the Employer or the Architect that the insurances required by clause 21.1.1.1 are in existence and that the limit of indemnity contained therein is £...........

★ (where possible) forward to the Employer or the Architect a summary of the insurance cover offered by the Contractor

★ forward a copy of the current premium receipt

★ inform the Employer or the Architect where he or his representative may inspect the original insurance policy.

Clause 21.1.3   In the event that the Contractor or any sub-contractor does not effect all or any of the insurances required under clause 21.1.1.1, then clause 21.1.3 permits the Employer to effect such of those insurances as he chooses. The costs incurred by the Employer may be deducted from monies due to the Contractor in Interim Certificates or the Final Certificate. The Employer will only be aware of any default of the Contractor when there has been no affirmative response to a request from the Employer for the Contractor to demonstrate the existence of the insurances. The Contractor will, therefore, know when the Employer is making enquiries and will be aware that failure to effect the insurances could result in the Employer doing so at the cost of the Contractor.

Damage to property other than the Works

Clause 21.2   Certain aspects of potential damage to property other than the Works are not required to be covered by the insurances effected by the Contractor under clause 21.1.1.1. Provision is made in clause 21.2 for the Employer to arrange for the Contractor to effect a further insurance intended to protect the Employer to some extent against claims for damage to property other than the Works that is caused, briefly, by interference with the foundations of adjoining buildings. The range of types of damage that is covered by the insurance and the number of exclusions means that the protection afforded to the Employer is limited.

Such insurances can only be effected where there is a provisional sum in the Contract Bills to cover the cost of such insurance and where the item fully describes the requirements of the Employer. Thus, the Architect must issue an instruction to the Contractor authorising the expenditure of the provisional sum and requiring the insurance to be effected. This arrangement also permits the Employer to change his mind and not have the insurance.

Where there is a provisional sum for clause 21.2 insurances in the bills of quantities, the Contractor must request instructions on this insurance immediately after the award of the contract. There are two reasons for proceeding with this matter with some urgency. Firstly, it is the initial operations of a contract (eg demolition, piling, excavation) that are most likely to cause damage. Secondly, a site inspection must be made by the prospective insurer in order to assess the risks and to settle the amount of the premium required. The request for instructions should be put in a letter to the Architect. Such a letter should:-

★ remind the Architect that there is a provisional sum in the bills of quantities or the Contract Bills for clause 21.2 insurance

★ request an instruction as to whether or not such insurance is required

★ inform the Architect that his instruction must be given urgently if the insurance is to be effected before commencement of the Works

★ inform the Architect of the identity of any proposed insurers and request that he or the Employer approve the proposed insurers.

Strictly, the Contractor should not commence the Works until the instruction of the Architect has been received and (if so required) the clause 21.2 insurance effected.

If the Contractor holds a Contractor's All Risk insurance, certain of the problems outlined in the previous paragraphs could be avoided, for the insurers may be able to deal with a clause 21.2 insurance by way of a simple endorsement to the existing insurance policy. This has many advantages to both the Employer and the Architect, and the Contractor would be able to expedite the settlement of the terms and the commencement of the insurance cover by requesting an instruction from the Architect in a different form. Such a letter should:-

★ remind the Architect that there is a provisional sum in the bills of quanitities or Contract Bills for clause 21.2 insurance

★ request an immediate instruction as to whether or not such insurance is required

★ make an offer to arrange such insurance through the normal Contractor's All Risks insurance of the Contractor

★ (if possible) forward a copy of the insurer's normal policy wording

★ request approval of the proposed insurers.

The latter point in each of the requests for instructions is required by clause 21.2.2 which also provides that the policy and premium receipt be held by the Architect.

If the Contractor does not effect the clause 21.2 insurance in accordance with the instruction of the Architect, then the Employer may do so. All that will happen then is the amount of the provisional sum will be a deduction from the Contract Sum in computing the final adjusted Contract Sum (the final account). There would be no addition to the Contract Sum.

Excepted risks

Clause 21.3   In clause 21.3 it is made clear that the Contractor is not required to either indemnify the Employer or insure the Works, the site, or any property against loss or damage that may be caused by nuclear accidents, sonic booms, etc., all of which are presumably uninsurable. The Contractor is only excused from indemnifying the Employer and from effecting insurance. It would appear that the basic liability for all loss or damage to persons and property remains with the Contractor. Presumably this is an oversight in the drafting of JCT 80 that will be corrected in due course, since it is clear that the Contractor is not expected to be responsible for loss or damage caused by these contingencies.

In the text of the present clause, it would appear that a reference to clause 20.1 in the opening words has been accidently omitted. As presently drafted, it would appear that in respect of injury to persons, the Contractor retains an obligation to indemnify the Employer and insure against the risk of injury or death to persons caused by nuclear accidents, sonic booms, etc.

The Conditions do not state what is to happen in the event of loss or damage by the excepted risks or state whether the Contractor is to proceed with reinstatement or whether an instruction of the Architect is needed.

It is believed that under statutory law, some compensation may be available from government, but, again, the Conditions do not set out any procedures for claiming such compensation.

INSURANCE AGAINST DAMAGE BY FIRE ETC.

Clause 22

The arrangements for effecting insurance in respect of damage to the Works and unfixed materials and goods by 'Clause 22 Perils' are set out in clauses 22A, 22B and 22C. The text of these clauses is essentially the same as those in the 1963 Edition. The clauses are alternatives and only one will apply to any particular contract. The basis of choice is simple; clause 22A applies where the Contractor undertakes to insure; clause 22B applies, **for the Local Authorities Editions,** where the risk remains with the Employer, but with no obligation to insure, and, **for the Private Editions,** where the Employer undertakes to insure; and clause 22C applies if the work is concerned with alterations to an existing building and where the Employer undertakes to insure both the existing building and '...the Works...'. The bills of quantities will inform the Contractor at tender stage of the alternative that is to apply.

Builders should note that the range of the Clause 22 Perils to be insured against, whilst wide, is not comprehensive. Therefore the extent to which the general obligation of the Contractor to carry out and complete the Works under clause 2.1, and restated in clause 20.2 is similarly limited. Irrespective of which part of clause 22 is applicable there are a number of risks that remain wholly in the hands of the Contractor, eg theft; loss or damage to plant and temporary buildings. In consequence, the Contractor should **always** have in existence Contractor's All Risks insurance.

Where insurance is by the Contractor

Clause 22A.1

Where clause 22A applies, the insurance is required to be in the joint names of the Employer and the Contractor and is to be effected with an insurer approved by the Employer. These are quite simple matters; more difficult is the amount for which the insurer is required to indemnify the Contractor in the event of loss or damage. The Conditions require that the value insured be the '...full reinstatement value...' plus the percentage for professional fees entered in the Appendix.

The word 'reinstatement' in this clause is new and has been introduced to ensure that the contract of insurance between the Contractor and the insurer is properly worded. The requirement of the Employer is that the Contractor should be able to recover the cost of reinstatement of the partially constructed building to the condition existing immediately before the Clause 22 Perils damage. It is likely that the amount concerned would exceed the then intrinsic value of the building. Under the fire, etc., insurance clause of the 1963 Edition, the Contractor is required to insure the Works '...for the full value thereof...' and this phrase has been shown to mean the indemnity given by the insurer is limited to the lower of either the value of the building or the cost of reinstatement.

The change of wording removes this problem by making it clear that the indemnity must be for the cost of reinstatement of the partially constructed building. A problem for the Contractor and his insurer is ascertainment of the amount of the indemnity applicable at any particular time, for the amount concerned will vary during the course of the contract. The maximum indemnity would be required if the Works were to be totally destroyed immediately before Practical Completion, when the amount concerned could be the amount of the original Contract Sum, **plus** the costs of any emergency work and of removing debris; **plus** the effect of inflation since the original tender and during reconstruction; **plus** the percentage for professional fees entered in the Appendix.

While there is no prescribed timetable for the presentation of evidence that the insurances have been effected, it is in the best interests of the Contractor to present his insurance particulars to the Architect before commencement of the Works on site. Presentation of insurance particulars should be made by notice in writing to the Architect (copy to the Employer). Such notice should:-

★ inform the Architect that insurances under clause 22A have been effected with a specified insurance company

★ (when applicable) inform the Architect that this is by a special insurance policy and enclose the policy for retention by the Architect

★ (when applicable) inform the Architect that the insurances are automatically covered by the existing Contractor's All Risks policy held by the Contractor and give its identifying particulars

★ confirm that the interest of the Employer in the policy has been endorsed thereon and attach documentary proof

★ attach current premium receipt(s)

★ request the Architect or the Employer to approve the insurance company concerned; to confirm that he is satisfied the Contractor has effected the required insurances; and to return the premium receipt(s).

Clause 22A.2   Where clause 22A is applicable and the Contractor fails to effect the insurances required by the Conditions, then clause 22A.2 permits the Employer to arrange the requisite insurances. The costs incurred by the Employer in effecting such insurances may be deducted from monies due to the Contractor in Interim Certificates or the Final Certificate.

There is no apparent requirement for the Employer to inform the Contractor that he is making independent arrangements for insurances to be effected and that his costs will be deducted from Interim Certificates or the Final Certificate. Presumably, the JCT is of the opinion that failure of the Contractor to effect the insurances required by clause 22A is a fundamental breach of contract and that no notice is required.

Where the risk is with the Employer

Clause 22B.1   Where clause 22B is used and the contract is in the terms of the **Local Authorities Edition,** the risk of loss or damage by reason of Clause 22 Perils passes entirely to the Employer without any obligation to arrange insurance. The theory here being that most local authorities would carry the risk of such loss or damage themselves. The Employer - the Local Authority - may insure if he wishes, but it would appear not to affect the Contractor one way or the other.

Where clause 22B applies and the contract is in the terms of the **Private Edition,** the position is different in that, in addition to being entirely responsible for the risk of loss or damage by reason of Clause 22 Perils, the Employer is required to effect insurances against the specified risks.

The policy of insurance effected by the Employer is to be a '...proper policy of insurance... against... (loss or damage by the Clause 22 Perils)...'. One wonders why the policy is not required to be for the full reinstatement value as required when the Contractor takes responsibility for fire, etc. insurance. Perhaps a policy for less than the full reinstatement value is 'improper', thus leaving the Employer in breach of contract and permitting the Contractor to insure under clause 22B.1.3.

The Contractor may request the Employer to produce proof, in the form of policies and current premium receipt(s), that such insurances exist and this evidence should be requested in the early stages of the contract. This will be helpful in the event that some loss or damage by reason of Clause 22 Perils occurs, when the question of the ability of the Employer to pay for the restoration of damaged work may become pertinent.

Clause 22B.1.3   If the Employer should fail to effect the insurances required by the Conditions, then clause 22B.1.3 of the Private Edition permits the Contractor to arrange the requisite insurances. The costs incurred by the Contractor in effecting such insurances will be added to the Contract Sum following presentation to the Architect of proper receipts for the premiums (clause 30.6.2.15).

While the workings of clause 28 (Determination by the Contractor) will come into effect where the Employer is not able to fulfill his obligations to pay for the reinstatement work, it is thought to be desirable for the Contractor to take up the facility granted to him to insure on behalf of the Employer.

Clause 22C.1   Where clause 22C applies, the Employer assumes the entire responsibility for loss or damage to the Works by Clause 22 Perils. The Employer is required to insure the Works, the existing buildings, and their contents against the specified risks. The existing buildings and their contents would ordinarily be of considerably greater value than the 'Works' and would already be the subject of extensive insurances. For these reasons the Employer is the best person to arrange the proper insurances, perhaps by way of an extension to his existing policies.

The policy of insurance to be effected by the Employer is to be '...adequate insurance against loss or damage by the Clause 22 Perils'. Again, one wonders why the policy is not required to be for the full reinstatement value as required when the Contractor takes responsibility for fire, etc. insurance.

Where clause 22C applies and the contract is in the terms of the **Local Authorities Edition,** the Contractor is not entitled to request proof that the insurances required by clause 22C have been effected, nor is he entitled to arrange such insurances in the event of default by the local authority.

On the other hand, where clause 22C applies and the contract is in the terms of the **Private Edition,** the Contractor has certain rights to enquire into these matters. Clause 22C.1.2 permits the Contractor to request the Employer to produce proof in the form of a current premium receipt that such insurance exists. Because of the greater amount at risk in the form of existing buildings and their contents it is thought to be essential for the Contractor to obtain, before commencement of the Works, proof that such insurances do exist. In the event of discovery that such insurances do not exist, then the Contractor may feel it is desirable not to commence the Works. The Contractor is permitted to arrange the requisite insurances and the costs incurred in effecting such insurances will be added to the Contract Sum following presentation to the Architect of proper receipts for the premiums.

LOSS OR DAMAGE BY FIRE ETC.

Clause 22
Perils

In the event of loss or damage by reason of Clause 22 Perils, the detailed procedures for reinstating the work vary according to which of the alternative parts of clause 22 applies.

Loss or damage where clause 22A is applicable

Clause
22A.4.1

Where clause 22A applies and there has been loss or damage to the Works by reason of one or more of the Clause 22 Perils, then 'Upon acceptance of any claim...' (presumably by the insurers, the Conditions do not say) then the Contractor is required to reinstate the Works '...with due diligence'. No instruction of the Architect is necessary, the point being that under the indemnity given by the Contractor under clause 18.2 and in accordance with the general obligation of the Contractor referred to in clause 2.1, this is his contractual duty. The responsibililty to commence reinstatement occurs upon acceptance by the insurers of the insurance claim made by the Contractor. It is made clear in clause 22A.4.2 that the amount received by the Contractor from the insurance claim is all he is going to get. The Contractor must ensure that the amount accepted includes the costs of delay and disruption in addition to the costs of reinstatement and any professional fees involved. This could take a little while to settle and the Contractor must ensure that all the necessary estimates, etc. and other evidence necessary to facilitate a prompt ascertainment of the quantum of the claim by the Contractor and acceptance by the insurer are available soon after the loss or damage has occurred. Any undue delay in reaching a settlement of the claim could affect the extension of time awarded by the Architect.

The reinstatement of work after loss or damage by Clause 22 Perils is almost certain to have an effect on the progress of the Works and to cause delay in completion of the Works, thus becoming a 'Relevant Event' under clause 25 leading to an extension of time. (In this case there can be no claim against the Employer for reimbursement of loss and expense; this must be included in the settlement of the insurance claim.)

In order to secure an extension of time by reason of reinstatement after loss or damage by Clause 22 Perils, the notices required under clause 25 must be given 'forthwith'. When estimating the extent of any delay in the completion of the Works, allowance must be made for the time that will be required while insurers or, more accurately, their loss adjusters, investigate the incident and settle the quantum of the claim. In addition, further time may be required before progress of the Works becomes 'normal' again.

Finally, in regard to delay where clause 22A applies, where there has been loss or damage **not** caused by negligence of the Contractor, and the whole of the Works are delayed for a period recommended to be three months, then the Contractor may be able to determine his own employment under the contract. (See clause 28.1.3.2, page 142).

Clause
22A.4.2

The Contractor is entitled to have refunded to him the costs of reinstatement in instalments '...under certificates of the Architect...'. It is not clear what is meant here, since the reference is to 'certificates', not 'Interim Certificates' issued by the Architect for monthly payment purposes. A method of working these arrangements would be for the Contractor to reach a settlement with the insurers and to arrange that the insurers pay monies to the Contractor at monthly intervals against a statement by the Architect as to the amount of reinstatement work carried out. Because the insurance is in the joint names of the Employer and the Contractor, the Employer must be made party to these arrangements. The arrangement suggested should enable the Employer to see that his interest is protected.

Loss or damage where clause 22B is applicable

Clause 22B.2   Where clause 22B applies and there has been loss or damage to the Works by reason of one or more of the Clause 22 Perils, then the Contractor is required to give notice in writing 'forthwith' to both the Employer and the Architect. Such notice should:-

★ inform the Employer that the whole or a specified part of the Works have been damaged

★ specify the cause of the damage (eg fire) and remind the Employer that the damage is, therefore, at his sole risk

★ give a brief explanation of the extent of the damage

★ (if applicable) inform the Employer and the Architect that, as a result of the loss or damage, progress on the whole or a specified part of the Works has been suspended

★ invite the Architect, the Quantity Surveyor and the Employer to visit the site and ascertain the extent of the remedial work that is required

★ confirm that the Contractor will commence the removal of debris immediately and will commence reinstatement work upon the expiry of (say) seven days from the date of the notice.

The two latter points in the notice are necessary because the value of the reinstatement work carried out has to be included by the Quantity Surveyor in interim valuations, by the Architect in Interim Certificates, and paid for by the Employer when honouring those Certificates. There is no apparent need for an instruction of the Architect to be issued before the Contractor commences reinstatement and no apparent need for the Contractor to await acceptance of an insurance claim where the Employer is bound to insure. On both these matters, it would be sensible for the Contractor to give some notice to the Employer so that he could, for example, have his Architect instruct that some remedial work be omitted from the Works or have his Architect order the suspension of some parts of the Works. The value of all remedial work carried out is required to be ascertained by the Quantity Surveyor by valuing the work under the Valuation rules of clause 13 as if such work were a Variation instructed by the Architect.

It is made clear by clause 22B.2.1 that the Employer has to pay for both the remedial works and for the work properly carried out prior to the occurrence of loss or damage by Clause 22 Perils.

The reinstatement of the works after loss or damage by Clause 22 Perils is almost certain to have an effect on the progress of the Works and to cause delay in completion of the Works. Such matters qualify for extension of time and possible determination, as has been described in connection with clause 22A on page 66.

Loss or damage where clause 22C is applicable

Clause 22C.2   Where clause 22C applies and there has been loss or damage to the Works (no mention here of the existing structures and/or their contents) by reason of one or more of the Clause 22 Perils, then the Contractor is required to give notice in writing 'forthwith' to both the Employer and the Architect. Such notice must cover the same items as those detailed in the clause 22B notice given above in the previous section.

Clause 22C.2.2

In addition, both the Employer and the Contractor are given the opportunity, within twenty-eight days of the occurrence of the loss or damage, to determine the employment of the Contractor under the contract. This could be an appropriate course of action where, for example, both the Works and the existing buildings are so damaged by fire that both would require to be rebuilt on a scale quite outside the capability of the Contractor. Should the Contractor wish to determine his own employment under the contract, then written notice to the Architect must be given. Such notice should:-

★ refer to the notice informing the Architect of the occurrence of loss or damage

★ inform the Architect that the Contractor wishes to determine his own employment under clause 22C.2.2.1

★ give seven days notice of that determination.

Within seven days after receipt of the notice of determination, either party may dispute the notice of determination by arbitration under the arbitration agreement. Since the dispute will arise after the 'termination or alleged termination of the Contractors employment', the matter qualifies for immediate arbitration. Where the notice of determination is accepted, or where an Arbitrator has upheld the notice of determination, then the provisions of clause 28.2 (Determination by the Contractor) apply.

Clause 22C.2.3

Where there is no notice of determination, or where an Arbitrator decides the notice was **not** just and equitable, then the Contractor is required to reinstate the loss or damage and carry on and complete the Works. There is no apparent need for an instruction of the Architect before the Contractor can commence the reinstatement work. Strangely, however, instructions of the Architect are required in this case in regard to the removal and disposal of debris. The Contractor does not appear to have to await settlement of any insurance claim by the Employer before commencing reinstatement work. The value of all remedial and reinstatement work carried out is required to be ascertained by the Quanity Surveyor by valuing the work under the Valuation rules of clause 13 as if such work were a Variation instructed by the Architect.

It is made clear by clause 22C.2.1 that the Employer has to pay for both the remedial works **and** for the work properly carried out prior to the occurrence of loss or damage by the Clause 22 Perils.

The reinstatement of the work after loss or damage by Clause 22 Perils is almost certain to have an effect upon the progress of the Works and to cause delay in the completion of the Works. Such matters qualify for extension of time and possible determination as has been described in connection with clause 22A on page 66.

Postscript to clauses 22B and 22C

In all cases where the Employer takes responsibility for damage to the Works by fire, etc., the Contractor should take special care to ensure that the Conditions have not been amended so as to place some or all of the burden of meeting reinstatement costs upon the Contractor. This could perhaps be by the imposition of fire precaution requirements that are, in the case of an insurance claim, quite impossible to have complied with.

The Contractor must in these cases be prepared to arrange his own fire insurance unilaterally and to allow for such costs in his tender.

Payment for the Work

In this Section, the financial arrangements between the parties are examined. These arrangements are in several distinct parts:-

★ the original sum (clause 14 - Contract Sum)

★ how the original sum may be altered (clause 3 - Contract Sum adjustments)

★ what events change the original sum (clause 13 - Variations and provisional sums; clause 26 - Loss and expense; clause 37 - Fluctuations)

★ payments on account and the final account (clause 16 - Materials on site; clause 30 - Certificates and payments).

THE CONTRACT SUM

Clause 14.1   The Contract Sum and its relationship to the Contract Bills is dealt with in clause 14.1. Under clause 2.1 the Contractor has agreed to carry out the Works according to the Contract Documents. Clause 14.1 states that the Contract Sum is based on the quality and the quantity of the work detailed in the Contract Bills. The former point restates what has already been referred to in connection with clause 8.1 and requires that the Contractor provide the materials and workmanship described in the Contract Bills; the latter point makes it clear that the Contract Sum is based only upon the quantities, rates and prices set out in the Contract Bills.

The Contractor should seek to ensure, before executing the Contract Documents, that the drawings offered to him for signature are, firstly, the same as those made available at the time of tender, and secondly, the same as those upon which the bills of quantities were based. A Contractor would be unwise to sign copies of drawings bearing a later revision suffix than the tender drawings. The Contractor must retain a copy of the drawings available at the time of preparing the tender so as to enable comparison with copies of subsequently revised issues. Clause B.3.1 of SMM 6 requires that bills of quantities contain a schedule of such drawings.

It does not matter whether the bills of quantities have been measured accurately from those drawings, since an error in this respect will be corrected under clause 2.2.2.2. What does matter is that the Contract Drawings properly represent what the Contractor believes he has undertaken to build. The proper, accurate and detailed checking of these matters prior to the execution of Contract Documents could well be productive. Whenever the actual work properly carried out is different from that measured in the Contract Bills, whether by reason of an error in description or quantity, a discrepancy or divergence, an instruction of the Architect, or a variation, the required adjustment to the Contract Bills is an addition to or a subtraction from the Contract Sum. It is clear, therefore, that the arithmetical computation of the Contract Sum (ie the priced, extended, bills of quantities) is critical and the Contractor must ensure that it is correct before executing the Contract Documents.

The modern concept in these matters is that the Contract Sum should be the amount of the tender submitted by the Contractor, irrespective of the total of the priced bills of quantities. However, the Contractor is recommended to ensure that his priced bills of quantities do equate to his tender and that amounts included for preliminaries and in respect of any lump sum adjustment are carefully and accurately apportioned within the proposed Contract Bills. The Valuation rules of clause 13 now provide for the inclusion of amounts in respect of such preliminary costs and lump sum adjustments (clauses 13.5.3.2 and 13.5.3.3). Clearly, a proper strategy in the 'spreading' of these amounts within the bills of quantities could significantly improve the recovery of the Contractor following the Valuation of Variations.

Clause 14.2   Clause 14.2 provides that the Contract Sum can only be adjusted by the application of the Conditions. The Contract Sum can be adjusted to correct errors in quantity or description or method of measurement, as has already been mentioned, but not to correct errors in rates or prices or other calculations inserted by the Contractor into the Contract Bills. The Contractor is precluded by this clause from raising any argument as to the sufficiency of any of his prices in the Contract Sum. Note the words used here - 'Contract Sum' - presumably mean that while the offer by the Contractor comprises only a tender or priced bills of quantities, it remains open for discussion or correction. It should be noted that approaches to Local Authorities for an adjustment to the tender or priced bills of quantities may have the effect of disqualifying the tender.

When executed by the parties the priced bills of quantities, extended and totalled to equate to the Contract Sum, become the Contract Bills and any errors are no longer open for correction.

Adjustments to the Contract Sum

Clause 3   Clause 3 is entirely new and provides authority for all adjustments to the Contract Sum (including those referred to in the preceding paragraph and reimbursement of loss and expense under clause 26) to be included in the next Interim Certificate or the Final Certificate. The amount of the adjustment need not be wholly agreed or ascertained; any partial agreement or ascertainment must be included. This new clause tidies up the anomaly that existed in the 1963 Edition where some additional payments to the Contractor were not expressly stated to be included in Interim Certificates. It also seems to be to the general advantage of the Contractor by reducing an otherwise unplanned adverse cash flow. Since it represents a significant change in the payment procedures it may be necessary for the Contractor to apply pressure on the Quantity Surveyor and the Architect to ensure that all the monies the Contractor is now entitled to be paid under this new clause are included in interim valuations and Interim Certificates.

VARIATIONS

Clause 13   Clause 13 deals comprehensively with Variations and includes both the definition of a Variation and the Valuation of that Variation. Much of clause 13 mirrors material from the 1963 Edition but there are some significant changes and the clause has been redrafted into a more logical sequence.

Getting properly paid under building contracts for work carried out as a consequence of instructions of the Architect for varied and additional works has always been a source of discontent among builders. Under JCT 80 such discontent should at least be reduced, since there is now provision for a more liberal approach to the use, or rather, the non-use of bill rates for the purpose of valuing Variations and provision is made for the inclusion of certain preliminary costs into the Valuation.

Variations to the Works

Clause 13.1.1   The definition of a Variation to the Works is set out in clause 13.1 and is concerned with a Variation in or on the Works. An amendment to the terms of the contract itself is a different matter altogether and is outside the scope of this paper. Clause 13.1.1 reproduces in tabular form the wide definition of clause 11(2) of the 1963 Edition. The Architect is specifically permitted by clause 13.1.1.3 to change materials already delivered to the site and to order that work already executed be demolished and removed from the site. Provided the work has been properly carried out in accordance with the Contract

Documents and any subsequent instruction of the Architect then the Employer will be required to pay for the original materials or work, for the replacement materials or work and for the removal or demolition of the original work. Naturally, this does not apply where the materials or work are not in accordance with the Contract Documents; in such a case the instruction of the Architect would be issued under clause 8.4 (see page 37).

The wide definition of 'Variation' reinforces the need previously expressed in this book for the Contractor to have in his possession copies of the Contract Drawings. These must be kept in safe custody, not on the site where they will be lost or destroyed sooner or later. Only the diligent comparison of each issue of drawings with the Contract Drawings will enable the Contractor to be sure he has identified all the changes from the work described in the Contract Bills.

Variations to the obligations and restrictions of the Employer

Clause 13.1.2   Reference has already been made in the discussion on clause 2.2 (page 17) to the provision of clause B.8 of SMM 6 which requires that any obligations or restrictions to be imposed by the Employer are to be set out in the bills of quantities. SMM 6 sensibly recognises that the Employer should be able, through the bills of quantities, to impose upon the Contractor his own requirements as to, say, the order of completion, or the use of parts of the site. Thus, the minimum of interference to the existing business of the Employer should occur during the presence of the Contractor on the property of the Employer.

Clause 13.1.2 provides that, in the case of any change to four particular classes of obligation or restriction imposed by the Employer, such a change (provided that change arises from an instruction of the Architect) becomes a Variation for the purpose of clause 13 and the financial effect can, therefore, be ascertained by the application of the Valuation rules of clause 13. The four classes of obligation and restriction are concerned with access to and use of the site, working space, working hours, and the order of the completion of the Works.

Under clause 4.1 the Contractor has certain rights to object to the content of an instruction of the Architect requiring a variation to the obligations or restrictions of the Employer. (See the notes on clause 4.1 page 22).

The 1963 Edition did not deal with these matters, perhaps on the historical basis that the Employer should not seek to change an implied term of the contract, namely, the absolute freedom of the Contractor to execute the Works in any manner of his choosing.

Apart from the four classes of obligation or restriction of the Employer referred to above, the Conditions do not anticipate any other changes in those items appearing in the preliminaries sections of the bills of quantities.

The text of clause 13.1.2.1 refers to '...access to the site...' (meaning, it is assumed, access to the site of the Works over some adjoining land in the possession or ownership of the Employer), and to '...use of any specific parts of the site...'. Neither expression is wide enough to embrace any change in the right of the Contractor to possession of the whole of the site expressed in clause 23.1.

Obligations or restrictions of the Employer are referred to in several clauses of the Conditions and in SMM 6, and in each case reference is made to the 'site', although there is no definition of 'site'. Therefore, when the tender of the Contractor is accepted and there are within the bills of quantities obligations or restrictions imposed by the Employer, the Contractor must, prior to the execution of the Contract Documents, ensure that the items in the bills of quantities are complete in their own right, or that they are defined in conjunction say, with a marked up drawing or drawings that are incorporated into the Contract Documents.

Exclusion from Variation

Clause 13.1.3   Clause 13.1.3 is also entirely new and states that the term 'Variation' does not include the situation where the Architect wishes to have work carried out by a Nominated Sub-Contractor that was measured in detail in the Contract Bills and priced by the Contractor for execution by himself or by a Domestic Sub-Contractor. In other words, the Architect is prohibited from issuing instructions that would remove work from the Contractor and pass it to a Nominated Sub-Contractor.

That is not to say that such a situation cannot arise. Only that it does not come under the definition of 'Variation' and the financial effect cannot be ascertained by reference to the Valuation rules of clause 13. Should the Architect wish a Nominated Sub-Contractor to carry out work measured in detail in the Contract Bills and priced by the Contractor for execution by himself or a Domestic Sub-Contractor, then the Architect must operate under the rules of clause 35.1.

The definition of a 'Nominated Sub-Contractor' is contained in clause 35.1 and clause 35.1.4 provides that a sub-contractor can '...by agreement...' between the Contractor and the Architect be nominated by the Architect to carry out any work. Where the Contract Bills do not state that the work in question is to be carried out by a Nominated Sub-Contractor, then the agreement of the Contractor may be subject to payment by the Employer to the Contractor of a sum representing compensation for loss of profit, etc on the work the Contractor expected to carry out himself or to have carried out by a Domestic Sub-Contractor. The Contractor should take care to ensure that he has the clear agreement of the Employer to pay compensation, for such a payment does not appear to be permitted by the Conditions and would not automatically be included in the final adjusted Contract Sum.

Clause 35.1.4 provides that the Contractor must not unreasonably withhold his agreement to the nomination of a sub-contractor in this situation. If agreement was withheld by the Contractor, then the reasonableness of that action by the Contractor could become the subject of immediate arbitration. For this to happen the Architect must issue an instruction omitting the work concerned from that to be executed by the Contractor and nominating a sub-contractor to carry out the same work. If the Contractor challenges that instruction under the provisions of clause 4.2 and pursues the matter to arbitration, then the dispute becomes subject to immediate arbitration. (Articles 5.2.2 - 'on the question whether or not the issue of an instruction is empowered by the Conditions...'.)

If an Arbitrator were, however, to find that it **was** unreasonable for the Contractor to have withheld his agreement, then the Contractor becomes responsible for any effect on the progress of the Works or delay in the completion of the Works by reason of non-compliance with the original instruction upon its first issue. The Contractor must take account of this possibility before initiating arbitration.

Authority of Architect to require Variation

Clause 13.2   Clause 13.2 empowers the Architect to issue instructions requiring a Variation. The text is the same as the 1963 Edition. In the opening words, 'The Architect may issue instructions requiring a Variation...' the word 'may' applies to 'variation' meaning that variations are not compulsory. If the Architect requires a Variation, he **must** issue an instruction. The Architect may also sanction a Variation not arising from his own instructions. This could arise where, perhaps, a verbal instruction of the Architect has not been confirmed under the rules laid down in the Conditions.

The reference in this clause is to the issue of instructions and, by clause 4.3 all instructions must be in writing, including instructions requiring a Variation.

In the final sentence of clause 13.2 it is made clear that a Variation will not vitiate the contract. Vitiate means to render of no effect, or to invalidate completely or in part (especially to destroy or impair the legal force of a deed). While Variations are contemplated by the parties to the contract, these must always be within the general ambit of the description of the Main Contract Works set out in the Articles of Agreement and shown upon the Contract Drawings. However, there is presumably a point where a Variation so changes the character or nature of the Works that it goes beyond the contemplation of the parties. In such a situation the Contractor would be able to dispute the authority of the Architect to issue such an instruction under the provisions of clause 4.2 and, if necessary, take the matter to arbitration.

Provisional sums

Clause 13.3   Provisional sums are introduced in clause 13.3 and the Architect is required to issue instructions before the execution of any work to which provisional sums apply. The provisional sums can be in the Contract Bills or in the documents related to any Nominated Sub-Contract. There is no mention in the present clause of prime cost sums (PC sums), since they only apply in respect of Nominated Sub-Contractors and Suppliers. The rules for the treatment of such sums are fully detailed in clauses 35 and 36. The instructions issued by the Architect for the expenditure of provisional sums can include the nomination of a sub-contractor or supplier, and in such a case the provisions and procedures of clauses 35 and 36 apply equally to such nominations.

A 'provisional sum' is not defined in the Conditions but the expression is referred to in clause A.8 of SMM 6 and this would seem to be adequate for the purpose. A provisional sum will appear in the bills of quantities (or in the documents related to any nominated sub-contract) in respect of any work for which insufficient information is available at the time of preparation of the bills of quantities to enable that work to be measured or described in detail.

There is no clearly laid down timetable for the issue by the Architect of instructions for the execution of any work to which provisional sums apply. This is perhaps understandable by reason of the nature of such work.

Where an instruction for the expenditure of a provisional sum is required, then the Contractor must request the Architect to issue his instructions by making written application at the appropriate time. The written application may be considereed as a notice from the Contractor to the Architect. Such a notice should:-

★ identify the provisional sum by reference to the Contract Bills

★ request that the Architect issue his instructions in regard to the expenditure of that provisional sum

★ (if appropriate) inform the Architect of the date by which his instruction must be received if the execution of the work so instructed is not to cause an effect on the regular progress of the Works or cause delay in the completion of the Works.

The last point in the notice is necessary in order to introduce the general question of delay and extension of time. The late issue of an instruction in regard to the expenditure of provisional sums could have an effect on the progress of the Works and cause delay in the completion of the Works, thus becoming a 'Relevant Event' under clause 25 leading to an extension of time. It could also become a 'matter' under clause 26 giving rise to a claim for reimbursement of loss and expense. The notice referred to in the preceding paragraph should not be regarded as the only notice with which to raise the question of a late instruction. The proper disciplines of contract management and the more formal notice requirements of clauses 25 and 26 must always be applied, although a more imaginative approach will be necessary in the case of provisional sums because of the nature of the work.

Valuation of Variations

Clause 13.4   The Valuation of Variations is dealt with in clause 13.4. By clause 13.4.1 all Variations, whether arising automatically under the Conditions (eg for the correction of errors in the Contract Bills, clause 2.2.2.2), or instructed or subsequently sanctioned by the Architect, and work carried out by the Contractor under the instructions of the Architect as to the expenditure of provisional sums, are required to be valued by the Quantity Surveyor. The process is described in the Conditions as the 'Valuation' and is to be made under the Valuation rules detailed in clause 13.5, unless otherwise agreed.

Provision is expressly made for the Contractor and the Employer (not the Architect on his behalf) to agree a special method of Valuation or a lump sum for any specific Variation. Where there is time to reach agreement and the Contractor wishes, for example, to agree a lump sum for varied work, then a letter to the Employer (copies to the Architect and the Quantity Surveyor) would suffice. Such a letter should:-

★ identify the instruction of the Architect or the Variation

★ offer to carry out the work for a specified sum

★ specify the document and/or drawings considered in preparing the offer

★ state whether the offer is 'fixed price', or subject to partial, full or formula fluctuations

★ (where a lump sum is **not** quoted) propose the method of measurement and Valuation to be adopted

★ request the Employer to give his agreement to the offer by the Contractor.

The Contractor should note that, provided the instruction of the Architect or Variation has been properly issued, he must commence to comply with that instruction or Variation. The Contractor is not permitted to demand acceptance by the Employer of any quotation he may have given before commencing to carry out the work. Any offer of alternative means of Valuation is merely an endeavour to shorten the valuation process for final account purposes.

Valuation of Variations to works by Nominated Sub- Contractors

The Valuation of Variations to the sub-contract works of any Nominated Sub-Contractor (including work arising out of instructions as to the expenditure of provisional sums contained in the Nominated Sub-Contract documents) is also to be carried out by the Quantity Surveyor. Provision is expressly made for the Contractor and the Nominated Sub-Contractor (with the approval of the Architect - no mention of the Employer in this case) to agree a special method of Valuation or a lump sum for a specified Variation; otherwise the Valuation rules of the Nominated Sub- Contracts NSC/4 or NSC/4a are to apply.

Alternative methods of ascertaining the final adjusted sub-contract sum are contained in both Nominated Sub-Contracts. Firstly, a lump sum tender with adjustments for Variations (clause 16 of Sub-Contracts NSC/4 and NSC/4a) or, secondly, where the sub-contract work is to be wholly measured or remeasured upon completion (clause 17 of Sub-Contracts NSC/4 and NSC/4a). In either case, sub- contract Valuation rules are included that are almost identical to the Valuation rules of JCT 80.

Exception to the use of Valuation rules

Clause 13.4.2   An exception to the application of the Valuation rules occurs in clause 13.4.2 and is applicable where a tender by the Contractor for work that is covered by a PC sum appearing within an instruction of the Architect as to the expenditure of a provisional sum has been accepted. In such a case, the valuation of the work is to be on the basis of valuation inherent in the tender by the Contractor and **not** according to the Valuation rules set out in clause 13.5.

It is convenient at this point to draw attention to the distinction between work done as a consequence of a PC sum included within a provisional sum instruction with the apparently similar circumstances dealt with in clause 35.2, that is to say, work done as a consequence of a PC sum in the Contract Bills.

Clause 35.2 applies where the tender of the Contractor for work covered by a PC Sum and described in the Contract Bills as being reserved for a Nominated Sub- Contractor, has been accepted. In such a case, clause 35.2.2 provides that the Valuation rules of clause 13.5 apply. For the purpose of applying those rules, reference is made to the tender documents of the Architect for the PC Sum work, not the main Contract Documents. This procedure has presumably been adopted to ensure that any Variations are valued under the same rules that would be applicable if an independent Nominated Sub-Contractor had been appointed to carry out the work. The procedure detailed in clause 13.4.2 reflects the less formal enquiry and tender procedures normally occurring when dealing with provisional sum work.

Valuation rules

Clause 13.5   The Valuation rules are set out in clause 13.5. There are some important changes of principle and careful consideration of the rules is required to obtain the full benefit of them. As was the case in the 1963 Edition, the Valuation rules are to be applied successively to each Variation until one or another is found to be appropriate for use in the particular case. In all cases where the Variation is to be measured (ie not to be valued on daywork or otherwise), clause 13.5.3.1 provides that the method of measurement shall be that of the Contract Bills; that is to say, SMM 6, unless otherwise stated in any particular item.

Valuation of measured Variations

Clause 13.5.1   The Valuation of the measured Variation is ascertained, firstly (clause 13.5.1,1), where the character, conditions and quantity of the work are similar - by the use of bill rates. Secondly (clause 13.5.1.2), where the character of the work is similar, but the conditions and/or quality of the work differ - on the basis of bill rates plus allowances for those differences. Thirdly (clause 13.5.1.3) where the character of the work is different - a fair valuation is to be made.

The references to work being of a similar character and being executed under similar conditions are repeated from the 1963 Edition. A new reference is added to these rules concerning significant changes of quantity. No guidance has been given in the interpretation of 'significant' changes; indeed, it would appear that the actual arithmetical extent of a change of quantity may be of no consequence. What, perhaps, the Contractor and the Quantity Surveyor will be looking for are Variations that make a significant change in the method of carrying out the work, or in the use of different plant or, in the quantity discounts available in the purchase of materials. Where a 'significant' change in quantity has been established, clause 13.5.1.2 provides that the Valuation shall include a fair allowance for the difference. The expression 'a fair allowance' should give rise to considerable debate between the Quantity Surveyor and the Contractor since it does appear to be capable of wide interpretation.

The Contractor should note that the arguments will flow in both directions, since he must be prepared for the bill rates to go down where there has been a significant **increase** in the quantity of any particular item.

Except to the limited extent of being present when Variations are to be measured, the Contractor has no part to play under the Conditions in the establishment of the amount of the Valuation. The Contractor will want to establish his case to have revised rates applied to varied work at the earliest opportunity and should, therefore, examine each instruction received and every Variation. If he is of the opinion that bill rates do not apply for the work in question, then a notice should be sent to the Quantity Surveyor (copy to the Architect). The notice should:-

★ identify the instruction issued by the Architect or the Variation that results in the changed quantities or conditions of working

★ inform the Quantity Surveyor that in the opinion of the Contractor the rates in the Contract Bills do not apply since

EITHER:

★★ the work will not be carried out under similar conditions to similar work set out in the Contract Bills and give a brief (one sentence) explanation of the changed conditions, or

★★ the work now required significantly changes the quantity of work set out in Contract Bills and give a brief (one sentence) description of the work with the changed quantity and

★★ request that the Quantity Surveyor therefore make his Valuation on the basis of bill rates with a fair allowance for the changed conditions and/or changed quantities as permitted by clause 13.5.1.2

OR

★★ the work is not of a similar character to work set out in the Contract Bills and give a brief (one sentence) note of the dissimilar work

★★ request that the Quantity Surveyor, therefore, make his Valuation on the basis of fair rates and prices without regard to any prices in the Contract Bills as permitted by clause 13.5.1.3

★★ request the Quantity Surveyor to agree that in his opinion the work is being carried out under the changed conditions, or, the quantities of the work have significantly changed, or that the work is not similar

★ offer to provide the Quantity Surveyor and/or Architect with such additional information as may be available to substantiate the request by the Contractor.

The position will sometimes arise where the original bill rate for any particular item of work is found to be incorrect. Since it is not the intention of the Contractor or Employer that either of them should significantly gain or lose financially as a consequence of any Variation, presumably the expression 'a fair allowance' could be interpreted liberally enough to enable a proper financial adjustment to be made. This remains to be seen. There is no apparent provision for the Contractor to make representations to the Quantity Surveyor as to the amount of any 'fair allowance' to be made. Similarly, the Quantity Surveyor is not apparently under any obligation to inform the Contractor of any 'fair allowance' he may be proposing until it is presented to him as part of the Final Account documentation.

Valuation of omissions

Clause 13.5.2   Where in the case of a measured Variation, work is to be omitted, clause 13.5.2 provides that the rates and prices set out in the Contract Bills will determine the amount to be omitted.

Addition for preliminaries etc

Clause 13.5.3   Once a technical Valuation of the measured Variation has been made the Quantity Surveyor has also to make allowance for any percentage or lump sum adjustments included in the Contract Bills (clause 13.5.3.2) and for preliminaries (clause 13.5.3.3). There should be no trouble with the former item, as it is common practice for the Contractor to make such adjustments in settling the tender sum. No guidance is given on the manner of calculating the effect of the adjustment. The intention is presumably to apply the adjustment as a percentage on or off all the rates and prices in the Contract Bills, the percentage being calculated by expressing the adjustment as a percentage of the Contract Sum **less** preliminaries, PC sums, provisional sums and any lump sum adjustment. There are other methods of allocating such sums and the Contractor should take care to ensure, before signing the Contract Documents, that the agreed calculation represents his actual requirements.

Preliminaries will probably prove more difficult. These are amounts to be added that represent costs automatically and directly incurred by carrying out the varied work. Obvious examples are insurances, trades foremen, plant, temporary buildings, etc. Preliminary costs incurred by the Contractor that arise because of an extended contract period are not considered here. The Valuation rules do not permit the Quantity Surveyor to include in his Valuation items that relate to disruption of the regular progress of the Works or that concern claims for direct loss and expense. These are ascertained under the provisions of clause 26 on the basis of actual loss and/or expense.

Reference has already been made to the importance of carefully and correctly setting out within the Contract Bills the preliminary costs for the contract. Such a breakdown of preliminary costs must be capable of analysis into those additional costs incurred directly as a result of carrying out the varied work and those that relate to the consequent disruption and delay.

Valuation by daywork

Clause 13.5.4   Where the additional or substituted work forming the Variation cannot be properly measured and valued, then the Valuation may be made on a daywork basis. The texts of clauses 13.5.4.1 and 13.5.4.2 insofar as they relate to the principle of a defined prime cost plus percentage additions are practically the same as those of the 1963 Edition. The rules for presentation of 'vouchers' (daywork sheets) contained in the proviso to clause 13.5.4.2 have changed. The daywork sheet **must** now contain the workmens names, and, in addition to the materials consumed, must now give details of the plant employed upon the work concerned. These matters are normally contained in daywork sheets used by contractors.

The Conditions do not incorporate a proper timetable for the verification, signature and return to the Contractor of his daywork sheets. Also there is no provision enabling the Clerk of Works (if appointed) to verify and sign daywork sheets.If this procedure is to be followed then arrangements must be made outside the contract.

Effect of Variation on other work

Clause 13.5.5   Where the carrying out of any work resulting from a Variation or a provisional sum instruction '...substantially changes the conditions...' under which other items of work have to be carried out, then that change in the other affected work is treated as if it were a Variation required by the Architect and valued under the Valuation rules. The Contractor should note that the word used here to describe the change in conditions - 'substantial'. Where a measured Variation has been valued under the Valuation rules of clause 13.5.1, varied work carried out in 'similar' conditions is to be valued at bill rates. In this case there has to be a 'substantial change' in the conditions under which the affected work is carried out before a new Valuation can be made of the work concerned.

There is considerable scope for discussion about the distinctions between these expressions. Where there has been a substantial change in the conditions under which the work is carried out, then the contractual requirement for the Valuation of that change is automatic. There is no requirement for the Contractor to demonstrate that he has incurred additional cost, although the Quantity Surveyor may require some demonstration that additional cost has been incurred, or that additional risks or liabilities have been imposed upon the Contractor.

There is no requirement for the Contractor to give notice that he requires a new valuation of the affected work under clause 13.5.5, although it would seem prudent for the Contractor to give notice to the Quantity Surveyor (copy to the Architect) that he requires such a Valuation. Such notice should:-

★ refer to the instruction of the Architect or Variation that results in the other (affected) work

★ identify the (affected) work and give a brief (one sentence) explanation of the substantial change in conditions under which the (affected) work now has to be carried out

★ request the Quantity Surveyor to agree that in his opinion the (affected) work is being carried out in substantially changed conditions

★ request the Quantity Surveyor to make a Valuation of the (affected) work under the provisions of clause 13.5.5

★ offer to provide the Quantity Surveyor and/or Architect with such additional information as may be available to substantiate the request by the Contractor.

Final review of Valuation

Clause 13.5.6   Clause 13.5.6 permits the Quantity Surveyor to make a 'fair valuation' in respect of any Variation, if after the proper application of the Valuation rules detailed in clauses 13.5.1 to 13.5.5, the amount of the Valuation does not reasonably represent the value of work done or liabilities assumed. The application of the provisions of this clause seems to be fraught with difficulties. For example, it does not apply to additional, substituted or omitted work, ie measured Variations and daywork.

There is no requirement for the Contractor to give notice that he requires a fair Valuation to be made under clause 13.5.6 as the Valuation so far proposed by the Quantity Surveyor is inadequate. It would seem prudent for the Contractor to give notice to the Quantity Surveyor (copy to the Architect) that he requires a fair Valuation to be made. Such notice should:-

★ refer to the instruction of the Architect or Variation to which the disputed Valuation refers

★ give a brief explanation of the problem(s) encountered in carrying out the work

★ give a brief statement as to the reasons why the Valuation made under clauses 13.5.1 to 13.5.5 is inadequate

★ request that the Quantity Surveyor make a Valuation of the work concerned under clause 13.5.6

★ offer to provide the Quantity Surveyor and/or Architect with any further information or details as may be required to substantiate the request by the Contractor.

Exclusion of loss and expense

Following clause 13.5.6, there is a proviso that is applicable to all the Valuation rules detailed in clause 13.5. The proviso states that no allowance is to be made in any Valuation under clause 13.5 for any effect of the Variation on the regular progress of the Works, nor is any allowance to be made for any item of loss and expense that may be reimbursable under any other Condition. The first part of this proviso is clear enough, for reimbursement of loss and expense incurred when carrying out Variations causes disruption to the regular progress of the Works is made under clause 26.2.7. The purpose of the second part is not so clear. It appears to allow inclusion in the Valuation of **any** loss or expense that is not reimbursable under any other Condition, providing it arises from the execution of a Variation and falls within one or other of the Valuation rules.

It seems that these provisions for the valuation of Variations, when interpreted as a whole, will make it much easier for the Contractor to achieve his first objective when carrying out varied and additional work. That is, to be promptly paid a fair sum for the work that properly reflects the costs incurred in carrying out that work.

Contractor to be present at measurement

Clause 13.6   The right of the Contractor to be present when measurements for the purpose of Valuations are taken is contained in clause 13.6. The Quantity Surveyor is to give the Contractor the opportunity to be present when measurements are to be taken. No reference is made to such opportunity being subject to any notice, reasonable or otherwise. The clause is unchanged from the 1963 Edition and is a relic from even older versions of the Standard Form when site measurement was the rule. There must be doubts as to its effectiveness when many of the measurements are taken from drawings in the offices of the Quantity Surveyor, which may be hundreds of miles from both the site and the office of the Contractor. It is regretable that the Standard Form has not been brought up to date to reflect current practice.

Valuation to be included in Interim Certificates

Clause 13.7   Finally, clause 13.7 (when read in conjunction with clause 3) ensures that the Valuation of each Variation is included in Interim Certificates. Again, it matters not whether the Valuation has been wholly or partly calculated, and, especially, there is no requirement for such Valuation to have been agreed.

REIMBURSEMENT OF LOSS AND EXPENSE

Loss and expense incurred as a result of disruption to the regular progress of the Works is reimbursed to the Contractor under the provisions of clause 26. While this clause has been substantially rewritten by comparison with the 1963 Edition, there are few changes of great importance.

The comments made when discussing clause 25 in relation to the analysis and allocation of Relevant Events apply equally to the 'matters' referred to in clause 26 for the Conditions seem to require the Contractor to specify in notices to the Architect a ground that appears in clause 26.2. It does not seem to be sufficient to merely describe the delay as a 'matter' under clause 26 using a blanket approach. As will be seen in the discussion on clause 26.1 (page 84), the Contractor is recommended to submit further notices when circumstances change and there would seem to be no reason why such a notice should not include a correction to the identification of the 'matter' specified in an earlier notice.

Generally

Clause 26.1   The conditions precedent could usefully have been drafted on a tabular basis similar to clause 25. For convenience the conditions precedent are listed here in a logical sequence and comment is made upon them individually. There are six conditions precedent to consideration by the Architect of a claim for loss and expense under clause 26, and these are set out in clauses 26.1 and 26.1.1 as follows:-

★ has the Contractor incurred, or will he incur, loss and expense?

(Actual loss and actual expense are meant. Not calculated losses, not estimated costs, not amounts included in bills of quantities for preliminaries. The Contractor should be prepared to produce for inspection invoices and books of account.)

★ has the loss and expense arisen because of a material effect on the regular progress of the Works?

(The Architect will not accept any responsibility for losses arising from errors in pricing, failure of Domestic Sub-Contractors and suppliers or bad management by the builder, etc.)

★ has the effect on the regular progress of the Works arisen from one of the items listed in clause 26.2 (the 'list of matters')?

(Inclement weather, lack of labour or materials etc do not count.)

★ will the loss and expense be reimbursed under any other clause in the contract?

(The loss and expense could be reduced by the proper application of the Valuation rules of clause 13, or by payments made as a result of an insurance claim (clause 22), or by the separate assessment of loss and expense following the discovery of antiquities (clause 34).)

★ has the Contractor made written application to the Architect stating that loss and expense has been, or will be, incurred?

(Not verbal comments in the course of conversation on site, not to the Quantity Surveyor, the Employer or the Clerk of Works; not even the recording of such matters in site meeting minutes would necessarily be sufficient.)

★ has the written application of the Contractor been made to the Architect in good time?

(That is to say, '...as soon as it has become, or should reasonably have become, apparent (to the Contractor) that the regular progress of the Works or any part thereof has been or was likely to be affected...(by one of the list of matters)'. After completion or non-completion of the Works is too late; upon receipt of an unsatisfactory Final Account is too late.)

The notice by the Contractor

The requirement, then, is for written application to be made by the Contractor upon realisation that any incident or event falling within the list of matters in clause 26.2 has caused, or will cause, '...the regular progress of the Works or any part thereof...to be materially affected...' **and** that loss and expense has been, or will be, incurred. Such an application is a notice to the Architect and should:-

★ state that the regular progress of the Works has been, or will be materially affected

★ give an explanation (one paragraph) of the circumstances or causes of the disruption of the regular progress

★ state that in the opinion of the Contractor such circumstances or causes are within the list of matters given in clause 26.2

★ specify the 'matter'

★ state that as a consequence of the causes or circumstances described, the Contractor has incurred, or will incur, loss and expense in completing the Works

★ state that in the opinion of the Contractor such loss and expense should be reimbursed under the provisions of clause 26

★ state that in the opinion of the Contractor such loss and expense would not be reimbursed under any other Condition

★ request the Architect to agree that the progress of the Works has been materially affected by the matters described

* request that the Architect immediately inform the Contractor of any further information he may require in order to consider the application by the Contractor

* request that the Architect or Quantity Surveyor ascertain the amount of the loss and expense incurred by the Contractor

* request that the Architect or Quantity Surveyor immediately inform the Contractor of any further details he may require in order to make such an ascertainment.

Duty of the Architect to consider notices

In respect of each written notice or application by the Contractor, the Architect has to decide whether or not the progress of the Works has been materially affected by the matters referred to in the application. If progress has been so affected, then the Architect must ascertain, or may instruct the Quantity Surveyor to ascertain, the resulting loss and expense incurred by the Contractor. The Architect is required to consider **all** notices claiming reimbursement of loss and expense where the regular progress of the Works has been disturbed or disrupted by reason of one of the 'matters' listed in clause 26.3, even where no extension of time has been requested by the Contractor or allowed by the Architect.

The Architect is only permitted to consider the matters referred to in the written application of the Contractor, irrespective of the merits of any other matter not so included.

Clauses 26.1.2 and 26.1.3   By clause 26.1.2, the Architect may request the Contractor to provide 'such information as should reasonably enable the Architect' to make such a decision. The qualifying words used here - 'should reasonably enable' - are important for the intention is presumably to prevent the Architect from **not** making a decision by prevaricating over the extent of the information provided by the Contractor. In addition the Architect or Quantity Surveyor, when ascertaining the amount of the actual loss and expense incurred by the contractor may, by clause 26.1.3, request the submission of 'such details of (his) loss and/or expense as are reasonably necessary for such ascertainment'. Similar qualifying words are used in regard to the reasonableness of the details requested and this should further prevent delay in the ascertainment of any loss and expense.

The Architect or Quantity Surveyor are enabled to make an ascertainment of the loss and expense 'from time to time', thus making it clear that the Contractor is entitled to interim payments of his reimbursement of loss and expense. These are not dependent upon full or agreed ascertainment of the amount concerned (see clause 3). The clear entitlement to interim payment of loss and expense is an important change from the 1963 Edition as is the computation of any loss and expense. The written notice by the Contractor has to state '...that he has incurred or is likely to incur direct loss and/or expense...' and the reference to loss and expense **likely to be incurred** is thought to make it clear that interest and financing charges will automatically be recoverable following ascertainment of the loss and expense. This provision seems to have anticipated the decision of the Court of Appeal in the case between *F.G. Minter and the Welsh Health Technical Services Organisation.*

There is no timetable laid down in the Conditions that expressly states when the Architect has to make a decision on the merits or otherwise of the application for reimbursement of loss and expense by the Contractor. Indeed, there does not appear to be any requirement for the Architect to make his decision known to the Contractor. This omission from JCT 80 requires correction. Should the Architect decide that the matters referred to in the application of the Contractor have **not** materially affected the progress of the Works then there is no immediate remedy open to the Contractor other than continued dialogue with the Architect. The matter can eventually be arbitrated upon, but not until after Practical Completion of the Works. The Contractor should not forget the existence of clause 26.6 which provides that the Contractor may take other action to secure recompense for loss and expense incurred. For example, to consider taking action under Common Law, since such action is not precluded by the Conditions.

It will be apparent that in order to protect properly his position, the timing and content of the written application by the Contractor is most critical. In discussing the practical effects of clause 25 (where the procedural matters concerning extension of time are set out in greater detail than in the present clause) it was suggested that the introduction of JCT 80 should stimulate a review of the procedures of the Contractor. The comments made there, in relation to the identification of Relevant Events, apply equally to this clause, since the pleas for extension of time and claims for recovery of loss and expense will often be pursued in parallel.

Finally, in regard to notices, etc. under clause 26, there is no apparent requirement in the Conditions for the written notices or applications of the Contractor to be updated in the event of any change in the circumstances. The Contractor is recommended to monitor continuously the situation and submit such further written notices as are necessary to keep the Architect informed of the up to date position. Obviously, the Contractor will want to revise his written applications or notices in any case when there has been any material change in the information alreeady given. Where the pleas for extension of time and claims for reimbursement of loss and expense are pursued in parallel, then the reviews required under clause 25 will undoubtably prompt an automatic review of the requests for reimbursement of loss and expense.

The list of matters

Clause 26.2   The matters giving rise to claims for reimbursement of loss and expense are detailed in clause 26.2. There are three new matters, otherwise they are practically the same as those of the 1963 Edition. The following schedule gives a brief description of each matter and some explanatory notes applicable to the new and changed items.

Table VIII Clause	Brief description and comments
26.2.1	**'the Contractor not having received in due time...instructions, drawings, details or levels...for which he specifically applied in writing...', etc.** In order to justify claims for reimbursement of loss and expense under this clause, it would appear that requests must specifically have been made to the Architect for each item of information. To have shown the dates by which information is required upon the master programme, or upon an information required schedule, is not sufficient to satisfy the requirements of this clause. Specific written application must be made everytime. When discussing the master programme earlier in this paper (clause 5.3.2 page 30) reference was made to the effect of incorporating 'float' within the master programme of the Contractor. Since the effect on the regular progress of the Works caused by the late receipt of information correctly requested from the Architect is in part measured by reference to the Completion Date (that is to say, the Date for Completion entered in the Appendix, or such later date as may be fixed by the Architect under clause 25), it will be obvious

(Table VIII continues overleaf)

(Table VIII continued)

that any extended period of float within the master programme would seriously distort the assessment of the disruption to the regular progress of the Works.

A mistake here could seriously affect the extent of disruption acknowledged by the Architect.

26.2.2   **'the opening up...of any work...or the testing of any of the work materials or goods in accordance with...(instructions of the Architect issued under)...clause 8.3 (including making good...)' etc.**

Naturally, no claim can be made where the Contractor has produced work, materials or goods **not** in accordance with the Contract Documents.

26.2.3   **'any discrepancy...or divergence...'etc.**

26.2.4.1   **'the execution of work...by the Employer...' etc.**
(See the discussion on clause 29 (page 152) for the methods by which the Employer can have such work carried out.)

26.2.4.2   **'the supply by the Employer of materials...' etc.**
A new provision applicable where the Contract Documents provide for the Employer to supply some or all of the materials for the Works, and where such supply (or, rather, non-supply) materially affects the regular progress of the Works.

26.2.5   **'Architect's instructions...issued in regard to the postponement of any work...' etc.**

26.2.6   **'failure of the Employer to give in due time ingress or egress from the site...' etc.**

An entirely new provision dealing with the obligations or requirements of the Employer to which several references have already been made in this paper. The words used here are 'ingress' (meaning capacity or right of entrance) and 'egress' (meaning the right or liberty of going out); thus making it clear that this clause has nothing to do with possession of the site, but **is** concerned with land or buildings adjoining the site which are under the control or are owned by the Employer over or through which the Contractor must pass an order to execute the Works.

The question of loss and expense will only arise where a new restriction on access occurs, or where a restriction specified in the Contract Bills and accepted by the Contractor is not met by the Employer and that action materially affects the regular progress of the Works.

26.2.7   **'Architects instructions...requiring a Variation or ...in regard to the expenditure of provisional sums...'.**

An entirely new provision permitting the reimbursement of loss and expense incurred by reason of the execution of Variations, etc. causing disturbance to the regular progress of the Works.

When considering the Valuation of Variations under clause 13, reference was made to the proviso of clause 13.5 which excluded from the Valuation of Variations any sums for loss and expense arising from execution of Variations and expressly causing disturbance to the regular progress of the Works. Such sums are included in the ascertainment of direct loss and expense reimbursed under this clause.

Any loss and expense arising from the execution of Variations but not causing the regular progress of the Works to be materially affected is still to be valued under clause 13.5.

Relationship of extension of time to loss and expense

Clause 26.3   Clause 26.3 introduces a new factor into the contract. In the 1963 Edition there was no positive connection between clause 23 (Extension of time) and clause 24 (loss and expense...). That is to say, the admission of a claim for reimbursement of loss and expense was not dependant on the award of extension of time. It has always been thought that the unmistakeable segregation of the two clauses was to the general advantage of the Contractor. Under clause 26.3 of JCT 80 the Architect is required, for certain of the Relevant Events, to state what extensions of time have been awarded if that information is necessary for the purpose of ascertaining the loss and expense incurred by the Contractor. This seems to be perilously close to making the award of extension of time a condition precedent to the admission of a claim for reimbursement of loss and expense.

The Contractor must beware of any attempt by Architects and Quantity Surveyors to interpret clause 26.3 as saying that the admission of a claim for reimbursement of loss and expense is conditional upon the award of an extension of time. Clause 26.3 does not say this.

The Relevant Events for which extension of time have been awarded and where the Contractor is permitted to request details of the award are:-

★ compliance with instructions of the Architect, but only where those instructions relate to:-

★ ★   discrepancies and divergencies

★ ★   Variation instructions issued under clause 13.2

★ ★   expenditure of provisional sums in the Contract Bills and in any Nominated Sub-Contract

★ ★   postponement of work

★ opening up for inspection

★ late instructions, etc.

★ work by the Employer or persons employed by him, or materials or goods supplied by him

★ failure by the Employer to give access, etc.

The obligation of the Architect to give details of the award to the Contractor is limited to those situations where it is necessary for the purpose of ascertaining the loss and expense. There is no express timetable either for the request by the Contractor or the statement by the Architect. The Conditions do not deal with the situation where there is disagreement as to the necessity for the information. Arbitration is presumably the only recourse in such a case.

Loss and expense by Nominated Sub-Contractors

Clause 26.4   If a Nominated Sub-Contractor makes written application for the reimbursement of loss and expense incurred by disruption to the regular progress of the sub- contract works by reason of the 'matters' detailed in clause 13.1.2 of Sub-Contract NSC/4 or NSC/4a, then the Contractor is required under clause 26.4.1 to pass a copy of the written application to the Architect. If satisfied that the progress of the sub-contract works has been materially affected by one or more of those matters, then the Architect or Quantity Surveyor will ascertain the amount of the loss and expense of the Sub-Contractor.

These provisions do not apply where the disruption of the regular progress of the sub-contract works is due to some default by the Contractor. In such a case, the amount of any claim is to be ascertained and agreed between the Contractor and the sub-contractor. Otherwise the 'list of matters' and rules for ascertainment of loss and expense for a Nominated Sub-Contractor are substantially the same as the main contract, including those provisions requiring the Architect to state the details of the extension of the sub-contract periods for those Relevant Events repeated in the 'list of matters'.

Payment of loss and expense

Clause 26.5   Clause 26.5 (when read in conjunction with clause 3) ensures that ascertained amounts of loss and expense are included in Interim Certificates. Again, it matters not whether the ascertainment is in whole or in part and there is no requirement for such ascertainment to have been agreed.

Other rights of the Contractor to recover loss and expense

Clause 26.6   The preceding notes on clause 26 provide for recovery by the Contractor of loss and expense by the processes set out in the Conditons. Clause 26.6 permits the Contractor to take other action outside the contract against the Employer with a view to recovering his loss and expense. In principle, the alternatives involve proceedings through the courts and are normally actions for the award of damages arising from breach of contract by the Employer or his agent, the Architect.

Any Contractor contemplating taking alternative action must, firstly, obtain proper legal advice and, secondly, carefully consider why he has been unable to recover loss and expense (damages) through the contract. It is believed that in the ordinary course of events it would be easier to show loss and expense in the context of the contract than to show damages in the neutral concept of breach of contract. For example, if the Contractor has been unable to satisfy the conditions precedent of clause 26.1 in order to justify his claim for reimbursement of loss and expense, then it is not likely that he will be able to show by evidence in a court of law that he is entitled to damages for breach of contract by the Employer.

RECOVERY OF FLUCTUATIONS

Clause 37   The extent to which fluctuations in costs are to be recovered by the Contractor and the methods to be adopted to ascertain those amounts are identified by the appropriate deletions in the Appendix. Clause 37 provides that the parties should decide which of the alternative clauses 38 (Contributions, Levy and Tax Fluctuations), 39 (Labour and Materials Cost and Tax Fluctuations), or 40 (use of Price Adjustment Formulae) shall apply. Clause 38 applies if no other has been identified. Clauses 38, 39 and 40 are published separately from the contract and each is complete in its own right, including the detailed procedures for calculation and payment of the amounts due to the Contractor. Clause 37.1 enables the chosen fluctuation clause to be incorporated into the contract by reference only should the parties so agree without the need for physical attachment to the contract. There will be no problem with this procedure provided the chosen clause remains unamended.

For the purpose of this book, since the wording of the limited fluctuations clause 38 (Contributions, Levy and Tax Fluctuations) is included almost verbatim in the full fluctuations clause 39 (Labour and Materials Costs and Tax Fluctuations), the following commentary will be in relation to clause 39, followed by brief comment dealing with the significant differences between that clause and clause 38.

Full fluctuations

Clause 39   Clause 39 is intended to provide for full recovery of fluctuations in cost. The text falls into several distinct sections:-

★ the principles of recovery

★ incorporation into sub-contracts

★ the procedures for calculation and payment (notices, evidence, exclusions, definitions)

★ the percentage addition.

Several sections of the 1963 Edition are reproduced in clause 39. However, there are several changes leading to recovery by the Contractor of a greater proportion of his actual increased costs than was the case previously.

The principles of price adjustment under clause 39 are unchanged from the 1963 Edition. That is to say, the Contractor is entitled to recover the amount of his actual additional costs, no more, no less.

Briefly the fluctuations recoverable by the Contractor are:-

★ **IN RESPECT OF LABOUR:** where there are increases in the minimum wage rates fixed by a wage fixing body, plus the consequential additional costs arising from the operation of an incentive bonus scheme, together with any additional expenses payable where the expense is calculated by reference to the increased wages and bonus (clause 39.1.2).

★ **IN RESPECT OF FARES AND TRANSPORT CHARGES:** either, where there are increases in the cost of fares reimbursable to workpeople under the rules of a recognised wage-fixing body, or, where there are increases in the transport charges of the Contractor (clause 39.1.6).

★ **IN RESPECT OF CONTRIBUTIONS, LEVIES AND TAXES:** where there are increases in the contributions, levies and taxes on the employment of labour (but not payments to CITB) payable by the Contractor and imposed under or by an Act of Parliament (clause 39.2.2).

★ **IN RESPECT OF CONTRIBUTIONS, LEVIES AND TAXES:** where any new contribution, levy or tax on the employment of labour payable by the Contractor is introduced (clause 39.2.2).

★ **IN RESPECT OF CERTAIN MATERIALS:** where there are increases in the market prices of those materials, plus increases in duty or tax (but not Value Added Tax) payable on the procurement of those materials and any new duty or tax on the procurement of those materials is introduced (clause 39.3.2).

★ **IN RESPECT OF DOMESTIC SUB-CONTRACTORS:** where there are increases in labour, certain materials, etc., that become properly payable under the relevant fluctuation provisions included in the sub-contract (clause 39.4).

Changes in the cost of labour

Clause 39.1   The actual conditions for the establishment of increases in the cost of labour are set out in clause 39.1. By clause 39.1.1, the Contractor declares that the basis of pricing the cost of labour in the Contract Bills is:-

★ the rates of wages, etc., promulgated by any appropriate wage-fixing body at the date of tender

★ any incentive bonus scheme payments, holiday scheme credits, employer's liability and third party insurances

★ together with allowances for the appropriate rates of contributions, levies and taxes properly payable by the Contractor as an employer at the Date of Tender and relative to the cost of labour so declared.

Promulgation means the date of publication of the new rate of wages by the wage - fixing body; not the date upon which the new rate of wages is payable. A 'wage- fixing body' is defined in clause 39.7.4; the present clause anticipates the National Joint Council for the Building Industry, but recognises that there may be others. The Date of Tender is defined in clause 39.7.1 as ten days before the date for return of tenders to the Employer (or his Architect).

The provision for recovery of increased costs on incentive bonus scheme payments is entirely new. Some care is required by the Contractor when considering this matter and calculating his tender rates, for it would seem to be quite possible to have an incentive bonus scheme that does not qualify for recovery of increased costs. This is because the reference in clause 39.1.1.4 is to an incentive scheme 'under the provisions of Rule 1.16' of the National Working Rule Agreement. In order to qualify for recovery of increased costs, the scheme must satisfy the objects, general principles, etc. set out in the Appendix to the National Working Rule Agreement, and one supposes that it would be in order for the Employer to require confirmation that it does so.

Clause 39.1.2   In the event that an appropriate wage-fixing body promulgates new rates of wages after the date of tender, clause 39.1.2 provides that the Contractor be paid:-

★ the increased cost of wages, plus

★ any increased cost of 'other emolument' (eg bonus, overtime, etc) and expenses (eg tool money), plus

★ any increase in holiday credits, plus

★ the consequential increase in the cost of:-

    ★★   employer's liability insurance

    ★★   third party insurance

    ★★   any contribution, levy or tax payable by the Contractor as an employer

to the extent that the increased costs relate to 'workpeople'. Workpeople are defined in clause 39.7.3 as those employees whose wages are governed by a recognised wage -fixing body, and are described in clauses 39.1.1.1 and 39.1.1.2 as employees who are actually employed upon the site by the Contractor or are employed by the Contractor in his own workshops etc., while producing materials or goods or manufactured articles for the Works. This description is wider than that appearing in the 1963 Edition and is a sensible extension to the range of matters for which recovery by the Contractor is possible.

The Conditions give no clue as to the means of calculating the amount of consequential increases referred to in the preceding paragraph.

Clause 39.1.3   Clause 39.1.3 is entirely new and provides that where there are persons employed upon the Works whose wages are not covered by a recognised wage-fixing body (eg site agent, trades foremen, surveyors, tea ladies, etc), then payment is made to the Contractor of an amount equal to the increases in wages, bonuses, expenses and the consequential increases in contributions, levies and taxes that would have been made if those persons were craftsmen. Certain qualifications regarding the eligibility for recovery of such persons are detailed in clause 39.1.4. To effect recovery under this clause, the Contractor is required by clause 39.5.5 to submit to the Architect or Quantity Surveyor each week a list of the employees for whom such amounts are payable.

The amount of increased wages, bonuses, expenses, contributions, levies and taxes recovered under clause 39.1.3 is bound not to meet the actual increased costs incurred by the Contractor. Allowance must therefore be made for this shortfall in recovery in the tender calculations.

Clauses 39.1.5   Clauses 39.1.5 and 39.1.6 are entirely new and provide for recovery by the Contractor
and 39.1.6   of increased costs of fares or of costs of transport of the operatives or other workmen of the Contractor. By clause 39.1.5 the Contractor declares that the basis of pricing the cost of transport of workpeople is, **either** by reference to a list of transport charges attached to the Contract Bills, **or**, by reference to the rules of a recognised wage-fixing body and current or promulgated at the Date of Tender. Where the Contractor prices on the basis of transport charges there is no need to foresee any increases. On the other hand where the basis of pricing is the reimbursement of fares, then the promulgated increases of the wage-fixing body must have been included. Where the Contractor requires the increases to be calculated by reference to a 'Basic List of Transport Charges', such a list must be completed and attached to the Contract Bills prior to signature of the Contract Documents. The particulars to be entered on the 'Basic List of Transport Charges' are not specified in the Conditions. Presumably the list could merely comprise a schedule of the possible vehicles required and a hire charge per hour, or per day. Where there are increases in the transport charges or where a recognised wage-fixing body promulgates new rates of reimbursement of fares to workpeople, clause 39.1.6 provides that the increases be paid to the Contractor.

Changes to the rates of contributions, levies or taxes

Clause 39.2   The actual conditions for the establishment of increases in the rates of contributions, levies or taxes and for the identification of new contributions, levies and taxes are detailed in clause 39.2. The meaning of contributions, levies and taxes is set out in clause 39.2.8. It is made clear that it is the **type** of contribution, levy or tax that matters. Provided that the contribution, levy or tax is imposed by an Act of Parliament and is payable by the Contractor as an employer and as a direct consequence of the employment of labour, then any increase in such contributions, levy or tax is recoverable under the contract and it matters not what it is called or how it is collected. The meaning given is deliberately drawn widely so as to avoid argument between the parties to the contract upon the introduction of any new contribution, levy or tax.

By clause 39.2.1, the Contractor declares that the basis of pricing in the Contract Bills is the rates of contribution, levy and tax ruling at the 'Date of Tender'. The Contractor is not required to have foreseen any increases; only the contributions, levy and taxes payable at the Date of Tender should have been allowed.

Where there are increases in the rates of contribution, levy or tax, clause 39.2.2

90

provides that the amount of the increases to the Contractor to the extent that they relate to 'workpeople' and to other persons employed upon the Works. In respect of those other persons, the description, principles and comments in considering clause 39.1.3 generally apply to the present clause.

Special attention should be drawn to the position of contributions to pension schemes and 'contracted-out' employment. All contributions paid by the Contractor as an employer in respect of his employees, and which are commonly described as National Health Insurance Scheme contributions, naturally come within the meaning of contributions under this clause and such contributions provide both the basic state pension and the additional earnings related state pension. Where 'workpeople' or others employed upon the Works are 'contracted-out' of the state pension scheme arrangements by a decision of the Contractor as an employer (ie the employee is a member of the private occupational pension scheme of the Contractor), then clauses 39.2.7 (in the case of workpeople) and clause 39.2.3 (in the case of others employed upon the Works) provide that payment be made to the Contractor of an amount equal to that which would have been payable were such workpeople not so contracted out. In the case, therefore, of 'workpeople' and others employed upon the Works who are members of the private occupational pension scheme of the Contractor the Contractor will receive some contribution towards his share of increased pension fund contributions. The amount recovered will not normally be sufficient to cover the actual increased costs incurred by the Contractor and, again, allowance must be made in the tender for this shortfall in recovery.

Where, however, workpeople are 'contracted-out' of the state pension scheme arrangements by a decision of a wage-fixing body (ie the employee is a member of an industry occupational pension scheme, for example, that operated by the Joint Industry Board for Plumbing Mechanical Engineering Services), the Contractor recovers any increase in contributions to the industry occupational pension scheme under the provisions of clause 39.1, changes in the cost of labour that occur in consequence of a change in the rules or decisions of a wage fixing body.

It is made clear in clauses 39.2.4 to 39.2.6 that where the Contractor receives refunds and premiums in his capacity as an employer and the amount of such refund or premium changes, then the resulting increase or decrease is payable to the Contractor or allowed to the employer as the case may be. An example of a 'refund' in the sense referred to here would have been the old Selective Employment Tax where manufacturers had this refunded. A 'premium' would perhaps occur where there are (or were) Regional Employment Premiums or Subsidies.

Changes in the cost of materials

Clause 39.3   The conditions for the establishment of increases in the cost of materials are set out in clause 39.3. By clause 39.3.1 the Contractor declares that the basis of pricing the cost of materials, etc in the Contract Bills is the market prices of the materials current at the Date of Tender and specified in the list of basic prices attached to the Contract Documents. There is no requirement for the Contractor to have foreseen any increases, only the costs of materials (including duties and taxes) at the Date of Tender should have been allowed.

The materials, etc. to be listed are now described as 'materials, goods, electricity and...(if so agreed)...fuels'. The definitions of 'materials' and 'goods' appears in clause 39.7.2 where it is made clear that the listed materials can include timber used in formwork but not consumable stores, plant or machinery. The bills of quantities will inform the Contractor whether or not payment will be made by the Employer for increases in the cost of fuels. The Conditions give no clue to explain why the reference to fuels is an optional clause, nor is there any guidance as to the reasons for settling the option one way or the other. The references to electricity and fuels are new. Increases in charges for electricity and fuels (when applicable) are payable where the electricity or fuel is used in carrying out the Works, including that used in the temporary site installation of the Contractor.

A change from the 1963 Edition that will have a more significant effect is the new provision requiring the list of materials and basic prices to be produced by the Contractor who, therefore, has the opportunity at least to include **all** materials, etc; for only those listed rank for recovery under the contract. Clause 39.3.1 requires only that the list be attached to the Contract Bills, but in practice such a list will in all probability be required to be submitted by the Contractor with the tender. To judge from the model form appearing in Sub-Contract Tender NSC/1, Architects and Quantity Surveyors will not require to know the identity of the supplier nor will they require substantiation of the market prices. The list should include electricity (rates per unit, any three phase supply) and, if applicable, fuels (petrol, lubricating oil, diesel, gas oil). Since it was the incompleteness of the list of materials that so reduced the amount of recovery under the arrangements of the 1963 Edition, the materials and goods to be listed should obviously be as complete as possible, while remaining consistent with the economics of eventually producing the detailed application. A Contractor having sophisticated computer systems to produce the data automatically may have a longer list of materials than a Contractor who has to produce the data manually. The Contractor must not forget to include the materials and goods of his domestic sub-contractors and must ensure that those rates and prices are those applicable at the Date of Tender under the main contract.

The Contractor should verify, before signing Contract Documents where clause 39 applies, that his list of materials and basic prices has been attached to the Contract Bills.

Where there are increases in the market prices of the materials, etc listed, clause 39.3.2 provides that the increases be paid to the Contractor. It is made clear in clause 39.3.3 that increases in the rates of duty or tax (but **not** including Value Added Tax) are recoverable by the Contractor.

Changes in sub-contract prices

Clause 39.4 Where the Contractor sub-lets work to a Domestic Sub-Contractor, clause 39.4.1 requires that the sub-contract agreement shall include like provisions to clause 39 (including the percentage addition). Clause 39.4.2 provides that increases properly payable under the sub-contract fluctuation clause shall be added to the (main) Contract Sum. The Domestic Sub-Contract issued by the NFBTE and others for use in conjunction with JCT 80 contains the like provisions required by this clause. There is no reference to Nominated Sub-Contractors, for clause 39.6.2 expressly excludes Nominated Sub-Contractors from the operation of clause 39. Fluctuations in the prices of Nominated Sub-Contractors are dealt with by reference to the fluctuation arrangements set out in each Nominated Sub-Contract.

It will be seen that by the wording of clause 39.4.1, the Contractor assumes a positive obligation to include matching fluctuation arrangements in every Domestic Sub-Contract. If the Contractor does not include the matching fluctuation arrangements in Domestic Sub-Contracts, then he would not be entitled under the main contract to recover any increases in the prices of Domestic Sub-Contractors. This is because the Contractor would technically be in breach of his contract with the Employer for not so including the matching fluctuation arrangements; the penalty for this breach being the inability of the Contractor to recover increases under the main contract.

When negotiating the final terms of any Domestic Sub-Contract, the Contractor must ensure that the basis of the tender or quotation of the sub-contractor is rates and prices for materials at the Date of Tender under the main contract, or he must face the penalty of recovering reduced, or even no increases at all in respect of that sub-contractor.

Establishing the entitlement to payment

Clause 39.5   The detailed procedures for the calculation of increases payable to the Contractor are set out in clause 39.5. Clause 39.5.1 requires that the Contractor give notice to the Architect of each and every event causing a change in the following:-

★ rates of wages, emoluments and expenses (including holiday credits)

★ transport charges or the rates for reimbursement of fares

★ contributions, levies and taxes including the introduction of new ones

★ refunds of contributions, levies or taxes, or premium receivable by the Contractor as an employer

★ cost of materials, etc. including duties and levies thereon

★ upon the occurrence of any of the five events listed above where these are relative to the work carried out by each and every domestic sub-contractor.

Such notice should be sent to the Architect (copy to the Quantity Surveyor) and should:-

★ refer to the requirement to give notice under clause 39.5.1;

AND IF IN REGARD TO LABOUR:-

★ ★ inform the Architect that the specified wage-fixing body have promulgated increases in the rates of wages, other emoluments and expenses applicable to the specified trade engaged upon the Works

★ ★ inform the Architect that there has been an increase in the rates of contribution, levy or tax upon the employment of labour engaged upon the Works and payable by the Contractor and/or any sub-contractor

★ ★ inform the Architect of the introduction of a new contribution levy or tax upon the employment of labour engaged upon the Works and payable by the Contractor and/or any sub-contractor

OR IF IN RESPECT OF FARES:-

★ ★ inform the Architect that the specified wage-fixing body have promulgated increases in the rates of fares reimbursable to the specified trade engaged upon the Works and payable by the Contractor and/or any sub-contractor

OR IF IN RESPECT OF TRANSPORT CHARGES:-

★ ★ inform the Architect that the rate or amount of transport charges in the list of basic transport charges has increased

OR IF IN RESPECT OF MATERIALS:-

★ ★ inform the Architect that there has been an increase in the market prices of the specified materials included in the list of materials and basic prices

★ ★ inform the Architect that there has been an increase in the rates of duty or tax on the procurement of the specified materials included in the list of materials and basic prices and payable by the Contractor and/or any sub-contractor

★ ★ inform the Architect of the introduction of a new duty or tax on the procurement of the specified materials included in the list of materials and basic prices and payable by the Contractor and/or any sub-contractor

OR IF IN RESPECT OF A DOMESTIC SUB-CONTRACTOR:-

★ ★ confirm that the sub-contract agreement contains provisions to the like effect of clause 39

★ ★ forward to the Architect a copy of the notice and substantiating documentary evidence received from the sub-contractor

AND IN EVERY CASE:-

★ ★ refer to documentary evidence in substantiation of the increase (eg promulgation notice; press release by Department of Health and Social Security (DHSS); press release by HM Customs and Excise, budget speech, letter from supplier etc), and give the effective date of the increase

★ ★ enclose a copy of the documentary evidence

★ ★ inform the Architect what records will be made (eg wage sheets, analysis of invoices), and submitted to the Architect and/or Quantity Surveyor to demonstrate the amount payable to the Contractor

★ ★ request the Architect to instruct the Quantity Surveyor to include the relevant amounts in future interim valuations in accordance with clause 30.2.2.4.

The Domestic Sub-Contract contains identical provisions to those of the main contract requiring that the sub-contractor give notice to the Contractor of the same events. Hence, it should only be necessary to pass such notices to the Architect.

The Nominated Sub-Contracts NSC/4 and NSC/4a also contain identical provisions requiring that the sub-contractor give notice to the Contractor of the same events, although there does not appear to be any obligation on the Contractor to pass such notices on to the Architect. For the benefit of good relations with the Architect and Nominated Sub-Contractors, it may be as well if such notices were passed on to the Architect.

By clause 39.5.2 the submission of notices where payment is required by the Contractor for any fluctuation in cost covered by clause 39 is a condition precedent. That is to say, no notice, no payment. The reason for such a firm clear statement is that the Architect may have no other way of knowing of the occurence of any fluctuation in cost and will not necessarily be able to keep his client informed as to the probable final account for the project. The notice must also be given within a reasonable time after the occurrence of the event. That is to say after the issue of the promulgation notice, not the commencement of payment of the new rates of wages. This again, is so that the Architect may keep the Employer informed as to his liabilities under the contract. In the case of materials suffering an extraordinary large increase, it may be possible for the Architect to specify an alternative, cheaper, material if he discovers the facts in time.

The traditional method of calculating the amount of increased costs payable to the Contractor has been the laborious analysis of wage sheets and invoices. In clause 39.5.3, provision is made for the Contractor and Quantity Surveyor to agree that in regard to any particular fluctuation, a different (eg simplified, where the traditional method involves costs out of proportion to the amount recoverable) method of evaluating the amount due to the Contractor may be employed, or even a lump sum where this is expeditious to both sides. The agreement is to be made with the Quantity Surveyor, no mention being made of the Architect. The Contractor is advised to write to the Quantity Surveyor stating:-

★ the amount of the agreement

★ the scope of the materials concerned

★ any restraint on the timing of increases taken into account.

Clause 39.5.4 (when read in conjunction with clause 3) permits increased costs to be included in interim valuations. Again, the amounts to be included need not be wholly ascertained, partial ascertainment is sufficient. In particular there does not have to be agreement as to the amounts to be included.

Clause 39.5.5 is entirely new and requires the Contractor to supply the Architect or Quantity Surveyor with evidence and calculations to justify his claim to payment under this clause. The evidence is limited to that which the Quantity Surveyor 'may reasonably require' to ascertain the amount due to the Contractor but the evidence and the calculations have to be presented 'as soon as reasonably practicable'. To qualify for inclusion in full in interim valuations, the Architect and Quantity Surveyor will require to be satisfied that monies are due to the Contractor. If the evidence required by this clause is inadequate or late, the Contractor will find that there is a shortfall in the amounts included in interim valuations. There is a specific requirement for the Contractor to submit a weekly list of the other persons employed upon the Works previously referred to (clause 39.1.3) and which are to be included in his increased cost claims. Similar lists are to be submitted for each and every Domestic Sub-Contractor. The Domestic Sub-Contract includes an identical requirement to the present clause covering submission of such lists to the Contractor.

There is a clear statement in clause 39.5.6 to the effect that no profit is allowed on increases payable under this clause. In the preceeding parts of this clause, this principle is apparent by reference to the amounts of increased costs to be paid as the **net** amounts of such increases.

Clause 39.5.7 is entirely new and provides for the limitation of payment of increased costs where Practical Completion has not been achieved at or before the defined term 'Completion Date' (that is to say, the Date for Completion entered into the Appendix or such other date as may be fixed by the Architect under clause 25). Such limitation operates only where clause 25 is included in the contract without amendment **and** where the Architect has made his award of extension of time (or not as the case may be) under clause 25 on all matters for which written application has been made by the Contractor. If these two pre-conditions are satisfied and the Contractor is indeed out of time achieving Practical Completion, then clause 39.5.7 provides that no amount is to be included in Interim Certificates or the Final Certificate in respect of increased costs arising from an event occurring **after the Completion Date.** There is no change to the right of the Contractor to the inclusion in Interim Certificates or the Final Certificate of amounts in respect of increased costs arising from an event occurring **before** the Completion Date even though the actual increased cost may not be incurred until **after** the Completion Date. It is important that the procedures of the Contractor for recording and substantiation of increases continue to be operated during any disqualifying period, for it may be that the Completion Date will still change as a consequence of further representations or by arbitration.

Clause 39.6   There are certain specified items of work to which clause 39 does not apply. This does not mean that increases in the costs of that work are not refunded to the contractor, only that for those particular items, the amounts due to the Contractor are calculated on a basis that automatically includes the correct amount of increased costs.

The items concerned are set out in clause 39.6.1 to 39.6.3 and are as follows:-

> ★ **daywork** - where the basis of valuation provides for use of rates of wages and prices of materials current at the time the daywork is carried out.

> ★ **Nominated Sub-Contractors and Suppliers** - where the sub-contract NSC/4 and NSC/4a or the contract of sale with Nominated Suppliers each contain their own rules for the calculation of increased costs and the amounts so calculated are reimbursed to the Contractor.

> ★ **work executed by the Contractor for which a prime cost sum is entered in the Contract Bills** - because the basis of valuation of such work contains its own rules for the calculation of increased costs.

An exception to this pattern is in clause 39.6.4 which provides that any increase in Value Added Tax does not qualify for payment under this clause. This is because Value Added Tax is excluded from the Contract Sum under clause 15. As a general rule, the Value Added Tax on all materials and services may be treated as an input tax to the Contractor and will thus be recovered by the Contractor from H.M. Customs and Excise irrespective of the actual rate of Value Added Tax. This means that the Contractor does not incur any additional costs, so that the exclusion of this item from the fluctuation clauses is entirely logical.

Percentage addition

Clause 39.8   Clause 39.8 provides for the Contractor to be paid a percentage addition on the net amount of increased costs payable under clause 39. The addition is intended to provide some measure of recovery for those items for which there is no express recognition within clause 39. It is **not** intended that the percentage addition should represent a contribution towards the increased costs of the overheads of the Contractor. In theory, therefore, one could envisage a correlation between the amount of the percentage addition and the extent of the list of materials and basic prices (ie the higher the percentage addition, the shorter the list of materials and basic prices). Unfortunately, it does not work out this way in practice, for the Employer normally chooses the amount of the percentage addition and often this is at an inadequate figure of 5 to 10 per cent.

Postscript to clause 39

The preceeding remarks lead naturally to a consideration of the effectiveness of clause 39 in regard to its implied aims. The Contractor must consider how much of the actual increased costs that he incurs will be recovered under the provisions of the clause. This consideration must then be reflected in an allowance in the tender to make provision for any shortfall in recovery. It is beyond the scope of this book to consider any detailed calculation in this regard. What can be done is to identify the obvious areas of cost where, as a direct consequence of the detailed provisions of this clause, the full increased cost will not be recovered.

No recovery at all is made on:-

The cost of calculating fluctuations.

Overheads and profit.

Consumable stores and small tools.

Site establishment costs.

Standing bonuses.

Bonus schemes not complying with the National Working Rule Agreement.

Materials not appearing on the list of materials and basic prices.

Fuels, where stated to be not applicable.

Inadequate recovery will be made on:-

Others employed upon the site.

Employers pension scheme contributions where contracted-out.

Materials purchased in small loads.

Limited fluctuations

Clause 38

Clause 38 provides for full recovery of fluctuations in the rates of contributions, levies and taxes on the employment of labour and in the rates of duties and taxes on the procurement of materials. In reality, the only amounts payable are those arising under or by virtue of an Act of Parliament. The extent of increased costs and recovery under this clause is extremely limited, which causes it to be referred to as 'Fixed Price'.

As has already been mentioned, the various matters ranking for recovery under clause 38 are also recoverable under clause 39 and the vast majority of the text of clause 38 appears in clause 39. Table IX shows those parts of clauses 38 and 39 where the text is identical except for the clause references.

Table IX Description	Clause 38 Reference	Clause 39 Equivalent reference
Contribution, levy and tax fluctuation	38.1	
Calculation of Contract Sum; type; and rate of contribution	38.1.1	39.2.1
Increases or decreases	38.1.2	39.2.2
Persons employed on site, not workpeople	38.1.3 38.1.4	39.2.3 39.1.4
Refunds and premiums	38.1.5,6 & 7	39.2.4,5 & 6
Contracted-out employment	See notes below	39.2.7
Meaning of contribution	38.1.9	39.2.8
Materials, duties and taxes	See notes p 99	39.3
Domestic sub-contractors	38.3.1 & 2	39.4.1 & 2
General (notices, payment, evidence, exclusions, definitions etc)	38.4.5 & 6	39.5.6 & 7
Percentage addition	38.7	39.8

The differences to be commented on will, therefore, be seen to be limited to the treatment of contracted-out employees and to the of treatment of duties and taxes on materials. Otherwise the comments made when discussing clause 39 are equally applicable to the equivalent parts of clause 38.

Contracted-out employees

Clause 38.1.8   Where employees (both 'workpeople' and others employed upon the Works) are contracted-out of the state pension arrangements (whether by the decision of the Contractor or by a decision of a wage-fixing body) clause 38.1.8 provides that payment be made to the Contractor of an amount equal to that which would have applied had such employees not been contracted-out. This means that no monies are payable in regard to any further increase in contributions to private occupational pension schemes. This is logical, for increases in contributions to schemes that are in excess of the increases in ordinary contracted-in employment cannot arise by any government action. The contributions of the Employer to private occupational pension schemes must provide benefits not less than those of the state scheme and while the contributions can by agreement between the employee and the employer exceed the minimum legal requirement, this would clearly not be an increase imposed by an Act of Parliament.

Employees to which this situation applies will normally be those referred to in clause 38.1.3 (persons employed upon the site, but not 'workpeople') and who will be members of the private occupational pension scheme of the Contractor. The Contractor will, therefore, receive some contribution towards his share of the increased pension fund contributions, but the amount recoverable will not normally be sufficient to cover the actual increased costs incurred. The Contractor must make allowance in his tender for this shortfall in recovery.

Duties and taxes on materials

Clause 38.2   The actual conditions for the establishment of increases in the duties and taxes on materials are set out in clause 38.2. By clause 38.2.1 the Contractor declares that the basis of pricing the cost of materials in the Contract Bills is the market prices of the materials current at the Date of Tender and specified in the list of materials attached to the Contract Documents. There is no need for the Contractor to have foreseen any increases, only the current rates of duty and tax at the Date of Tender should have been allowed.

The materials etc. to be listed are now described as 'materials, goods, electricity and...(if so agreed)...fuels'. The definition of 'materials' and 'goods' appear in clause 38.6.2, where it is made clear that the listed materials may include timber used in formwork but not consumable stores, plant or machinery. The bills of quantities will inform the Contractor whether or not payment will be made by the Employer for increased duties and taxes on fuels. The Conditions give no clue to explain why the provision relating to fuels is optional, nor is there any guidance as to the reasons for settling the option one way or the other. The references to electricity and fuels is new. Increases in charges for electricity and fuels (when applicable) are payable where the electricity or fuel is used in carrying out the Works, including that used in the temporary site installations of the Contractor. There will be attached to the Contract Bills a list of materials and goods that defines the materials, etc., on which increases in rates of duty and tax will be payable.

The present clause does not expressly state who is to prepare the list of materials and goods, although in all probability the list will be required to be prepared and submitted by the Contractor with his tender. The list should contain electricity (both single and three phase) and, if applicable, fuels (petrol, lubricating oils, diesel, gas oil). The Contractor must not forget to include the materials and goods of his Domestic Sub-Contractors.

The Contractor should verify before signing Contract Documents where clause 38 applies, that the list of materials etc has been attached to the Contract Bills, and that it is as complete as possible.

Where there are increases in the rates of duty or tax on the materials, goods, electricity or fuels specified in the list of materials etc., clause 38.2.2 provides that the increases be paid to the Contractor.

Formula fluctuations

Clause 40   Clause 40 provides for payment to the Contractor of fluctuations in costs by the operation of a formula that uses as the basis of calculation the value of work completed each month. The concept of the fluctuations clauses 38 and 39 previously considered is that the Contractor demonstrates **actual** increases in cost, and then recovers those amounts from the Employer. In clause 40, the amounts recovered from the Employer are calculated by reference to predetermined rules and, therefore,can only be considered as increases in cost **deemed** to have been incurred by the Contractor. Most Contractors who have operated the formula fluctuation clause agree that the amounts recovered do in practice give reasonable recovery of the increased costs incurred. This is principally because the formula operates on the full amount (or 90% where the main contract is in the terms of the Local Authorities Editions) of the Contract Sum inclusive of preliminaries, overheads and profit.

The mechanics of the formula method

Clause 40.1   It would be helpful perhaps to provide a brief explanation of the working of the formula method. The key are the 'Work Categories' developed by the Property Services Agency and which represent a typical mix of labour, plant and materials resources in each of 48 elements of building work. The Contract Bills are analysed into the Work Categories where possible. Those items not allocated to work categories are totalled together and become an amount known as the 'Balance of Adjustable Work' and which is expressed as a proportion of the amount that has been allocated to Work Categories. Each Interim Valuation is similarly analysed into Work Categories. Fluctuations are then calculated for payment to the Contractor by the arithmetical comparison of the cost level indices applicable at the Base Month (effectively, one month before the Date of Tender) and those applicable to the month during which the work was carried out. Adjustments are made for the proportionate increase payable in respect of the Balance of Adjustable Work, and, applicable to Local Authorities Editions only, a deduction for the Non-Adjustable Element (Local Authorities take the view that the Contractor should not be entitled to increased costs on overheads; this has been set by them at 10%, and the total amount of increased costs payable, therefore, are subject to a 10% reduction).

There are no significant changes between clause 40 and the formula fluctuation provisions of the 1963 Edition. Such changes as there are arise entirely from the fact that certain matters referred to in the previous clause now appear in the Conditions in their own right, eg some definitions are included in clause 1.3; rules for retention are included in clause 30; immediate arbitration on the award of extension of time is included in the arbitration agreement.

The detailed operation of this clause is governed by the 'Formula Rules', which repeat the rules previously issued for use in conjunction with the formula fluctuations clause of the 1963 Edition. By clause 40.1.2, definitions included in the Formula Rules apply to clause 40.

After calculation of the amounts due to the Contractor, clause 40.1.3 provides that the amount so calculated be included in 'all certificates for payment'. Clause 40.1.4 permits any amount calculated and paid in an Interim Certificate to be adjusted in future Interim Certificates. The need for such adjustments are legion by the nature of the processes concerned with calculation of the monthly amounts and could include:-

★ work allocated to the wrong Work Categories

★ incorrect index numbers used

★ wrong specialist engineering index used

★ arithmetical errors.

Amendment to payment certificate procedure

Clause 40.2   An amendment to the payment certificate procedure of clause 30 is contained in clause 40.2. Clause 30 ordinarily provides that the Architect may instruct the Quantity Surveyor to carry out interim valuations. Where that discretion is not exercised, a valuation by the Quantity Surveyor is **not** a pre-requisite to the issue of a payment certificate by the

Architect. In clause 40.2, the discretion of the Architect in this matter is removed, thus a valuation by the Quantity Surveyor must be made prior to the issue of every payment certificate by the Architect. This is necessary because the proper operation of the Formula Rules requires that meticulously detailed valuations of the work carried out in each Work Category be made each month.

Materials and goods imported

Clause 40.3   The cost indices upon which the amount of fluctuations are calculated are based on data collected from British manufacturers and, therefore, such indices cannot represent the cost changes relative to goods manufactured abroad. Transport costs and currency changes are the most obvious items that would not be covered. Clause 40.3 neatly gets over the problem by providing that changes in the cost of imported materials and goods be adjusted by reference to 'market prices'. The Contractor is required to produce a list of imported goods and market prices for such materials, and the list is required to be attached to the Contract Bills. In practice, such a list will in all probability be required to be submitted with the tender. The Architect and Quantity Surveyor do not appear to want to know the name of the supplier nor to require substantiation of the market prices. The materials and goods to be listed are those imported by the Contractor, a Domestic Sub-Contractor or a supplier and incorporated into the Works without further treatment by either of them. The prices entered are those current at the Date of Tender and there is no requirement for the Contractor to have foreseen any increases. The Contractor should verify, before signing Contract Documents where clause 40 applies, that the list of imported materials, etc., and market prices has been attached to the Contract Bills.

Where there are increases in the market prices of the materials, etc listed, clause 40.3 provides that the increases be paid to the Contractor. Such changes in market prices can include changes in the rates of duties and taxes (but not Value Added Tax). The Conditions do not include any requirement for the Contractor to give notice of increases in market prices in such materials, etc. However, it would seem prudent for the Contractor to do so in order to facilitate payment. Such notice should be sent to the Architect (copy to the Quantity Surveyor) and should:-

- ★ refer to clause 40.3 and the list of imported materials, etc. and market prices

- ★ inform the Architect that there has been an increase in the market price of the (specified) materials included in the list of imported materials, etc. and market prices

- ★ refer to documentary evidence in substantiation of the increase (eg press release by HM Customs & Excise, letter from supplier/or importer, etc) and give the effective date of the increase

- ★ enclose a copy of the documentary evidence

- ★ inform the Architect what records will be made (eg invoice list; computer printout; etc) and submitted to the Architect or Quantity Surveyor to demonstrate the amount payable to the Contractor

- ★ request the Architect to instruct the Quantity Surveyor to include the relevant amounts in future interim valuations in accordance with clause 40.1.3.

The provisions of clause 40.3, if properly operated, should ensure that the Contractor recovers his total increased costs on imported materials etc.

Application to sub-contractors

Clause 40.4

The position of Nominated Sub-Contractors is dealt with rather laboriously in clause 40.4.1, which provides that the method of calculation of fluctuations set out in the tender of the Nominated Sub-Contractor and accepted by the Architect shall apply.

Where the Contractor elects to sub-let work to Domestic Sub-Contractors, clause 40.4.2 provides that the Domestic Sub-Contract may include provisions for formula adjustment, or that it may not if the Contractor and Domestic Sub-Contractor otherwise agree. Where it is desired to include formula fluctuations, the Domestic Sub-Contract issued by the NFBTE and others for use in conjunction with JCT 80 includes the matching provisions anticipated by this clause. Domestic Sub-Contract Formula Rules are also available.

There is no obligation for Domestic Sub-Contracts to contain formula fluctuation arrangements, since there is no direct correlation between the amounts received by the Contractor under the main contract and the amounts paid to a sub-contractor under the Domestic Sub-Contract. This makes it possible for the Contractor to arrange differing fluctuation arrangements where this is appropriate. For example, where a quotation from a Domestic Sub-Contractor is received after the commencement of the Works it is quite practicable to operate the formula fluctuations in a sub-contract by using a different base month from that in the main contract. Alternatively, a sub-contract may be 'fixed price' or subject to fluctuations on labour but 'fixed price' for materials etc.

Changes to the procedures

Clause 40.5

In clause 40.5 provision is made for the Contractor and Quantity Surveyor to agree to changes to the methods and/or procedures of the Formula Rules. The purpose of making any change is obscure, since the mechanics of carrying out the computations necessary to determine the amounts due are quite simple. Possibly this provision is to permit adoption of the Work Group Method used by the Property Services Agency. The agreement to change methods and/or procedures is, however, heavily qualified. The amounts payable to the Contractor as a result of the operation of the changed method are to be approximately the same as those that would have resulted from the application of the published method.

It is useful to compare the wording here '...agree any alterations to the methods and procedures...' with the wording in the traditional full fluctuations clause 39.5.3 '...agree...the net amount payable...'. In the latter case, it is clear that it is the **amount** that may be agreed and one can see economies in settling lump sums in lieu of laborious calculation. In the present clause it is equally clear that it is a change of **method** of calculating the amount due that may be agreed.

It is made clear in clause 40.5.2 that any agreement made by the Contractor and the Quantity Surveyor under clauses 40.5 and 40.5.1 does not affect any amount to be paid to any Domestic or Nominated Sub-Contractor. However, clause 37 of both the Nominated Sub-Contracts NSC/4 and NSC/4a, and the Domestic Sub-Contract contain provisions that allow an agreement between the Contractor and the Sub-Contractor in identical terms to the present clause. Consequently, if appropriate, the two agreements could proceed in parallel should the parties so wish.

Failure of the indices to appear

Clause 40.6

Failure of the indices to be published is anticipated in clause 40.6. The 'Monthly bulletin of indices' is published by Her Majesty's Stationery Office using data produced by the

Property Services Agency. The indices are used for the procedures applicable to the formula fluctuations method for a vast number of Government contracts as well and it is most unlikely that they will cease to appear. However, if indices do fail to appear, the Contractor remains entitled to be paid for fluctuations in his costs and the adjustments to be included in each Interim Certificate are to be made on a '...fair and reasonable basis...'. If, subsequently, publication of the indices should recommence, then any adjustment to the amounts provisionally assessed during the period of their cessation shall be treated as an adjustment under clause 40.1.2. Clause 40.6.3 requires the Contractor and the Employer, presumably the Quantity Surveyor on his behalf, to ensure that adequate records are kept so as to enable the adjustments to be made. The Conditions doe not anticipate the situation where publication of the indices has not recommenced before the Final Certificate is to be issued.

Clause 40.7   Clause 40.7 provides for the limitation of payment of increased costs where Practical Completion has not been achieved at or before the Completion Date (that is to say, the Date for Completion entered in the Appendix, or such other date as may be fixed by the Architect under clause 25). Such limitation operates only where clause 25 is included in the contract without amendment, **and** where the Architect has made his award of extensions of time or not, as the case may be, under clause 25 on all the matters for which written application has been made by the Contractor. If these two pre-conditions are satisfied and the Contractor is indeed out of time in achieving Practical Completion, then clause 40.7.1.1 provides that formula adjustments included in subsequent Interim Certificates or the Final Certificate shall only be made on the basis of the indices applicable to the month during which the Completion Date occurred. This is known as the 'freezing' of the indices. It is important that the procedures of the Contractor and the Quantity Surveyor for carrying out valuations in such a way that work done can readily be analysed into Work Categories continue to be operated, since it may be that the Completion Date will still change as a consequence of further representations by the Contractor or by arbitration.

Examples and model forms of price adjustment using the formula method can be found in the Property Services Agency booklet 'Guide to application and procedure' of the Price Adjustment formulae for building contracts. The labour, material and plant resources used in the calculation of the price level indices for the Work Categories are set out in the Property Services Agency booklet 'Description of the indices'.

In theory it is possible for a comparison to be made of the actual labour, material and plant resources anticipated at tender stage by the Contractor for each category with the resources incorporated into the indices. This enables some adjustment to be made to the tender to provide for the consequent over or under recovery of fluctuations by the Contractor. Such calculations are often impracticable in the hurly burly of tendering. It may be worthwhile for builders to carry out an historical survey of the resources detailed in the indices and their own cost experiences. Such calculations may well expose a consistent over or under recovery of fluctuations and a coarse adjustment factor for tenders could be revealed.

MATERIALS ON AND OFF THE SITE

Materials on site are dealt with in clause 16.1 and materials off-site in clause 16.2. The texts are unchanged from the 1963 Edition which is strange, in view of the comments made in legal circles in regard to ownership of unfixed materials that arose from the Romalpa case. Clauses 16.1 and 16.2 are 'vesting clauses' and seek to protect the position of the Employer in the case of liquidation or bankruptcy of the Contractor.

Materials on site

Clause 16.1 Materials and goods brought on to the site may not be removed without the permission of the Architect. This is presumably to prevent the Contractor having materials delivered to the site and removing them again after payment by the Employer. The reference in this clause is to materials and goods only. There is no mention of plant, equipment, or temporary works.

The value of materials and goods brought on to the site may be included in Interim Certificates provided the conditions set out in clause 30.2.1 are satisfied. That is to say, the materials and goods must be '...reasonably, properly and not prematurely...delivered and ...protected...'. There is, therefore, wide scope for Quantity Surveyors and Architects **not** to include the whole value in an Interim Certificate. Where an Interim Certificate containing amounts for materials on site has been paid by the Employer, clause 16.1 provides that the materials and goods become the property of the Employer. This is fine where the goods belong to the Contractor, but if the materials or goods still belong to the supplier or manufacturer because the contract of sale between the Contractor and supplier contains, say, a provision to the effect that ownership only passes upon payment in full, and the Contractor has not paid, then the Employer is not fully protected. This would in practice only matter in the event of liquidation or bankruptcy of the Contractor.

The entire responsibility for loss or damage to materials on site remains with the Contractor at all times, whether the materials have been paid for by the Employer or not. The only exception is where there is loss or damage by one of the 'Clause 22 Perils' and where under clause 22B or 22C that risk is taken by the Employer.

Materials off site

Clause 16.2 The Architect is obliged to include in Interim Certificates the value of materials properly on the site, whereas for materials off site the Architect may or may not include the value of such materials and goods in Interim Certificates at his discretion. Such discretion is governed by a schedule of conditions set out in clause 30.3 and which have to be complied with by the person holding the materials or goods. The conditions themselves are examined in the discussion on clause 30.3, commencing on page 118.

Where the Architect has exercised his discretion and the Contractor has been paid, the materials and goods become the property of the Employer, and the holder of the materials and goods must not move them, except for delivery to the site, while at all times remaining at the risk of the Contractor as regards loss or damage. As will be seen in the advice offered when discussing clause 30.3, the Contractor can protect his position by obtaining indemnities and/or certificates from his supplier to deal inter alia with these points. In clause 16.2 it is made clear that the Contractor retains responsibility for storage, handling and insurance of the materials or goods.

PAYMENTS TO THE CONTRACTOR

Clause 30 The procedures for payments to the Contractor are set out in clause 30, 'Certificates and payments'. It is evident that the increased length of this clause arises, firstly from the tabular presentation of the material and, secondly, from the inclusion of a substantially extended section setting out matters to be included in the final adjusted Contract Sum (the final account).

Interim Valuations and Interim Certificates

Clause 30.1 Clause 30.1.1.1 provides that the Architect will issue Interim Certificates and that the Contractor is entitled to be paid within 14 days of the date of issue of each Interim

Certificate. Clause 5.8 required that all certificates be issued to the Employer with a copy to the Contractor and this means that it is no longer necessary for the Contractor to present payment certificates of the Architect to the Employer. This small change will be welcomed, for in theory the Contractor will receive his money earlier.

Clause 30.1.1.2 is entirely new and grants to the Employer an express right to deduct or set off from monies due to the Contractor in an Interim Certificate such amounts as may be due to the Employer under the Contract. The deduction can be made from any monies due to the Contractor whether these are in respect of work carried out by the Contractor or any Nominated Sub-Contractor or that become payable by reason of a reduction in the Retention held by the Employer. The most obvious example of such a right being liquidated and ascertained damages (clause 24.2.1) but there are several others:-

* ★ the cost to the Employer of the failure of the Contractor to comply with instructions of the Architect (clause 4.1.2)

* ★ the cost to the Employer of insurance following the failure of the Contractor to insure (clauses 21.1.3 and 22A.2)

* ★ the cost to the Employer of completion of the contract following determination of the employment of the Contractor (clause 27.4.4)

* ★ the amount of any deduction made by the Employer under the Construction Industry Tax Deduction Scheme (clause 31.6.1)

* ★ the amount of direct payments to Nominated Sub-Contractors following the failure of the Contractor to make payment (clause 35.13.5.3)

* ★ any amount not recovered by the Employer under the indemnity given by a Nominated Sub-Contractor in Agreement NSC/2 or NSC/2a and arising from the cost of rectifying defects in the sub-contract works discovered after final payment has been made to the sub-contractor (clause 35.18.1.2)

* ★ the amount of the additional cost of the employment of a substitute Nominated Sub-Contractor following the valid determination of his own employment by a Nominated Sub-Contractor (clause 35.24.6)

* ★ the amount of any expenses incurred by and loss and/or expense caused to the Employer by reason of the determination of the employment of a Nominated Sub-Contractor (clause 29.4 of Sub-Contract NSC/4 or NSC/4a and incorporated into the Conditions by clause 35.26).

The right of the Employer to deduct amounts due to him is limited in certain respects. Clause 30.1.1.2 only permits deductions to be made from Interim Certificates (deductions from the Final Certificate are authorised by clause 30.8 (see page 115)). The deduction can only be made where the Conditions expressly permit such deduction to be made. No deduction can be made from Retention monies until they have been included in an Interim Certificate. Where the deduction proposed to be made by the Employer arises because of a failure by the Contractor to pay to Nominated Sub-Contractors amounts included in a previous Interim Certificate, then the right of the Employer to make such a deduction is further limited. Where any Interim Certificate includes or comprises reductions in the amounts of Retention held by the Employer, then, irrespective of the amount due to the Employer by reason of default of the Contractor, the maximum deduction that may be made by the Employer is the amount in that certificate which represents the reduction in the Retention held by the Employer in regard to work carried out by the Contractor. This prohibits the Employer from making a deduction that would interfere with the retention he holds in regard to work carried out by an Nominated Sub-Contractor. In other words, the retentions of Nominated Sub-Contractors remain inviolate.

The foregoing comments are concerned with amounts due to the Employer by reason of some default by the Contractor. It may be that the deduction made by the Employer from monies due to the Contractor is the direct result of some default by a Nominated Sub-Contractor under the contract. Clause 21.3.1.2 of Sub-Contract NSC/4 or NSC/4a anticipates that the Employer could make such a deduction and the Contractor is permitted to reduce his payment to the Nominated Sub-Contractor by a similar amount.

Where the Employer makes a deduction from a payment to the Contractor, clause 30.1.1.3 requires that he inform the Contractor of the reason for making the deduction. This is admirable as far as it goes but the Conditions give no timetable for the issue or receipt of the notice. It can be argued that the Employer should give notice of the deduction prior to payment of the balance, or that the explanation should accompany the payment.

The Quantity Surveyor has been given a new responsibility under clause 30.1.2 to make interim valuations. The valuations are to be made at the discretion of the Architect generally, except that where the formula fluctuation clause 40 applies, they are compulsarily at monthly intervals. This is necessary in order to facilitate the operation of the formula fluctuation procedures.

The programme for the issue of Interim Certificates is detailed in clause 30.1.3 and the associated Appendix entry. The normal arrangement anticipated by the Conditions is that certificates be issued monthly, but there is no mention of the timing of the issue of the first Interim Certificate. It is important for the Contractor to consider the question of timing of the first Interim Certificate for it settles the programme of certificates for the remainder of the contract. The Contractor is recommended to explore with the Employer the actual mechanics of making payment to the Contractor. For example, a local authority computer may produce cheques only at specific times in any week or month, or it may be that the payment has to be approved by a committee that only meets once a month. In such cases the Contractor should endeavour, in conjunction with the Architect and Quantity Surveyor, to arrange that the timing of the issue of Interim Certificates be geared to the procedures of the Employer. It may then be that payments could be received within two or three days of the issue of the Interim Certificate, thus optimising the cash flow of the Contractor.

The important point to note is that the date of issue of the first Interim Certificate establishes the date of issue of all future Interim Certificates, for the Conditions envisage their regular issue at the agreed intervals (normally monthly), come what may. The Architect's holiday, for example, is not a valid reason for failing to issue an Interim Certificate. The fact that the Contractor has not carried out much work since the issue of the last Interim Certificate is not normally a valid reason for failing to issue a further Interim Certificate.

The Conditions do not deal adequately with the position where the Architect does not issue an Interim Certificate. The right of the Contractor to determine his own employment under clause 28 arises only from failure by the Employer to honour an Interim Certificate, **not** the absence of an Interim Certificate. Where, by reference to the programme for the issue of Interim Certificates set out in the Conditions at the Appendix, the Contractor does not receive his copy of an Interim Certificate at the proper time, notice should be given to the Architect (copy to the Employer). Such notice should:-

★ inform the Architect that copy of Interim Certificate No... has not been received

★ identify the date upon which it should have been issued

★ request that the Architect issue the Interim Certificate as a matter of urgency.

Should the Contractor still not receive a copy of the Interim Certificate within a few days after the notice, then it would appear that the only recourse for the Contractor is to commence arbitration proceedings. This is a matter upon which the Contractor is entitled to immediate arbitration, article 5.2.2 '...whether or not a certificate has been improperly withheld...'. However, even an immediate arbitration will take some time to establish and proceed to a hearing, so it is doubtful how this procedure will help.

While the Conditions do not permit the Contractor to suspend the execution of the Works, the failure of the Architect to issue a payment certificate would surely constitute a fundamental breach of contract of such proportions that suspension of the Works may be justified.

It may be that there are other legal procedures that may be taken against the Employer and the Architect. The Contractor will require to obtain proper legal advice on these matters.

In addition to the normal monthly certificates, clause 30.1.3 provides for additional Interim Certificates to be issued:-

★ at the end of the monthly period during which the Certificate of Practical Completion is issued

★ as and when further amounts are due to the Contractor

★ and upon the issue of the Certificate of Completion of Making Good Defects.

The Interim Certificate issued at the end of the month during which Practical Completion occurs will, firstly, ensure that one half of the Retention held by the Employer is promptly paid to the Contractor and, secondly, where formula fluctuations apply, enable the increased costs relative to the monthly period during which Practical Completion occurs to be properly calculated using the correct valuation amounts. The Interim Certificate issued upon the completion of making good defects will ensure that the second half of the Retention held by the Employer is promptly paid to the Contractor. Clearly, the proper date for the issue of such certificates can be determined readily and in their absence a notice to the Architect,similar to that referred to previously should be sent by the Contractor. The eventual remedy by the Contractor in the continued absence of such certificates is the same, arbitration, with the same problems.

The remaining group of additional Interim Certificates is intended to provide a means of making payments to the Contractor during the Defects Liability Period and arising from final Valuation of Variations, for loss and expense due to disruption, etc; for early final payments to Nominated Sub-Contractors etc. The issue of these additional Interim Certificates is not subject to any firm timetable and during the negotiations between the Contractor and the Quantity Surveyor leading to the establishment of the amount of further monies due to the Contractor, the Quantity Surveyor must be requested to recommend to the Architect that a further Interim Certificate be issued. Much will depend on the amount and frequency with which such monies are identified. It is difficult to see what can be done to force the issue of such an Interim Certificate.

The amounts due in Interim Certificates

Clause 30.2   Two new expressions, the 'gross valuation' and the 'Retention' are introduced in clause 30.2. The items to be included in the 'gross valuation' are set out at some length in clauses 30.2.1, 30.2.2 and 30.2.3. The Retention is now considered in a slightly different concept by comparison with the 1963 Edition, for 'Retention' is specifically the amount calculated by the application of the 'Retention Percentage' to the various parts of each and every valuation according to the rules laid down in clause 30.4. Clause 30.2 provides that the amount stated to be due to the Contractor in any Interim Certificate is the gross valuation, **less** Retention and **less** the total of the amounts included in previous certificates. There is no reference to the amounts actually paid to the Contractor by the Employer. The reason for this is that the amount actually paid by the Employer is not the direct concern of either the Architect or the Quantity Surveyor; it is solely a matter between the Contractor and the Employer. The Conditions purport to set out the remedies available to the Contractor in the event of non-payment by the Employer. These are not really very effective as will be seen in the discussion on clause 28, page 140. The final part of clause 30.2 permits the gross valuation to be made up to seven days before the date of the Interim Certificate. The purpose is presumably to enable the Quantity Surveyor to complete his recommendation and to send it to the Architect, although the time scale does not permit any lengthy enquiries by the Architect. Work carried out and materials supplied **less** than seven days before the Interim Certificate **may** be included in it, but need not be.

The amounts to be included in the gross valuation and the Interim Certificate are set out in clauses 30.2.1 (work subject to Retention); 30.2.2 (work **not** subject to Retention); and 30.2.3 (deductions). Briefly, these are:-

Clause 30.2.1 (ie subject to Retention)

★ the value of:-

★★ work properly executed (including Domestic Sub-Contractors, work carried out as a result of instructions as to the expenditure of provisional sums, and work carried out where the tender of the Contractor for work covered by a PC sum has been accepted)

★★ variations ascertained by reference to clause 13.5 (including daywork, lump sum adjustments, preliminaries etc)

★★ formula fluctuation additions

★★ materials on site (properly, not prematurely, and protected)

★★ materials off site (for which the Contractor has submitted indemnities and other documents)

★ the amounts directed for payment to Nominated Sub-Contractors which are themselves subject to Retention

★ the profit of the Contractor on the amounts directed for payment to Nominated Sub-Contractors. (Note that the rules for valuation of profit where the nomination is in consequence of the expenditure of a provisional sum are given in clause 30.2.1.5).

Clause 30.2.2 (ie not subject to Retention)

★ the amount of cost actually incurred by reason of:-

★ ★   fees or charges payable to local authorities or statutory undertakers (clause 6.2)

★ ★   instructions of the Architect amending errors in setting out (clause 7)

★ ★   instructions of the Architect to inspect or test materials (clause 8.3)

★ ★   royalties and patent rights (clause 9.2)

★ ★   defects and the like rectified at the cost of the Employer (clauses 17.2 and 17.3)

★ ★   insurances to property other than the Works (clause 21.2.3)

★ any loss and expense ascertained and caused by:-

★ ★   disruption, etc. (clause 26.1)

★ ★   antiquities (clause 34.3)

★ the amounts of:-

★ ★   any final payment to a Nominated Sub-Contractor (clause 35.17)

★ ★   any increased costs due under the cost fluctuation clauses (clauses 38 and 39)

★ the amounts directed for payment to Nominated Sub-Contractors which are themselves not subject to Retention.

Clause 30.2.3 (ie deductions)

★ any amount allowable:-

★ ★   by the Contractor under the cost fluctuation clauses (clauses 38 and 39)

★ ★   by a Nominated Sub-Contractor under the cost fluctuation clauses of a Nominated Sub-Contract.

There is no reference in this clause or elsewhere in the Conditions to the need for the Contractor to make an application for payment. The Contract Bills may contain an item requiring the Contractor to make applications for payment to the Quantity Surveyor and to supply a greater or lesser amount of detail in that application. Such a requirement in the Contract Bills should be complied with since the requirement does not become in-validated under clause 2.2.1, which refers only to items in the bills of quantities not over-riding or modifying the Conditions. A requirement for the Contractor to make applica-tions for payment cannot be made a condition precedent to the issue of an Interim Cer-tificate since that **would** override the Conditions and would be rendered invalid by clause 2.2.1. The Contractor would remain entitled to an Interim Certificate, whether or not he had made an application for payment. There could well be a dispute over the amount of the Interim Certificate if the Contractor does not make an application, but the Ar-chitect must issue an Interim Certificate.

The Conditions do not expressly contemplate the position where the Contractor is dissatisfied with the amounts included in an Interim Certificate. Where the Contractor is seriously aggrieved by the amount of an Interim Certificate, notice should be given to the Architect (copy to the Quantity Surveyor). Such notice should:-

★ refer to the Interim Certificate in question

★ inform the Architect of the dissatisfaction of the Contractor of the amount included

★ give a brief (one sentence) explanation of the reason for the dissatisfaction (eg work complete but not included, materials properly delivered but not included, Valuation of Variations inadequate etc)

★ request that the Architect immediately issue an adjusted certificate.

Should the Contractor not receive an adjusted certificate and should he still feel aggrieved, then his only recourse would appear to be arbitration. Under the arbitration agreement the Contractor is entitled to immediate arbitration, article 5.2.2 '...whether a certificate is not in accordance with the Conditions...' (ie it does not reflect the values properly due to the Contractor). If the Architect has not issued an adjusted Interim Certificate, then the Employer must honour the original Interim Certificate. It would be iniquitous if this were not so, for by its nature, the dispute is not concerned with work that **has** been included in the Interim Certificate; the dispute is in relation to work that has **not** been included in the Interim Certificate.

Where a Nominated Sub-Contractor is aggrieved with the amount included in an Interim Certificate, then he has, subject to certain conditions, a similar right to objection and arbitration.

Retention

Clause 30.4   The precise rules for calculating the amount of Retention the Employer may deduct and retain are set out in clause 30.4. There is no obvious reason for the use of the word 'may' in this clause, but the inference is that deduction of Retention is not obligatory. The Retention Percentage will have been communicated to the Contractor at tender stage since it is an Appendix entry and will thus be detailed in the bills of quantities. It is made clear that Retention is the **amount** calculated by applying the Retention Percentage according to the rules in clause 30.4.1.

The method of calculating the amount of retention is set out in clauses 30.4.1.2 and 30.4.1.3. Where work that is subject to Retention has not reached Practical Completion, the full Retention Percentage is deductible. Where work has reached Practical Completion, but a Certificate of Making Good Defects has not been issued, then one half of the Retention Percentage is deductible. **No** Retention is deductible on any other work, for example, where a Certificate of Making Good Defects has been issued, nor where the work is **not** subject to Retention.

It is intended that work by Nominated Sub-Contractors should be treated in exactly the same way as outlined in the preceding paragraph, that is to say, the Nominated Sub-Contractor will be paid one-half of the Retention in the first valuation after practical completion of the sub-contract works and may, (there are a number of conditions, see the notes on clause 35 (page 161)), be paid the remaining Retention twelve months later. The Contractor is not expected to finance the payment of Retention to Nominated Sub-Contractors. The amounts concerned will be included in Interim Certificates under the main contract. There is no such concession for Domestic Sub-Contractors, unless the Contractor and the Domestic Sub- Contractor shall so agree. The Domestic Sub-Contract issued by the NFBTE and others contains optional provisions for such agreement.

The calculation of the amounts of Retention to be held by the Employer in respect of the Contractor and each Nominated Sub-Contractor can be a burdensome exercise. By clauses 30.4.2, 30.5.2.1 and 30.5.2.2 the Quantity Surveyor will provide the Architect, the Employer, the Contractor, and each Nominated Sub-Contractor concerned with a statement showing the relative amounts the Employer is holding in respect of the Contractor and each Nominated Sub-Contractor.

So far as can be ascertained the statement will show the amounts contained in each Interim Certificate that are subject to full, half and nil retentions. Builders may not be agreeable to those amounts being circulated to all Nominated Sub- Contractors as these amounts are priviliged or confidential information.

Clause 30.5 Some further rules on the treatment of Retentions are set out in clause 30.5. Reference has already been made to the right of the Employer to set off monies due to him from amounts included in Interim Certificates. In clause 30.5.4 that right is restated and it is made clear that it exists in regard to amounts included in Interim Certificates for payment of Retentions to either the Contractor or any Nominated Sub-Contractor. Where the Employer exercises his right to make such a deduction from Retentions, he is required to inform the Contractor of the amount so deducted from either the 'Contractors retention' or the retention of Nominated Sub- Contractors. The statement of Retentions, for the Interim Certificate concerned, prepared by the Quantity Surveyor will be the basis of the information to be given by the Employer.

Employer a trustee for Retention

In clause 30.5.1 it is made clear that the interest of the Employer in the Retention held by him on behalf of the Contractor and each Nominated Sub-Contractor is fiduciary as trustee. This means that the Employer becomes a trustee and holds the Retention on trust for the Contractor. The word 'fiduciary' describes the relationship between the trustee (the Employer) and the beneficiary (the Contractor) in regard to the trust fund (the Retention). That is to say, the Conditions place the Employer in a position of power and confidence with respect to the Contractor and the Retention. As a trustee, the Employer assumes certain duties prescribed by the law. He is obliged to administer the Retention fund in accordance with various rules of law and to act in the sole interest of the Contractor. The clause is intended to ensure that the Contractor will always be paid the Retention, even in the event of liquidation or bankruptcy of the Employer.

In order to be wholly effective, the Retention must have been set aside by the Employer in a separately identifiable fund (the trust). Therefore, a new clause 30.5.3 appears in the Private Editions of JCT 80 entitling the Contractor or any Nominated Sub-Contractor to request that the Employer positively assumes the role of trustee by having the Retention put into a separate bank account in the joint names of himself and the Contractor. This is a significant change from the 1963 Edition and has been introduced because the absence of a separate trust fund would probably have meant that the Contractor would not have access to funds held by the liquidator or trustee in bankruptcy of an insolvent Employer. Clause 30.5.3 does not appear in the Local Authorities' Editions since a Local Authority cannot become bankrupt.

Upon the commencement of a contract under one of the Private Editions of JCT 80, the Contractor must consider in each case whether he is to ask the Employer to create a separate trust fund for the Retention and so secure for himself and Nominated Sub-Contractors protection for that Retention in the event of insolvency or liquidation of the Employer. Where the Contractor does decide that the Employer should be requested to create a separate trust fund for Retentions in a separate bank account, then the Contractor is required by the Conditions to give notice to the Employer upon the receipt of each payment. Such notice to the Employer (copy to the Architect) should:-

★ draw attention to clause 30.5.3 of the Conditions

★ request that the Employer place in a separate bank account the amount of Retention held in respect of Interim Certificate No...

★ (upon the first request) request that the Employer certify to the Architect (copy to the Contractor) when the separate bank account has been created and giving a note of its number and designation

★ request that the Employer certify to the Architect (copy to the Contractor) when the Retention has been placed in the separate bank account:-

The text of the present clause indicates that any Nominated Sub-Contractor can similarly request the Employer to place Retention into a separate bank account. It is not clear from the Conditions whether one request from either the Contractor or a Nominated Sub-Contractor is sufficient to ensure that the Employer sets aside **all** Retentions whether held in respect of the Contractor or all the Nominated Sub- Contractors.

The final adjustment of the Contract Sum

Clause 30.6

The procedures and rules for the calculation of the final adjustment of the Contract Sum (the Final Account) are set out in clause 30.6. The clause has been redrafted by comparison with the 1963 Edition but the principles are unchanged. There is, however, a more extended listing of items to be included in the final account.

Clause 30.6.1.1 requires the Contractor to present to the Quantity Surveyor the documents necessary to permit him to compute the final account. The description of the documents to be produced by the Contrctor is very widely drawn and must be taken to mean that if the Contractor wants to be paid then he **must** produce the necessary documents. In particular, such documents must include the final accounts for Nominated Sub-Contractors and invoices, etc for Nominated Suppliers. The Contractor is to produce the final account documents within a reasonable time after Practical Completion of the Works. Clearly, delay by the Contractor in producing such documents would prevent the operation of the next stage of the final account process, the issue of the Final Certificate, and this would only penalise the Contractor.

A statement of the final Valuation of Variations is to be passed to the Contractor within a period recommended to be six months after Practical Completion of the Works. It is made clear in clause 30.6.1.2 that this is subject to the Contractor delivering the necessary final account documents to the Quantity Surveyor within a reasonable time. The final Valuation of Variations is to be prepared by the Quantity Surveyor and sent to the Contractor by the Architect. The statement sent to the Contractor will include the final accounts of Nominated Sub-Contractors but the Architect will send the relevant parts to each Nominated Sub-Contractor. The Conditions do not envisage, either in the present clause or in clause 13, any formal arrangement for the agreement of such Valuations by the Contractor and the Quantity Surveyor. In particular, there is no express provision dealing with the situation where the Contractor and the Quantity Surveyor are not able to agree the amount of the Valuation.

Items to be included in the final account

Clause 30.6.2

The amounts to be included in the final adjustment of the Contract Sum are detailed in clause 30.6.2. Briefly, these are:-

Deductions

- ★ PC Sums and amounts for named Nominated Sub-Contractors from the Contract Bills, together with the profit of the Contractor on those sums

- ★ provisional sums and work described as provisional in the Contract Bills

- ★ the amounts of:-

  - ★ ★ those items in the Contract Bills that are omitted in the measurement of Variations

  - ★ ★ those items in the Contract Bills that are omitted in the Valuations of affected work consequential to a Variation

  - ★ ★ any allowance by the Contractor under cost or formula fluctuation clauses

- ★ (in case anything has been forgotten) '...any other amount which is required by this contract to be deducted from the Contract Sum...'.

Additions

- ★ the final accounts of Nominated Sub-Contractors plus the profit of the Contractor on those amounts

- ★ the final adjusted tender sum for work carried out by the Contractor as a consequence of the offer by the Contractor to carry out work reserved for Nominated Sub-Contractors in the Contract Bills, plus profit at the rate stated in the Contract Bills on the PC Sum

- ★ the amounts properly payable by the Contractor in respect of Nominated Suppliers, plus the profit of the Contractor on those amounts

- ★ the amounts of costs actually incurred by reason of:-

  - ★ ★ fees or charges payable to local authorities and statutory undertakers (clause 6.2)

  - ★ ★ instructions of the Architect amending errors in setting out (clause 7)

  - ★ ★ instructions to test or inspect materials (clause 8)

  - ★ ★ royalties and patent rights (clause 9.2)

  - ★ ★ defects and the like rectified at the cost of the Employer (clauses 17.2 and 17.3)

  - ★ ★ insurances to property other than the Works (clause 21.2.3)

  - ★ ★ (Private Editions only) insurances to the Works etc consequential to default by the Employer (clauses 22B and 22C)

- ★ the amounts of the Valuation of those items:-

  - ★ ★ added in the measurement of Variations and ascertained by reference to clause 13.5, ie including daywork, lump sum adjustments, preliminaries, etc.

113

★ ★   added in the Valuation of other affected work consequential to a Variation (clause 13.5.5)

★ ★   carried out as a result of instructions as to the expenditure of provisional sums

★ ★   carried out and which were described as provisional in the Contract Bills

★ any loss and expense ascertained and caused by:-

★ ★   disruption, etc (clause 26.1)

★ ★   antiquities (clause 34)

★ the amounts of any increased costs due under the cost or formula fluctuation clauses

★ 'any other amount which is required by the Contract to be added to the Contract Sum'.

The Contractor is entitled (clause 30.6.3) to receive a copy of the calculations of the final adjusted Contract Sum prepared by the Quantity Surveyor before the issue of the Final Certificate by the Architect.

The position in regard to final account documents is, therefore, that the Contractor is to receive, firstly, the Valuation of Variations by the Quantity Surveyor not later than the expiry of the Period of Final Measurement stated in the Appendix (recommended to be six months after Practical Completion of the Works). Secondly, the computation of all the remaining items to be included in the final adjustment of the Contract Sum not later than the expiry of the period for issue of the Final Certificate stated in the Appendix (recommended to be three months) after the later of, either, the end of the Defects Liability Period or, the issue of the Certificate of Completion of Making Good Defects.

This means that the Contractor cannot receive the complete final account documentation earlier than nine months after Practical Completion of the Works and perhaps a lot later. The Conditions do not actively contemplate the position where the Contractor is dissatisfied with the amount of the final adjusted Contract Sum prepared by the Quantity Surveyor. Where the Contractor is aggrieved by the amount of the final adjusted Contract Sum no formal action can be taken until the recommendations of the Quantity Surveyor have materialised into the Final Certificate. The amounts contained therein can then be disputed and settled by arbitration (see clause 30.9.2). In the meantime the Contractor can be holding discussions with both the Architect and the Quantity Surveyor in an endeavour to have the under-valuations corrected.

Penultimate certificate

Clause 30.7   A new type of Interim Certificate is introduced in clause 30.7. This special Interim Certificate will include all the amounts of the final payments to Nominated Sub- Contractors consequent to settlement of their respective final accounts. The sole reason for this special Interim Certificate is to ensure that in the event of the Contractor failing to make the final payments to Nominated Sub-Contractors, the Employer is able to operate the direct payment provisions of the Agreement NSC/2 or NSC/2a in the knowledge that he will be able to recover the amounts of those direct payments from the final payment to the Contractor.

The special Interim Certificate is to be issued at least twenty-eight days prior to the

114

issue of the Final Certificate, thus providing enough time for any notices sent by Nominated Sub-Contractors to the Employer to have effect before the Employer is required to make final payment to the Contractor. It is intended, therefore, that the Final Certificate will only deal with the balance of monies due to the Contractor.

The Final Certificate

Clause 30.8   The Final Certificate is issued under the provisions of clause 30.8 and is issued not later than the expiry of the period for issue of Final Certificate stated in the Appendix. In the Private Editions, the period is a maximum of three months; in the Local Authorities Editions, the period is a maximum of six months. However, the period only commences to run after the happening of the later of three other events:-

★ expiry of the Defects Liability Period

★ issue of the Certificate of Completion of Making Good Defects

★ receipt by the Quantity Surveyor of the documents necessary for the computation of the final adjusted Contract Sum.

The importance to the Contractor of attention to the systematic presentation of final account documents stressed previously is now apparent. Any delay will prevent the issue of the Final Certificate.

The Final Certificate will show two amounts; the amount of the final adjusted Contract Sum and the total of the amounts previously certified in Interim Certificates. It does **not** show the amounts previously paid by the Employer, for this is not the concern of the Quantity Surveyor or the Architect.

The difference between the final adjusted Contract Sum and the total of the amounts previously certified, less any deductions properly due to the Employer, becomes payable to the Contractor (or by the Contractor to the Employer, as the case may be) within fourteen days of the date of the certificate not the date of issue. The balance due to either party is described as a 'debt payable' and these words make it certain that a final payment can be properly the subject of High Court action in the event that payment is not made within the fourteen days prescribed. The rights of the Contractor to obtain full payment of any amounts unpaid from Interim Certificates are not prejudiced by the issue of the Final Certificate.

The Employer may deduct or set off from monies due to the Contractor in the Final Certificate, such amounts as are due to the Employer under the contract. The matters that permit the Employer to make deductions from the Final Certificate are the same as those referred to in the discussion on clause 30.1.2 (page 106). Clause 30.1.2 only permits the Employer to make deductions from Interim Certificates; the express right of the Employer to make such deductions from any balance due under the Final Certificate is in the words '...and subject to any deductions authorised by the Conditions...' of the present clause.

Effect of the Final Certificate

Clause 30.9   Clause 30.9 sets out the effects of the Final Certificate and these are unchanged from the 1963 Edition. That is to say, the Final Certificate is **not** conclusive in respect of all matters arising out of the contract. It is still further limited if the parties initiate arbitration proceedings under the arbitration agreement or take some other legal proceedings as a result of its issue. It does not apply to any matter that is already the subject of arbitration or other legal proceedings. Those matters that the Final Certificate **does** cover are finally and irrevocably settled by the issue of the Final Certificate. Clauses 30.9.1.1 and 30.9.1.2 use the words 'conclusive evidence' and this means that in any arbitration or other legal proceedings no evidence can be brought to contradict or qualify the decision of the Architect in that matter.

The conclusiveness of the Final Certificate is dealt with under two headings only:-

★ clause 30.9.1.1 - where materials and workmanship are to be to the satisfaction of the Architect, then such materials and workmanship **are** to the satisfaction of the Architect.

★ clause 30.9.1.2 - that all the necessary financial adjustments to the Contract Sum have been made.

The former point restates what has already been referred to in the discussion on clause 2.1 (page 15), and it would seem that where materials and workmanship are **not** stated to be to the satisfaction of the Architect, then the Final Certificate is **not** conclusive. In the case of such materials and workmanship, the Contractor remains liable to the Employer until the expiry of the period of limitation of the contract, and any proceedings relating to the quality of materials and workmanship provided by the Contractor would be concerned with breach of contract.

Regarding the financial adjustments to the Contract Sum, the matters for which the Final Certificate is conclusive are altogether more numerous. The Final Certificate will be conclusive, for instance, as to the Valuation of Variations (clause 13), the ascertainment of loss and expense (clause 26) and amounts arising under fluctuation clauses (clauses 38, 39 or 40). Where matters are not concerned with financial adjustment, for example, extensions of time (clause 25), or the date by which the Works should have been completed (clause 24), then the Final Certificate cannot be conclusive. In addition, certain financial matters between the Contractor and the Employer are not embraced by the Final Certificate. Any amounts, for example, liquidated and ascertained damages, due to the Employer are not covered by the Final Certificate for they never become matters for which an adjustment of the Contract Sum is required.

It will be seen from the foregoing remarks that the Final Certificate is not perhaps such an important document as it would appear upon first sight.

Besides the limited scope of its conclusiveness, there are two minor and one major overriding qualifications to the effect of the Final Certificate. Where there has been fraud, all or part of the Final Certificate is not valid. By fraud, one may presume that criminal fraud is meant and builders may perhaps at this point ponder on the distinction between 'fraud' (ie criminal) and a 'legitimate adjustment' (ie permitted by the Conditions or SMM, but perhaps termed sharp practice). The Final Certificate is also not valid to a greater or lesser degree by the 'accidental inclusion or exclusion of any work materials goods or figure...or any arithmetical error...'. The important thing here is that the error has to be accidental.

The major item that invalidates the conclusiveness of the Final Certificate arises from the commencement of any arbitration or legal proceedings. Where the proceedings have commenced before the issue of the Final Certificate, then the Final Certificate is amended or not, as the case may be, by the judgement or settlement in the proceedings concerned. In the event that the proceedings fail to make progress for a period of twelve months, then the position existing at the end of that period appears to become the conclusive Final Certificate. Where, say, there are five events that are subject to proceedings and four are resolved but the fifth has made no progress for some reason, then it would appear that the Final Certificate as issued becomes 'conclusive' for all the matters for which it would normally become conclusive evidence except for the four matters resolved. The fifth remains unamended. This is a rather remote circumstance for it should be possible to demonstrate some progress in a year, in even the most dilatory proceedings.

The most important point to bear in mind when disputing the effect of the Final Certificate is clause 30.9.3 which sets a time limit on the capacity of both the Contractor and the Employer to commence arbitration or legal proceedings. The Contractor and the Employer are prohibited from commencing arbitration or legal proceedings more than fourteen days after the issue of the Final Certificate. Clause 30.9.3 goes on to say that all those other matters for which proceedings have not started within fourteen days of the issue of the Final Certificate, the Final Certificate is automatically conclusive, provided that it is a matter for which the Final Certificate becomes conclusive evidence.

It must be stressed that clause 30.9.3 does not restrict the Contractor to give notice only on matters included in the Final Certificate. All that it does is to establish a time limit for the commencement of arbitration or legal proceedings. The proceedings can be on any matter arising out of the Contract. For example, the Contractor may already have commenced proceedings on some relatively narrow topic and there is nothing in this present clause to prevent new proceedings on a much broader basis, including the matters giving rise to the existing proceedings.

This little clause creates two major pitfalls for the unwary Contractor. Firstly, the time limit for the commencement of proceedings is fourteen days after **issue** of the Final Certificate. The Contractor may be aware of the impending issue of the Final Certificate and know its content and may, perhaps, have decided that he will, say, commence arbitration proceedings. But the Contractor must react exceedingly quickly to the arrival of the copy of the Final Certificate in his office if he is to be certain of giving notice within the fourteen day time scale given, for the time limit is fourteen days from issue, **not** receipt of the Final Certificate. The nature of the dispute must be very carefully defined in the notice of arbitration. If not drawn widely enough in its description of the dispute, it could be that the builder will find himself unable to argue his case correctly because of the constraints of his notice of arbitration. On the other hand, it is possible that a notice of arbitration drawn so widely as to render the Final Certificate totally ineffective could be open to rejection on the grounds that it is not precise enough.

Status of certificates of the Architect

Clause 30.10   In clause 30.10, it is made clear that, except to the limited extent referred to in the previous discussion on the Final Certificate, **no** certificate of the Architect is conclusive as to the quality of work, materials or goods provided under the contract. What in effect the clause is saying is that notwithstanding the Certificate of Practical Completion, the Certificate of Completion of Making Good Defects and the Final Certificate, all issued by the Architect, the responsibility for satisfying the Employer that the work, materials or goods are in accordance with the Contract Documents remains with the Contractor.

Strange as this may seem, the position is entirely consistent with the RIBA Conditions of Engagement. Section 1.33 requires only that the Architect '...inspect generally the...quality of the work and...determine in general if the work is proceeding in accordance with the contract documents', and, in Section 1.60, 'During his on-site inspections...the Architect...shall endeavour to guard the client against defects and deficiences in the work of the contractor...'. Section 1.34 expressly states 'The Architect shall not...be responsible for any failure by the contractor to carry out and complete the work in accordance with the terms of the building contract...'.

Employers would do well to note these responsibilities and duties of their agent supervising the work on their behalf.

PAYMENT FOR MATERIALS OFF SITE

Some rules concerning ownership and responsibility of materials paid for by the Employer have already been referred to in clause 16.2 (see page 104). The inclusion of amounts for materials off site in Interim Certificates is expressly authorised in clause 30.2 (page 108). The precise conditions to be complied with by the Contractor before the Architect is entitled to include monies in an Interim Certificate are set out in clause 30.3. The re-. quirements are extremely onerous and there can be little doubt that, if monies for materials off site should be paid to a supplier or a sub-contractor, then the Contractor is accepting a considerable risk for which there is no detectable renumeration or reward.

The discretion of the Architect

The Conditions permit the Architect to include in Interim Certificates amounts in respect of materials or goods (including manufactured articles) not at that time delivered to site. The materials concerned can be those ordered from any supplier by the Contractor or by a sub-contractor, or can have been manufactured or assembled by a sub-contractor or by a sub sub-contractor to a sub-contractor. The Sub- Contract NSC/4 or NSC/4a and the Domestic Sub-Contract DOM/1 each permit payment in respect of off-site materials to be made by the Contractor to a sub- contractor provided the sub-contractor has complied with the relevant conditions precedent set out in the main contract. There is no reference in clause 36 -Nominated Suppliers, nor in the JCT Form of Tender for Nominated Suppliers, to the possibility of payment to any Nominated Supplier for materials off-site.

The authority of the Architect to include amounts for off-site materials in Interim Certificates is discretionary only. There are a number of conditions precedent that must be fulfilled by both the Contractor and his sub-contractor or supplier before the Architect is able to consider exercising that discretion.

The duty of the Contractor

Clause 30.3

The conditions precedent are set out in clauses 30.3.1 to 30.3.9, and clause 16.2 contains certain further obligations that become operative **after** the Employer has honoured any Interim Certificate containing amounts for off-site materials. All the relevant conditions precedent set out in clause 30.3 must be complied with **before** the Architect is authorised to issue an Interim Certificate containing amounts for off-site materials.

Clauses 30.3.4, 30.3.5 and 30.3.6 do not all apply in any one case:-

★ clause 30.3.4 applies where the materials have been ordered from a supplier by the Contractor

★ clauses 30.3.4 and 30.3.5 apply where materials have been ordered from a supplier or a sub sub-contractor by a sub-contractor

★ clause 30.3.6 applies where the materials have been manufactured by a sub-contractor.

The Contractor should carefully consider whether the conditions precedent set out in clause 30.3 are sufficient to protect his own position in purely commercial terms. It may be that they do not. The Contractor should have no difficulty in imposing further conditions upon the supplier or sub-contractor before making the request for payment to the Architect.

To protect the position of the Employer and the Contractor, the Conditions appear to anticipate that a supplier or sub-contractor will produce to the Contractor (for onward transmission to the Architect) a document in which he certifies authoritatively that the relevant conditions precedent of clauses 30.3.1 to 30.3.9 have been fulfilled. Such a document would also show that any other requirements of the Contractor have been complied with. The document must be signed by a Director or authorised signatory of the sub-contractor or supplier, so that the document shall have full legal force and effect.

The conditions precedent

Clauses 30.3.1 to 30.3.9   The following table gives a brief description of the conditions precedent set out in clause 30.3 that must appear in such a document. Some comments are also offered by way of explanation or amplification of the various matters covered.

In respect of any particular parcel of materials or goods, the relevant conditions precedent to be fulfilled are:

Table X Clause	Brief description and comments
30.3.1	**the materials or goods are for incorporation in the Works.** (Note. Temporary materials, eg formwork, do not therefore qualify).
30.3.2	**the materials or goods are complete.** (Note. The materials or goods are to be complete, ie ready for delivery to the site and for installation in the Works. Thus, a quantity of steelwork, cut to length and with angle cleats fitted, for eventual use as a structural steel frame would qualify; a quantity of steel at a lift manufacturers factory would only qualify when the lift car had been fabricated).
30.3.3	**the materials or goods are set aside and marked with both the name of the main contract Works and with the name of the person in whom the ownership of the materials or goods has been vested.** That is to say:- ★ if on the premises of the Contractor, with the name of the Employer ★ if on the premises of a sub-contractor or of a supplier to the Contractor - with the name of the Contractor ★ if on the premises of a supplier or a sub sub-contractor to a sub-contractor with the name of the sub-contractor. (Note. This requirement is designed to ensure, in the event of bankruptcy or liquidation of the person holding the materials or goods, that the trustee in bankruptcy or the liquidator will be aware that the materials and goods are the property of some other person. **BUT BEWARE, THIS MAY NOT PROTECT THE CONTRACTOR COMPLETELY (See page 124).)**
30.3.4	**if ordered from a supplier by the Contractor or a sub-contractor, or from a sub sub- contractor to a sub-contractor, the contract of sale for the materials or goods is in writing and expressly provides that ownership of the materials or goods vests in the purchaser upon completion of manufacture or fabrication or after marking as required by clause 30.3.3.**
30.3.5	**if ordered from a supplier by a sub-contractor, the sub-contract is in writing and expressly provides that when ownership of the materials or goods vests in the sub- contractor by the operation of the contract of sale referred to in clause 30.3.4, then ownership automatically vests in the Contractor at the same time.**

(Table X continues overleaf)

(Table X continued)

30.3.6	**if manufactured or assembled by a sub-contractor, the sub-contract is in writing and expressly provides that ownership of those materials or goods vests in the Contractor upon completion of manufacture or assembly or after marking as required by clause 30.3.3.** (Notes. 1. Clauses 30.3.4, 30.3.5 and 30.3.6 are all concerned with the vesting of materials, goods or manufactured articles in the Contractor. 2. Contracts of sale between builders and sub-contractors and their suppliers or sub sub-contractors do not normally contain the express provisions required by clauses 30.3.4, 30.3.5, or 30.3.6. Neither the Sub-Contract NSC/4 or NSC/4a, nor the Domestic Sub-Contract DOM/1 seem to contain the express provisions required by clauses 30.3.4, 30.3.5 and 30.3.6. However, supplemental agreements in the forms suggested in the Appendix are thought to meet those requirements. 3. The supplemental agreements provide for the ownership of the materials or goods to pass from the supplier and/or the sub-contractor to the Contractor. Thus, the Contractor would be able to state authoritatively to the Architect that ownership of the materials or goods is in him, so satisfying the condition precedent set out in clause 30.3.8. 4. Except where the materials or goods have been ordered from a supplier by the Contractor, it would appear that in order to satisfy the conditions precedent of clause 30.3, two supplemental agreements are required; one from the supplier or the sub sub-contractor to the sub-contractor (Form B); and a second (Form A) from the sub-contractor to the Contractor.)
30.3.7	**the materials or goods are in accordance with the Contract Documents.** (Notes. 1. It is recommended that a representative of the Contractor visit the works or factory and count and examine the materials or goods claimed to be complete and in accordance with the Contract Documents. 2. The Contractor may not be able to say whether the materials or goods comply with the description of the materials in the Contract Bills or in any sub-contract document. For example, could the Contractor know whether the colour of some imported marble or granite is acceptable to the Architect? In appropriate cases the Architect must be invited to examine the materials or goods and approve them before including monies in an Interim Certificate.)
30.3.8	**the Architect is to be satisfied that ownership of the materials or goods has vested in the Contractor.** (Notes. 1. The Architect needs to be satisfied that this is the case so that he can assure the Employer that ownership of the materials or goods will vest in him when he has honoured the Interim Certificate containing amounts for materials off-site. The actual provision for setting out the requirement of the change of ownership is clause 16.2. 2. The Contractor would normally provide the reasonable proof required by this clause by presenting to the Architect the supplemental agreement given by the supplier or the sub-contractor. The supplemental agreement will also automatically provide confirmation that the relevant conditions precedent have been complied with. 3. The tense of the printed text of this condition precedent ('...property in the materials **is** in him...') makes it clear that ownership must have passed to the Contractor **before** the Architect may exercise his discretion to issue an Interim Certificate containing amounts in respect of materials off-site. It is not satisfactory for a supplier or a sub-contractor to state that ownership would pass on receipt of payment. This is self-evident, and misses the whole point of the exercise − to protect the Employer against loss).
30.3.9	**the materials or goods are insured.** (Notes. 1. The Conditions only require that the materials or goods are insured against Clause 22 Perils, ie fire, storm, etc. 2. The supplier or sub-contractor will have to attach to the supplemental agreement evidence that the insurances are in existence).

Other conditions by the Contractor

In addition to the conditions precedent set out in clauses 30.3.1 and 30.3.9, the Contractor may consider that, to protect his own commercial position adequately, some additional conditions should be imposed. Examples of such additional conditions are:

★ that the ownership of the components or raw materials incorporated into the materials or goods have been vested absolutely in the supplier or the sub-contractor and that the supplier or sub-contractor shall demonstrate this with documentary evidence.
(Note. A supplier or sub-contractor cannot agree ownership in the materials or goods is vested in the Contractor if the component materials have not themselves been vested in the supplier or the sub-contractor in the first place).

★ that the materials or goods should be insured under an 'All-Risks' insurance including theft, vandalism, damage during transportation and delivery, etc, and consequential losses.
(Note. This would give the Contractor some protection against the worst effects of delay to the progress of the Works if the materials or goods were required to be re-manufactured as the result of some accident or catastrophe befalling the supplier or sub-contractor).

★ that the materials or goods may be inspected by the Employer, Architect or Contractor upon reasonable notice.

★ that the supplier or sub-contractor retains full responsibility for the costs of storage, warehousing, maintenance, security, insurance, handling, transporting and unloading the materials or goods.

★ that payment by the Contractor to the supplier or the sub-contractor shall not constitute or imply acceptance by the Contractor or the Architect that the materials or goods are in accordance with the Contract Documents.
(Note. These three items are suggested so that there should be no doubt between the Contractor and the supplier or the sub-contractor as to the status of these matters.)

Ownership of the materials and goods

Several references have been made in the preceding comments to documentary evidence of the ownership of the materials or goods for which payment is desired. The necessity for documentary evidence is enshrined in clause 30.3.8 which requires that 'the Contractor provides the Architect with reasonable proof that the property in the materials is in (the Contractor)...'. This provision is necessary since upon payment by the Employer of any amount in respect of off-site materials, such materials are required by clause 16.2 to become the property of the Employer. The Contractor can provide reasonable proof by obtaining confirmation from the supplier or the sub-contractor that the property in the materials or goods or manufactured articles has indeed passed to the Contractor. Such confirmation, if passed to the Architect, should be sufficient to provide the reasonable proof required.

Care is necessary in securing and examining such evidence since it is usual for builders' merchants, manufacturers, and suppliers of materials to trade only on the basis of terms and conditions containing 'Retention of title' clauses. This means that in many cases the ownership of the materials or goods remains in the hands of the builders' merchant, manufacturer, or supplier until payment in full is received by them. In such a situation, the Contractor would be unable to show to the Architect that ownership had passed to the

Contractor. **IF OWNERSHIP HAS NOT PASSED, IN THE EVENT OF THE BANKRUPTCY, LIQUIDATION OR RECEIVERSHIP OF THE MANUFAC-TURER OR SUPPLIER, THE ADVANCE PAYMENT BY THE CONTRACTOR WOULD INVARIABLY BE LOST.**

A supplemental agreement in the terms suggested in the Appendices will enable the supplier or the sub-contractor to certify that the property in the materials or goods or manufactured articles has passed to the Contractor and provide proof that the supplier, or builders' merchant, or manufacturer of the components or raw materials has passed ownership to the supplier or the sub-contractor. The evidence required to demonstrate the latter point will vary according to the materials or goods concerned and the extent to which those goods remain separately identifiable. For example, a quantity of white glazed wall tiles always remains separately identifiable and could readily be removed from the premises of a supplier or a sub-contractor by the merchant, manufacturer, or supplier of the component. In such a case, the only satisfactory evidence would be a supplemental agreement from the builders' merchant, manufacturer, or supplier given to the supplier or sub-contractor and certifying that ownership of the component had been vested in the supplier or sub-contractor. On the other hand, cement, sand, aggregates and reinforce-ment, incorporated into precast concrete cladding units, will have lost their separate identity and, notwithstanding the terms and conditions of a builders' merchant, manufacturer or supplier, the materials would not be recoverable by them. In such a case, a written state-ment from the supplier or sub-contractor that ownership of the materials or goods is in him would probably suffice.

The procedure for obtaining payment

Where the Contractor or supplier or sub-contractor wish to have amounts for off-site materials included in an Interim Certificate and the Contractor requests that the Architect exercise his discretion, then it will be apparent that the process is complicated because of the various conditions precedent required by the Conditions to be fulfilled. Notwithstan-ding the variety and character of the conditions precedent, the fact remains that the Con-tractor is taking a risk when he pays a supplier or sub-contractor for off-site materials. The reason for this is that in the event of the loss of the materials or goods for any reason, then it is the Contractor who may be faced with buying the materials again, for he retains his obligation to complete the building. It would be preferable for the materials or goods to be delivered to the site, for this eliminates the majority of risk. It also avoids the necessity of getting the supplemental agreement from the supplier or sub-contractor and inspec-ting the materials or goods.

Where it is not practicable for the materials and goods to be delivered to the site, it is desirable for the Contractor to have already ascertained the willingness or otherwise of the Architect to exercise his discretion in the matter of payment for off-site materials. If the Architect is willing, then the supplier or sub-contractor should be requested to sub-mit the supplemental agreement and a schedule of the materials and goods concerned. The supplemental agreement will show whether the conditions precedent of clause 30.3 have been fulfilled. The schedule will detail precisely the materials and goods for which payment is requested, the location of the materials and goods, and the amount of the valua-tion of those materials or goods. The supplemental agreement must be accompanied by evidence that ownership of the materials and goods is in the hands of the supplier or sub-contractor and by evidence of insurances.

The conditions precedent required by clause 30.3 and the additional matters suggested in the earlier part of these notes have been drafted into model documents and are includ-ed as Appendices (pages 199 to 206). The documents appended are:-

Form A – 'Supplemental Agreement for Materials Off Site'

For use in all cases. To be completed by the person holding the materials or goods or by the person in whom they have been vested.

Form B – 'Supplemental Agreement for Materials Off Site'

For use in conjunction with Form A where the materials or goods have been ordered from a supplier to a sub-contractor or have been fabricated or assembled by a sub sub-contractor to a sub-contractor. If properly completed will provide the documentary evidence to substantiate that property in the materials or goods has vested in the sub-contractor, see clause 2.6 of Form A. To be completed by the holder of the materials or goods.

Form C – 'Schedule to Supplemental Agreement'

For use in all cases. To be completed by the holder of the materials or goods.

Upon receipt of Forms A, B (if required), and C, the Contractor should arrange, perhaps in co-operation or conjunciton with the Architect and/or Quantity Surveyor, for the materials or goods in question to be examined. If satisfied that the conditions precedent have been fulfilled, then the Architect must be requested to exercise his discretion and include in his next Interim Certificate an amount in regard to those materials or goods. Such a request can be a letter to the Architect and need only:-

★ refer to clause 30.3 of the Conditions dealing with off-site materials

★ request the Architect to include a (specified) amount in his next Interim Certificate representing the value of materials, goods or manufactured articles completed but not yet delivered to the site

★ enclose copies of the 'Supplemental Agreements for off site materials' Form A, or Forms A and B, and the 'Schedule to Supplemental Agreement' Form C

★ invite the Architect to examine the materials, goods or manufactured articles prior to including their value in his Interim Certificate

★ offer the opinion that the agreement(s) and Schedule constitute the reasonable proof required by clauses 30.3.8 and 39.3.9 that:-

★★ property in the goods is in the Contractor

★★ the relevant conditions of clauses 30.3.1 to 30.3.7 have been complied with

★★ the minimum insurance requirements of clause 30.3.9 have been satisfied.

The Architect has a part to play at this stage in the procedure since he may be required in due course to express his satisfaction of the quality of the materials or goods and the standard of the workmanship of manufactured articles. Where this is the case, it clearly is to the benefit of everybody concerned that the expression of the approval of the Architect should be secured as soon as possible.

Should the Architect decline to exercise his discretion and not include the value of materials off-site in any Interim Certificate, then there would appear to be little the Contractor and his sub-contractors or suppliers can do. The matter rests entirely in the hands of the Architect and his client.

Postscript I

Supplemental Agreements in the styles of Forms A and B remain valid and appropriate while the materials, goods or manufactured articles scheduled remain unchanged at the premises named in the Schedule, Form C. In every other case, that is to say, where some have been delivered to the site or, where further materials goods or manufactured articles have been procured or manufactured and added to those already in store, a further supplemental agreement is required with an accompanying schedule and valuation in respect of the new parcel of materials, goods or manufactured articles. It would seem to be sensible for the Contractor, sub-contractors and suppliers to present supplemental agreements automatically when making their regular monthly applications for payment.

Postscript II

The documents included in the Appendices (Forms A, B and C) have been prepared in an endeavour to find a satisfactory procedure that suits the particular requirements of JCT 80. **Before employing the model documents builders should consult their own legal advisers so as to be sure that their use is satisfactory.** There are two areas that require particular consideration:-

★ do the supplemental agreements effectively vary the terms of the sub-contract or contract of sale?'

(Notes. 1. Since the Sub-Contracts NSC/4, NSC/4a and DOM/1 and typical contracts of sale (including the compulsory conditions applicable to nominated suppliers set out in clause 36.4) do not seem to contain the express provisions for passing ownership required by clause 30.3, the supplemental agreements must be so drafted that there is a binding agreement between the contracting parties to vary the signed contract.

2. The usual documents offered to builders by sub-contractors and suppliers (ie vesting certificates) are probably not satisfactory for this purpose since, in effect, the certificate represents a unilateral variation to the terms of the contract and it is believed that this could prove to be ineffective in a court of law.

3. A supplemental agreement that is intended to vary the terms of a contract must apparently possess the same characteristics as a valid contract, that is to say:-

(a) there must be offer and acceptance

(b) the parties must be 'ad idem' (literally – one of mind, in a consensus)

(c) there must be consideration, or the document must be a 'deed', that is to say, executed under seal.

The supplemental agreements appended to this paper are believed to contain all three characteristics. In the case of item (c), it has been felt that the option of sealing the supplemental agreements is making the procedure unnecessarily burdensome.)

★ do the supplemental agreements adequately provide for ownership of the materials or goods manufactured articles to pass to the Contractor as required by clauses 30.3.4, 30.3.5 and 30.3.6?

(Notes. 1. The supplemental agreements included in the Appendices are believed to deal with this problem adequately.

2. The builder is reminded that when making any payment to a sub-contractor or supplier for materials not on the site, considerable risk is assumed for there can be no absolute guarantee that, in the event of the bankruptcy or liquidation to the supplier or the sub-contractor, the Contractor will be able to physically take possession of those materials or goods or manufactured articles.)

Postscript – III

It will be seen that the requirements of JCT 80 are comprehensive in their scope and will be difficult to administer. It is surprising that in preparing the Sub-Contracts NSC/4 and NSC/4a the JCT did not include the necessary provisions within the Sub-Contract Conditions to deal automatically with payment of materials off site. In this way, some of the legal, administrative and practical problems identified in the last few pages could have been eliminated.

Other Financial Matters

In this Section, certain other matters affecting the financial relationship between the Contractor and the Employer will be examined. In each case, the need for some contractual arrangement arises because the matters concerned are imposed upon the parties by statutory law. The statutes tell the parties **what** they are to do, the Conditions set out in detail the administrative procedures to tell the parties **how** to do it. The matters concerned are value added tax (clause 15 - value added tax - supplemental provision), and the construction industry tax deduction scheme (clause 31 - Finance (No.2) Act 1975 - statutory tax deduction scheme).

VALUE ADDED TAX

Clause 15

Value added tax is dealt with in clause 15 and in a set of supplemental provisions known as the 'VAT Agreement' and is incorporated into the contract by reference. Both clause 15 and the 'VAT Agreement' are virtually unchanged from those included in the 1963 Edition and will be considered together. They are both in amplification of the legislation and a thorough understanding of the Notices issued by HM Customs and Excise is necessary in order to be able to properly operate the scheme.

The VAT Agreement appears after the Appendix to the Conditions in the printed document. It has been separated from the Conditions for the simple reason that the Architect is not required to certify VAT due to the Contractor and because it is axiomatic of the VAT system that the **supplier** of goods and services (ie the Contractor) should decide whether such supplies are taxable. Thus, the VAT Agreement creates separate arrangements outside the normal valuation and certification procedures for the payment of VAT.

General principles

Clause 15.1

Clause 15.1 sets out some definitions relating to VAT. Clause 15.2 makes it clear that the Contract Sum is to be deemed as VAT exclusive and expressly provides that should any VAT become chargeable by the Contractor to the Employer then the rules for such payment are those detailed in the present clause and the VAT Agreement.

The principle of the VAT system is that where taxable goods and services are supplied, the VAT paid on goods and services purchased (the input tax) may be offset from the VAT collected from the goods and services supplied (the output tax). Thus, the trader pays to HM Customs and Excise the balance remaining after deducting the input taxes from the output taxes. For the construction industry at the present time, the majority of the goods and services (ie the buildings) are taxable, but the rate of VAT chargeable is 'zero'; as a result the input tax of the Contractor will normally exceed the output tax and, therefore, the nett difference is **refunded** by HM Customs and Excise to the Contractor.

Clause 15.3

Clause 15.3 is included in the Conditions in anticipation of some change in the arrangements outlined in the preceding paragraph. If the status of the supply of goods and services (ie buildings) made by the industry were to be changed so that they became classified as 'exempt' for value added tax purposes then the Contractor would not be able to offset the input taxes. Clause 15.3 makes it clear that in such a situation, the Employer would refund to the Contractor any input taxes not allowed to be offset.

The VAT Agreement

Clause 1

The clause numbers in the VAT Agreement are numbered independently from those in the Conditions. The first sentence of clause 1 sets out the basic principle of the treatment of VAT under the contract, namely that the Employer will pay to the Contractor any VAT properly chargeable on the goods and services (ie buildings) supplied to the Employer. The second sentence of clause 1 is new and establishes the statutory authority for the operation of the Authenticated Receipt procedure referred to in clause 1.4.

Provisional assessments

Clause 1.1   Clause 1.1 requires that the Contractor present to the Employer a provisional assessment of the amounts included in each Interim Certificate that are subject to VAT and the rates of VAT applicable to those amounts. The provisional assessment is best issued immediately after receipt of the interim valuation of the Quantity Surveyor, for the provisional assessment is required to be issued in relation to the amounts included in each Interim Certificate and is required to be issued before the date of issue of the Interim Certificate concerned. While the Contractor may have a good idea of the date of issue for each Interim Certificate, only upon receipt of a copy of the interim valuation of the Quantity Surveyor can he be aware with any degree of certainty what values are to be included in the Interim Certificate. Even so, the Contractor may not always be able to comply with the requirements of this clause, where the provisional assessment is to be given to the Employer **before** the issue of the Interim Certificate.

The provisional assessment is to include work that is both zero-rated and positively rated, if any, so that the preparation of a provisional assessment on a monthly basis should be built into the contract administration system of the Contractor.

Clause 1.2   Clause 1.2.1 requires the Employer to calculate the VAT due to the Contractor (if any) and pay that amount to the Contractor, together with the amount of the Interim Certificate.

Where the Employer does not agree to the provisional assessment of taxable work given by the Contractor, clause 1.2.2 sets out the procedures to be followed by the Employer and the Contractor. The Employer must make a written objection to the provisional assessment of the Contractor. The Contractor can either, withdraw the assessment where the Employer has been able to show that the Contractor has made an error of fact in making the assessment; or, may make a reassessment in the event that the Contractor has made some error of judgement in making the assessment; or, if satisfied with the original provisional assessment, the Contractor must confirm to the Employer that the original assessment **is** correct. Where the Contractor has either amended or withdrawn the assessment, then the obligation of the Employer to pay VAT to the Contractor is reduced or cancelled as the case may be. Where the Contractor has confirmed his original assessment, then the Employer remains obligated to pay the full amount of VAT to the Contractor.

The entire process of objection by the Employer, and withdrawal, reassessment, or confirmation by the Contractor is presumably required to be concluded before the expiry of fourteen days after the date of issue of the Interim Certificate concerned.

In the event of serious disagreement between the Contractor and the Employer over the amount of VAT due, the Contractor would be well advised to endeavour to reach agreement on a reasonable amount to be included in a provisional assessment and to be paid by the Employer in respect of any particular Interim Certificate, leaving the detailed arguments to follow the full appeal procedure set out in clause 3. This would avoid a complex accounting procedure that requires the amount of VAT calculated from the provisional assessment to be deemed to have been received by the Contractor − whether or not the Employer does in fact pay VAT. Where the Employer does not pay VAT calculated from the provisional assessment, the accounts of the Contractor would then show that the Employer had not paid the full amount of the Interim Certificate. Thus, the Employer is in breach of contract!!

There are two conflicting considerations applicable here; firstly, that of HM Customs and Excise – that any VAT due should be collected and paid over to them at the earliest opportunity; and, secondly, that of the Contractor who should not be required to pay monies to HM Customs and Excise that he is yet to receive from the Employer.

The final assessment

Clause 1.3
The Contractor is required by clause 1.3.1 to submit a written final statement of the VAT due to him from the Employer. The statement is to detail the relative values of work zero-rated and positively rated, if any, and must show the amounts off VAT already paid (or deemed to have been paid) by the Employer. The written statement is to be issued as soon as possible after the issue of the Certificate of Completion of Making Good Defects, but, clause 1.3.2 provides that the final statement may be issued before or after the Final Certificate. The reason for this provision is obscure but may be in anticipation of the difficulty the Contractor will have in getting decisions from HM Customs and Excise as to the taxable status of some items of work.

If the Employer agrees with the relative values stated in the final written statement and the rates of VAT ascribed thereto, then he is to calculate the VAT due to the Contractor and any balance due is to be paid to the Contractor within twenty eight days of submission of the final statement. Alternatively, where there is a balance due to the Employer, he is to notify the Contractor of this situation and the Contractor is to refund the overpayment of VAT within twenty eight days of the notification by the Employer.

Authenticated receipts

Clause 1.4
Under clause 1.4 the Contractor is required to issue an 'authenticated receipt' to the Employer in respect of each payment. An authenticated receipt is a special document permitted by HM Customs and Excise under the provisions of the Regulations governing the operation of VAT. It reflects the peculiar situation in the construction industry, where the Contractor, although responsible for the assessment and collection of VAT on behalf of HM Customs and Excise, has no direct control over the interim valuation of work carried out and cannot therefore say with certainty the amount of taxable work carried out. The authenticated receipt procedure permitted under the Regulations therefore allows the VAT to be paid by the Contractor to HM Customs and Excise to be limited to the amount received from the Employer. The original of the authenticated receipt is used by the Employer to justify his input tax to HM Customs and Excise and the copy of the authenticated receipt is used by the Contractor to justify his output tax to HM Customs and Excise. Clause 7 of the VAT Agreement sets out the remedies available to the Employer if the Contractor should fail to issue an authenticated receipt to the Employer.

Exclusion of liquidated damages

Clause 2
In clause 2, it is made clear that in any calculation of the value of work done under the contract for the purpose of assessing VAT, no allowance is to be made for the rights of the Employer to liquidated and ascertained damages. No mention is made of other types of damages that could arise following some breach of contract by the Contractor.

Appeal procedure

Clause 3
Where, following the issue of the final written statement of taxable values referred to in clause 1.3.1, the Employer disagrees with either the liability to pay VAT, or with the values of taxable work, or with the rates of VAT detailed by the Contractor, then clause

3.1 details the right of the Employer to challenge the assessment by the Contractor. The Employer must take action within twenty-eight days from receipt of the final written statement from the Contractor and in the first instance this consists of requesting the Contractor to ask HM Customs and Excise to give their decision on the amount of tax properly payable to the Contractor and thus refunded to him by the Employer, on the items concerned.

If the Employer is still dissatisfied then he may request that the Contractor appeal to the VAT Tribunal for the final decision. Such an appeal is subject to the conditions:-

★ the Employer must indemnify the Contractor against the costs of such an appeal

★ the Employer may be required to deposit with the Contractor a reasonable pre-estimate of such costs

★ the Contractor must have paid to HM Customs and Excise his assessment of the VAT due on the work

★ that the Employer shall have paid the same amount to the Contractor.

Clause 3.3 contains a simple procedure for corrections to the amounts payable one way or the other, after the VAT Tribunal has given its adjudication of the appeal.

Finality of assessments and payments

Clause 4   The first sentence of clause 4 provides that, after any settlement of balances due, either as a consequence of the final written statement by the Contractor, or as a result of a decision or appeal given by HM Customs and Excise, then as between the Contractor and Employer all matters in regard to VAT are finally settled. The second sentence of clause 4 provides that HM Customs and Excise may re-open the matter at any time and where, as a consequence, the amount of VAT applicable is revised, then such amount is to be paid to or refunded by the Contractor as the case may be.

VAT and arbitration

Clause 5   The position of VAT and an arbitration award is dealt with in clause 5. It would appear that where in an arbitration award the valuation of some item of taxable work is revised, then any adjustment in the amount of VAT is automatically revised. The resulting amount of VAT would then become payable to, or refunded by, the Contractor as the case may be.

Clause 6   Clause 6 makes it clear that the arbitration agreement to the main contract does not apply to the VAT Agreement. The reason for this is that the final adjudication in all matters regarding VAT is laid down in the statutory legislation, that is to say with the Commissioners of HM Customs and Excise, or with the VAT Tribunals.

Miscellaneous provisions

Clause 7   Should the Contractor fail to provide an authenticated receipt for any payment as required by clause 1.4, then clause 7 introduces some draconion powers to the effect that the Employer may suspend **all** payments under the main contract and the VAT Agreement. The power to suspend all further payments is subject to two conditions, both of which must apply. Firstly, the Employer must require the authenticated receipt in order to justify input taxes paid and, secondly, the Employer must have paid the provisional assessment by the Contractor, or must have paid the amounts agreed to be due after an objection under clause 1.2.

Clause 8   Finally, in connection with VAT, clause 8 deals with the situation where there has been a determination under clause 27 (Default by the Contractor). Where, as a consequence of the determination - perhaps by reason of the increased costs of completion by a substituted Contractor - the total amount of VAT to be paid by the Employer is greater than it would have been under the original contract, then clause 8 provides that the increased amount of VAT becomes part of the claim by the Employer against the Contractor under clause 27.

CONSTRUCTION INDUSTRY TAX DEDUCTION SCHEME

The statutory tax deduction scheme is introduced in clause 31, and is virtually unchanged from that included in the 1963 Edition. As was the case with VAT, this clause cannot stand on its own. It must be read in conjunction with the legislation and a detailed understanding of the Inland Revenue booklet IR 14/15 is necessary in order to be able to operate the scheme properly. The general procedure that has been established under the legislation is that in certain circumstances the Employer will operate a sort of PAYE scheme on behalf of Inland Revenue and will collect tax on their behalf.

Definitions

Clause 31.1   There are set out in clause 31.1 some definitions that are really only applicable to the present topic. A definition not appearing is that of 'tax'. The legislation considers 'tax' to be sums due to be paid to the Inland Revenue to be treated as income tax, corporation tax and Class 4 National Insurance Contributions.

Perhaps the only other points to be stressed are that the definitions of 'contractor' and 'sub-contractor' are far wider than anybody in the industry would normally expect. A 'contractor' for this purpose is any person carrying out business which includes construction operations and a 'sub-contractor' is any business carrying out construction operations for a 'contractor'. Thus, it will be seen that for all practical purposes the Employer will be a 'contractor' and the Contractor will be a 'sub- contractor'.

Status of Employer

Clause 31.2   There is an Appendix entry that will inform the Contractor if the Employer is a 'contractor' for the purpose of the scheme or not. In the event that the Employer is not a 'contractor' under the scheme, clause 31.2.1 provides that, in effect, the scheme is not applicable. Should the status of the Employer change during the course of the contract so that he becomes a 'contractor', then by clause 31.2.2 the Employer is required to inform the Contractor of that change and, thereupon, the provisions of the scheme and this clause comes into effect.

Status of the Contractor

Clause 31.3   The Contractor is required, by clause 31.3.1, to present to the Employer evidence that he holds a 'Sub-Contractors Tax Certificate' and that he is, therefore, entitled to be paid in full. Should the Contractor not be the holder of such a certificate, then he is required to inform the Employer of that fact. In either case, the information must be presented to the Employer not later than twenty one days before the first interim payment is due. In practice, the Contractor holding a certificate will present it or his certifying document to the Employer immediately following the acceptance of any tender.

The Employer has fourteen days in which to make known any dissatisfaction with the evidence submitted by the Contractor, so that it is desirable for the Contractor to consider the production of the requisite evidence as a notice to the Employer. Such notice should:-

★ refer to clause 31.3.1 requiring evidence of the status of the Contractor under the statutory tax deduction scheme:-

AND EITHER

★ enclose the 'Sub-Contractors Tax Certificate' of the Contractor and claim that the Contractor is, therefore, entitled to receive payment in full under the contract

★ request that after inspection the certificate be immediately returned by recorded delivery with confirmation by the Employer that payments will be made in full

OR

★ enclose a 'Certifying Document' containing all the particulars required by paragraph 90 of IR 14/15 and claim that the Contractor is, therefore, entitled to receive payment in full under the Contract

★ state that if after fourteen days, the Employer has not expressed dissatisfaction with the Certifying Document the Contractor will assume that payments by the Employer will be made in full

OR

★ inform the Employer that the Contractor does not hold a 'Sub-Contractor's Tax Certificate'

★ confirm that the Contractor will inform the Employer of the direct cost to the Contractor of materials used in carrying out the work contained in each Interim Certificate and will present that information to the Employer not less than seven days before the date each interim payment is due.

Where the Contractor is the holder of a Sub-Contractor's Tax Certificate in the form 714I or 714P, the certificate must be presented in person to the Employer. Presuming the Employer to be satisfied that the Contractor is indeed the holder of a Sub-Contractor's Tax Certificate, it would be as well if the Contractor were to confirm such satisfaction in writing and remind the Employer that he is entitled to receive payments in full.

Clause 31.4   Where the Contractor obtains a Sub-Contractor's Tax Certificate for the first time, notice shall be given by the Contractor, and if satisfied with the evidence presented, the Employer should make all future payments in full. Where the certificate of the Contractor expires, then he is to present evidence of his new 'Sub- Contractor's Tax Certificate' to the Employer and a notice similar to that given above would suffice. The details of the new certificate are required by clause 31.4.2 to be presented not less than twenty eight days before expiry of the old certificate. This will not be possible in practice, for the Inland Revenue will not issue a new one until the old one is within a few days of expiry. In the event that the certificate of the Contractor is withdrawn or cancelled, then the Contractor is required to inform the Employer of this fact. Payments will then only be made subject to the statutory tax deduction.

Vouchers by the Contractor

Clause 31.5   Where the Contractor is the holder of a Sub-Contractor's Tax Certificate in the form 714I or 714P and is, therefore, required to provide the Employer with vouchers (receipts)

in the form 715, then clause 31.5 requires that the Employer forward the same to the Inland Revenue. The point here is that the Contractor could find his status with the Inland Revenue prejudiced if the Employer were dilatory in passing the vouchers to the Inland Revenue.

Deduction from payments

Clause 31.6   Where the Contractor is not the holder of a certificate the Employer is required to make the statutory deduction. Reference to the regulations and to IR 14/15 shows that the tax deduction is to be made from the full amount of the payment, less **only** the direct cost to the Contractor and his sub-contractors of materials. The direct cost of materials requires a little extra consideration, for IR 14/15 makes it clear that 'materials' for this purpose includes the cost of fuel, plant and plant hire. Where materials or goods are manufactured or fabricated by the Contractor, a supplier, or a sub-contractor then the cost of manufacture and prefabrication is also included in the cost of materials. In all cases, the amounts concerned are the **cost** to the Contractor etc., not the amounts **charged** to the Employer. The Employer is required to check that the amount stated to be the cost of materials is not over stated. Thus, it will be seen that tax is to be deducted on labour, overheads and profit, and this fits in with the amplification of 'tax' previously given.

Clause 31.6.1 requires the Employer to inform the Contractor if at any time he is not satisfied that the Contractor is properly the holder of a certificate and that he proposes to make the statutory deduction from all future payments. Under the same clause, the Employer can require the Contractor to provide the Employer with the amount of the direct cost of materials within each Interim Certificate.

The cost of materials has to be delivered to the Employer not later than seven days before that Interim Certificate becomes due for payment. In giving the cost of materials, the Contractor indemnifies the Employer against loss (ie a claim from the Inland Revenue that he did not deduct sufficient tax). Where the Contractor does not give the required information, the Employer is permitted to make a fair estimate of the cost of materials but, in this case he is not so indemnified. The Contractor who is in the unfortunate position of suffering these deductions would be well advised to present the cost of materials with great care and accuracy, for, as will be seen, the deductions are subject to limited scope for correction.

Correction of errors

Clause 31.7   Any correction of the deduction by the Employer is dealt with in clause 31.7. Any error in the deduction or the accidental omission of any deduction is to be corrected by payment to the Contractor or refund by the Contractor as the case may be. Unfortunately, corrections cannot be made where there is a statutory limitation on making that correction. The principal statutory limitation that will concern the Contractor is that corrections of over or under deduction can only be made during any tax month; that is to say, in regard to any particular deduction no refund can be made by the Employer if the 5th of the following month has passed by. Where a Contractor suffers the statutory deduction, he obviously must react exceedingly quickly should he wish to dispute the amount of the deduction.

Relationship with the Conditions

Clause 31.8   As will already be apparent, the whole of clause 31 is necessitated by statutory legislation, and it is made clear, therefore, in clause 31.8 that the relevant legislation will override any provision in the Conditions should any conflict become evident.

Statutory tax deduction scheme and arbitration

Clause 31.9   Clause 31.9 provides that the arbitration agreement shall apply to any dispute or difference in relation to the operation of clause 31 - except where there is a dispute over purely taxation matters, in which case the appeal procedures laid down by the Inland Revenue become the means of settling the dispute. This means that any argument over the cost of materials could be settled by arbitration; while a dispute over the sufficiency of evidence to demonstrate whether or not the Contractor has a certificate would be settled by appeal to the Commissioners of the Inland Revenue.

Postscript to clause 31

Finally, it should be noted that where the Employer is a 'contractor' under the scheme and does not make the statutory deduction when he should have done so, the Inland Revenue can claim from the Employer the monies that he has not deducted. Of course, the Contractor is similarly liable to the Inland Revenue for monies not deducted from his sub-contractors. Failure to operate the scheme correctly can lead to criminal charges and imprisonment.

Termination of the Work

In this section the usual causes of determination will be considered (clause 27 - Determination by Employer, and clause 28 - Determination by Contractor) together with other, less likely, causes of cessation of the Works and determination (clause 32 - Outbreak of hostilities, clause 33 - War damage, and clause 34 - Antiquities).

GENERALLY

These observations are applicable irrespective of the party initiating the determination procedures:-

★ it is the employment of the Contractor that may be determined, not the contract itself. The reason for this is that the rights and duties of the parties (including in particular, the financial arrangements resulting from such determination) are set out in full in the Conditions.

★ the party considering determination must be absolutely certain of his ground before deciding to determine under either clause 27 or clause 28. Should it be found by an arbitrator or a court that there are no valid grounds for such determination, then the roles of the parties could be reversed. The effect being that the party determining may be found to have repudiated the contract and be liable to pay damages to the other for breach of contract.

★ the notices that give effect to the determination procedures must not be given 'unreasonably or vexatiously', thus giving each party some protection against an over zealous Contractor or Employer who is tempted to act on some correct, but trivial matter.

★ except where the determination arises from the bankruptcy, etc. of the Contractor, there are no express provisions dealing with the situation where, after a determination, there is a reconciliation between the parties and the employment of the Contractor is to be reinstated. The parties will presumably have to make appropriate contractual agreements to deal with that new situation.

★ the opening works of both clauses 27 and 28 state that the legal rights of the determining party are not prejudiced by the determination clauses of the contract. For example, repudiation of the contract is not dealt with in these clauses. The rights of the determining party in such a case are dealt with under Common Law.

★ determination of the employment of the Contractor is compulsory only in the case of bankruptcy or liquidation of the Contractor. In all other situations the aggrieved party 'may' initiate the determination procedures - it is not obligatory.

★ the actual notice of determination referred to in these clauses- not any preliminary notice that may be required- will determine the employment of the Contractor under the contract 'forthwith'. This presumably means upon the issue of the notice of determination, for there is no reference to receipt of the notice by the defaulting party. Where a preliminary notice has been given, the period of continued default commences upon **receipt** of that notice

★ should the defaulting party wish to dispute the fact of determination by the aggrieved party, then the defaulting party must commence arbitration proceedings under the arbitration agreement. The parties would be entitled to immediate arbitration for the restraints upon the operation of the arbitration agreement cease upon the '...alleged termination of the Contractor's employment under this Contract...' - Article 5.2.

The preceding observations are common to the two principal determination clauses. There is one point where clause 27 and 28 differ significantly. The rights of the Employer to determine under clause 27 provide for an almost instant determination of the employment of the Contractor upon repetition of an earlier default by the Contractor. No such provision appears in clause 28, where each default by the Employer is regarded as a **new** default, and the full, two notice, procedure must be followed. This is inequitable to the Contractor in the case of the one item under which repetition of an earlier default by the Employer is most likely to occur - his failure to honour Interim Certificates.

DETERMINATION BY EMPLOYER

Clause 27   Determination of the employment of the Contractor by the Employer under the contract is covered by clause 27. The text is virtually identical to that contained in the 1963 Edition.

Default of the Contractor

Clauses 27.1 to 27.4   Clauses 27.1.1 to 27.1.4 detail the actual circumstances of default by the Contractor that may give rise to the right to determine. Each of the circumstances detailed are subject to certain constraints and qualifications, as follows:-

★ **(clause 27.1.1)** where the Contractor wholly suspends the execution of the Works. That is to say, if there has been a complete, unplanned, cessation of work on the site. (Not enforceable, presumably, if the cessation arises from some lack of information from the Architect.)

★ **(clause 27.1.2)** where the Contractor is no longer proceeding regularly and diligently to complete the Works.
That is to say, if the progress of the Works is not pursued wholeheartedly and it becomes clear that completion will be seriously delayed as a consequence. (The Contractor has undertaken (clause 23.1) to proceed regularly and diligently. It is implied that the Architect has already awarded all the extensions of time he considers proper before initiating the determination procedure).

★ **(clause 27.1.3)** where the Contractor has not removed defective work or improper materials after a valid instruction of the Architect under clause 8.4 and the notice to comply required by clause 4.1.2.
The consequences of the refusal of the Contractor to remove defective work or improper material must be such that '...the Works are materially affected'. For example, a refusal to remove defective structural concrete would clearly be contemplated by this clause, whereas a refusal to remedy poor painting or landscaping would perhaps not, since the better remedy of the Employer would be under clause 4.1.2 where he may have the work done by others, still at the expense of the Contractor, but without the delay caused by the determination procedure.

★ **(clause 27.1.4)** where the Contractor assigns the contract or sublets any part of the Works without the written consent of the Architect.

★ **(also clause 27.1.4 but Local Authorities Editions only)** where the contractor fails to pay wages, etc. not in accordance with the National Working Rule Agreement.

Notices by the Architect and the Employer

For determination to occur as a consequence of the preceding defaults by the Contractor, two notices are required.

Firstly, upon the happening of the default, the **Architect** is required to give notice to the Contractor by registered post or recorded delivery. Such a notice should:

★ inform the Contractor that in the opinion of the Architect, the Contractor is in default

★ specify that default

★ remind the Contractor that if the default continues for fourteen days after receipt of the notice, then the Employer may determine the employment of the Contractor under the contract.

Upon receipt of the notice by the Architect, the Contractor must ask himself:-

★ is he indeed in default for one of the reasons detailed in clauses 27.1.1 to 27.1.4? (He may be in default for some other reason but this does not matter for the present purpose.)

★ has the Architect specified the same default? (The notice need only mention which of the four defaults detailed in clauses 27.1.1 to 27.1.4 is alleged to apply. There is no apparent obligation to set out the default in detail in the notice).

The Conditions do not contemplate a situation where the Contractor wishes to dispute the notice by the Architect and it would appear that there is no formal action that the Contractor can immediately take until such time as his employment has consequently been determined by the Employer, whereupon the arbitration agreement can be brought into operation.

Secondly, where the default of the Contractor continues for fourteen days after receipt of the notice by the Architect, or if the default by the Contractor is repeated at any subsequent time, then the **Employer** may within a further ten days give notice of determination of the employment of the Contractor. An important point to stress here is that the ten days for the second notice by the Employer commences either, in the case of the first default, within fourteen days of receipt by the Contractor of the first notice by the Architect, or, upon repetition of that default, at any time afterwards. In the case of repetition of the default, there is no need for the Employer to await a further notice from the Architect. In either case, the notice by the Employer to the Contractor must be sent registered post (or recorded delivery). Such a notice should:-

★ inform the Contractor that the default specified in the notice by the Architect has continued for a period of fourteen days

OR

★ inform the Contractor that the default specified in the notice by the Architect has been repeated

★ determine the employment of the Contractor under the contract.

Upon receipt of the notice by the Employer, the Contractor must ask himself:-

★ has his default indeed continued for fourteen days after receipt of notice by the Architect?

★ has the default truly been repeated?

★ has the notice by the Employer been given within ten days of the expiry of fourteen days from receipt of notice of the Architect OR of the repetition of the default?

If the response to one or all of these questions is 'No', then the notice of determination is invalid and should be challenged by the Contractor by notice in writing to the Employer (copy to the Architect). In addition, the notice by the Employer would be invalid if it were given unreasonably or vexatiously. Naturally, if the Contractor should cease his default during the fourteen days after receipt of the notice by the Architect any notice of determination by the Employer would also be invalid.

Finally, it would appear that if the Employer does not give notice within the prescribed ten days, ie within twenty four days after receipt by the Contractor of the notice by the Architect, then, according to the text of clause 27, he appears to lose his right to determine until, or unless, there is some repetition of the default by the Contractor.

Bankruptcy or liquidation of the Contractor

Clause 27.2   The financial failure of the Contractor is dealt with in clause 27.2. An individual or partnership become bankrupt, limited companies go into liquidation. Upon the bankruptcy or liquidation of the Contractor, the employment of the Contractor under the contract is automatically determined. No notice of determination is required, for the position here is that upon such bankruptcy or liquidation, a trustee in bankruptcy, receiver, or liquidator will be appointed who will in the ordinary course of events give notice to the Employer of the actual or imminent demise of the Contractor.

The Employer and the trustee in bankruptcy, receiver, or liquidator may agree that the employment of the Contractor be reinstated. This would occur where the trustee in bankruptcy, receiver, or liquidator could continue with the contract for a quite modest expenditure and thereby generate a significant recovery of monies for the creditors, perhaps by reason of achieving Practical Completion with the consequent reduction of Retention held by the Employer. The present clause does not set out any procedural requirements that would properly reinstate the employment of the Contractor and the parties would presumably have to make their own arrangements for restoring the contract to its former status.

Corruption by the Contractor

Clause 27.3   In the Local Authorities Editions only, clause 27.3 provides that the local authority 'shall be entitled to determine the employment of the Contractor under this or any other contract' if the Contractor engages in corrupt practices. The clause is designed around the terms of standing orders adopted by most if not all local authorities.

The powers granted to the local authority Employer are draconian. The local authority Employer does not appear to have to give notice and the Contractor does not have to be aware of the corrupt act. The right to determine applies to **all** contracts between the Contractor and the local authority concerned.

Consequences of determination

Clause 27.4 The arrangements between the parties following upon determination of the employment of the Contractor by the Employer are set out in clause 27.4, except where the employment of the Contractor has been reinstated by agreement between the Employer and the trustee in bankruptcy, receiver, or liquidator of the Contractor.

In the first place, the Employer still requires his building to be built, and clause 27.4.1 gives him express rights that should ensure completion of the Works. In particular, the Employer may use the plant, tools, equipment, etc. belonging to the Contractor and lying on the site. This is clear enough where plant, etc. belongs to the Contractor. Where the plant belongs to outside hirers, the use of such plant, etc. by the Employer is not free of charge, and he must make his own arrangements for its continued hire. This is because the Employer has no lien on it in the absence of a vesting clause relative to plant. Any payment made to hirers for the period either before or after the determination becomes part of the costs incurred by the Employer and will appear in the settlement of accounts. In regard to materials and goods already on the site, much will already have vested in the Employer by the provisions of clause 16.1. The Employer may purchase any further materials or goods necessary for the completion of the Works.

Where, following determination, the Contractor remains in business, clause 27.2.4.1 permits the Employer to require that the Contractor assign to him the benefit of all contracts of sale for the supply of materials and all sub-contracts. Since this is designed to facilitate completion of the Works, the Conditions require the assignment to be completed within fourteen days of the determination. A proper legal document will be required in order to give effect to such an assignment, for it is an express provision of the assignment that the supplier or sub-contractor shall be entitled to object to any further assignment by the Employer, eg to any replacement Contractor. Where the determination arises from or results in, bankruptcy or liquidation, there can be no such assignments, for clause 27.4.2.2 expressly provides that the Employer may pay such suppliers or sub-contractors for goods delivered and work done before determination and this would in effect create new preferential creditors, which are prohibited by the statutory law governing these matters.

Except where the determination arises from or results in bankruptcy or liquidation, the Employer is entitled by clause 27.4.2.2, to pay all suppliers and sub-contractors (Domestic or Nominated, assigned or not) for monies outstanding to them at the date of determination or incurred after the date of determination. It is made clear that where a Nominated Sub-Contractor is concerned, the obligations or discretion of the Employer to make direct payments under the provisions of any other contract (eg the Agreement NSC/2 or NSC/2a) are unaffected by any payment made under the present clause.

As and when required to do so by the Architect, clause 27.4.3 provides that the Contractor shall remove his temporary accommodation, plant, tools, equipment, etc. from the site. This could be immediately after determination, or after the Employer or substitute builder has completed the Works. Where the Contractor does not or cannot remove the temporary accommodation, etc. then the Employer may remove it and dispose of it.

138

If the Contractor has remained in business, any cash arising from such disposal will be taken into account in the settlement of accounts. Where, however, a bankruptcy or liquidation is concerned, any cash arising is to be paid over to the trustee in bankruptcy, receiver, or liquidator, for the property disposed of belongs to him and under the rules of bankruptcy and liquidation, such monies must be applied to the benefit of all creditors, not just one, the Employer.

The settlement of accounts following determination by the Employer is dealt with in clause 27.4.4. The opening words set out the basic concept that the Contractor will pay or allow to the Employer the direct loss and expense caused to him. The Conditions anticipate that such loss and expense will exceed any amounts due to the Contractor, for it is expressly provided that no payment will be made to the Contractor until the final settlement of accounts.

The Architect is required, within a reasonable time after completion of the Works, to certify or verify the costs incurred by the Employer in completing the Works and will presumably produce the final statement of accounts. The Conditions do not provide for the Architect or the Quantity Surveyor to do it.

The final statement of account will comprise the following items:-

★ the total amount of the final account as it would have been if the Works had been completed by the Contractor

LESS the total of:-

★ the amounts previously paid by the Employer

★ the amount of the costs incurred by the Employer in completing the Works (ie direct costs of labour, materials, sub-contractors, insurances, professional fees, and any substitute builder, etc)

★ '...any direct loss and/or damage caused to the Employer by the determination...'.

The words used here 'loss and/or damage' are important, for they are different to those used in other clauses where one party has a claim against the other, eg in clause 26, for example, where the claim by the Contractor is for reimbursement of 'direct loss and/or expense'. It is believed that by the use of the words 'loss and/or damage' it is made clear that the Employer is entitled to claim the entire loss or damage that he is able to prove in the courts under Common Law. There is no reference in this clause to liquidated and ascertained damages, for the right of the Employer to further liquidated and ascertained damages in respect of the period after determination of the employment of the Contractor appears to expire upon that determination.

The balance is payable to the Contractor by the Employer or to the Employer by the Contractor as the case may be. Where the determination is caused by, or results in, bankruptcy or liquidation of the Contractor, then the claim by the Employer for the balance due goes to the trustee in bankruptcy, receiver, or liquidator and the Employer then takes his chance along with all the other creditors. The balances due to the Contractor or Employer as the case may be are described as debts payable one to the other, so that they can readily become the subject of legal action for recovery of the debt.

DETERMINATION BY THE CONTRACTOR

Clause 28 Determination by the Contractor of his own employment under the contract is covered by clause 28. The text is virtually identical to that contained in the 1963 Edition.

Defaults of the Employer

Clauses 28.1.1 to 28.1.4 Clauses 28.1.1 to 28.1.4 detail the actual circumstances of default by the Employer or his professional advisers that may give rise to the right to determine. The circumstances detailed in the present clause are more numerous than those appearing in clause 27 and some of them are events one would not ordinarily describe as breaches of contract. The procedures for determination vary according to the nature of the default so that in the following discussion, the default and the relevant notices, etc. by the Contractor will be taken together.

Failure of the Employer to honour certificates

Clause 28.1.1 Clause 28.1.1 gives the Contractor the right to determine his own employment under the contract if the Employer '...does not pay the amount properly due...on any certificate...'. The word 'properly' here is new and has presumably been included to reinforce the right of the Contractor to receive payment in full, subject only to the **express** rights granted to the Employer elsewhere in the Conditions to deduct monies from the amounts stated in Interim Certificates as due to the Contractor.

The Employer will not be in default under this clause if he does not pay the amount due in an Interim Certificate provided the difference is an amount he is permitted to deduct under the Conditions. Those Conditions which grant an express right to the Employer to make such a deduction are listed in the discussion on clause 30.1.2 (page 106).

Where the Employer does not make the payment within fourteen days from issue of the certificate, and if the Contractor wishes to commence the determination procedure, then he must give notice to the Employer (copy to the Architect) by registered post or recorded delivery. Such notice should:-

★ identify the certificate number and the date of issue

★ inform the Employer that he has not honoured the certificate within fourteen days of the date of issue

★ inform the Employer that if payment is not received within seven days of receipt of the notice, then the Contractor will serve notice of determination of his own employment under the contract.

The Conditions do not anticipate any dispute between the parties as to the facts of such a notice by the Contractor, although one could imagine quite heated disputes where, perhaps, the Employer has made an 'improper' deduction from an amount due to the Contractor, or where the Contractor does not accept the quantum of a proper deduction. It would appear that the Employer can take no immediate formal action until such time as the Contractor has determined his own employment under the contract, whereupon the arbitration agreement can be brought into operation.

If payment is not received by the Contractor within a few days after the issue of the first notice, then, if the Contractor still wishes to proceed with determination, he must give a second notice to the Employer by registered post or recorded delivery. The second notice is to be sent seven days after the first notice and should:-

- ★ refer to the first notice and state the date the notice was received by the Employer

- ★ inform the Employer that, since he has not honoured the certificate of the Architect for a further period of seven days after receipt of the first notice by the Contractor, the Contractor forthwith determines his own employment under the contract

- ★ remind the Employer that such determination is without prejudice to any other rights or remedies he may have under the Conditions or at Common Law.

The position of the parties consequent to determination is dealt with in clause 28.2 and will be discussed there.

Interference by the Employer

Clause 28.1.2   Where the Employer '...interferes with or obstructs the issue of any certificate...' then clause 28.1.2 gives the Contractor the right to determine his own employment under the contract. What is envisaged here is some interference or obstruction to payment certificates, but it is clear from the words used - 'any certificate' - that this clause is intended to include any certificate to be issued by the Architect. The non- issue of a Certificate of Practical Completion would have the same effect as the non- issue of a payment certificate, for its absence would prevent the payment of monies properly due to the Contractor.

It is not easy to describe the actions that may be considered as interference or obstruction. Obvious examples would be where an Employer, suffering some temporary financial embarrassment, instructs his Quantity Surveyor not to make, or to delay the making of, an interim valuation, or instructs his Architect not to issue, or to delay the issue of, an Interim Certificate. Perhaps a Local Authority Employer would block the issue of a certificate because of some mishap in the financial arrangements with central government. More subtle forms of interference or obstruction include deliberate under valuation and certification of the work carried out. To justify taking action under this clause the Contractor has to demonstrate that the Employer has interfered with or obstructed the issue of a certificate, and by its nature such interference or obstruction will be difficult to detect and demonstrate. Perhaps the best test would be for the Contractor to ask himself - has the Employer taken any action that would prejudice the impartiality of the Quantity Surveyor or the Architect in the matter of issue of certificates?

If the Contractor is satisfied that the Employer is interfering with or obstructing the issue of certificates, and if he wishes to determine his employment under the contract, then he must give notice to the Employer or the Architect sent registered post or recorded delivery. The notice is to be sent to the Employer (copy to the Architect) and should:-

- ★ inform the Employer that certificates due under the Conditions are not being issued by the Architect because of interference or obstruction by the Employer

- ★ state (one sentence) the nature of the interference or obstruction

- ★ inform the Employer that, because of such interference or obstruction, the Contractor forthwith determines his employment under the contract

★ remind the Employer that such determination is without prejudice to any other rights or remedies he may have under the Conditions or at Common Law.

The position of the parties consequent to determination is dealt with in clause 28.2 and will be discussed there.

Suspension of the Works

Clause 28.1.3   Where the Contractor is not able to proceed with the whole or a substantial part of any remaining uncompleted portion of the Works for a prescribed period by reason of certain happenings (detailed in clauses 28.1.3.1 to 28.1.3.7), then the Contractor may determine his own employment under the contract. In the present clause the uncompleted Works must have been 'suspended', which is a word not referred to elsewhere in the Conditions. Presumably, it is the Contractor who suspends the execution of the Works but, strangely, he does not have to tell anybody of the suspension. The qualifying period of the suspension is recorded in the Appendex and the periods are recommended to be three months in the case of loss or damage by fire etc. (the Clause 22 Perils) and one month in all other cases. The parties may agree periods different from those recommended, but some period must be agreed and entered in the Appendix or else it would appear that this clause cannot be operated. The periods of delay have to be continuous. Separate periods totalling the prescribed period would not seem to qualify as grounds for determination.

Clauses 28.1.3.1 to 28.1.3.7 detail the actual circumstances of default by the Employer or his professional advisors that may lead to suspension of the Works and may give rise to the right to determine. Many of the circumstances detailed here (albeit slightly amended) have been referred to previously in the discussions on clause 25 (Extension of time) and 26 (Loss and expense..). The comments made there in regard to 'Relevant Events' and 'matters' are equally applicable where the same items reappear in the present clause. In effect clauses 25 and 26 provide the Contractor with a remedy in the case of interruption to the regular progress of the Works, and the present clause deals with the situation where work actually stops. Before contemplating action under this clause the Contractor should remember that he is required to proceed regularly and diligently with the Works (clause 23.1) and to use his best endeavours, etc. (clause 25.3.4). With these points in mind it would appear that the Contractor probably has to work himself to a standstill before a suspension could become properly effective for the purpose of this clause.
Certain of the circumstances merit special comment:-

★ **clause (28.1.3.2)** - loss and expense caused by Clause 22 Perils.
Note that loss or damage caused by negligence of the Contractor does not qualify.

★ **clause (28.1.3.3)** - civil commotion.
That is to say, an incident involving the population at large (ie not employees) and preventing the execution of the Works. 'Civil commotion' appears here in isolation without the other incidents referred to in clause 25.4.4. The reason being that the incidents not included in the present clause relate to the procurement of materials required for the Works. Presumably extended difficulties in securing materials would be dealt with by a change of supplier (if the materials are to be supplied by the Contractor), or by an instruction of the Architect (if the materials are to be supplied by a Nominated Supplier or Nominated Sub-Contractor). Damage to the Works by civil commotion is already covered by the reference in clause 28.1.3.2 to Clause 22 Perils.

★ **clause (28.1.3.4)** - instructions of the Architect.
Note that instructions given as the result of some negligence or default of the Contractor do not qualify; the purpose presumably being to prevent the Contractor from engineering a right to determine by precipitating an instruction that has the effect of suspending the Works.

★ **clause (28.1.3.5)** - late instructions of the Architect.
Mere lateness of instructions is not sufficient; the Contractor must have made previous written application for the instruction or drawing or detail and the application must have been made in good time. (See also clauses 25.4.6 (page 50) and 26.2.1 (page 84)).

Where there has been a suspension of the Works fitting all the conditions precedent, and if the Contractor wishes to determine his own employment under the contract, then he must give notice to the Employer or the Architect. The notice must be sent registered post or recorded delivery to the Employer (copy to the Architect). Such notice should:-

★ inform the Employer that the whole (or a specified part) of the Works has been suspended for a continuous (specified) period since (a named date)

★ state (one sentence) the reason for the suspension

★ inform the Employer that, because of such suspension, the Contractor forthwith determines his own employment under the contract

★ reminds the Employer that such determination is without prejudice to any other rights or remedies he may have under the contract or at Common Law.

The Conditions do not seem to contemplate a situation where the Employer wishes to dispute the fact of determination by the Contractor. It would appear that he should commence arbitration proceedings under the arbitration agreement. Since the employment of the Contractor under the Contract has been terminated, then the dispute is again subject to immediate arbitration.

The position of the parties consequent to determination by reason of suspension of the Works is dealt with in clause 28.2 and will be discussed there.

Bankruptcy or liquidation of the Employer (Private Edition only)

Clause 28.1.4 The financial failure of the Employer is dealt with in clause 28.1.4. The employment of the Contractor does **not** automatically determine upon financial failure of the Employer, notice of determination must be given by the Contractor. Of course, it may be that the Contractor has already set the wheels of determination in motion due to the failure of the Employer to honour a certificate. Where the Contractor is satisfied that the Employer has suffered financial failure and he has proper proof that this is so (eg a court order, or a letter from the receiver or liquidator. Heresay, or merely knowledge of an impending court hearing, is not sufficient) the Contractor will probably wish to determine his own employment under the contract and he must give notice to the Employer or the Architect. The notice must be sent registered post or recorded delivery and be sent to the Employer (copy to the Architect). Such notice should:-

★ set out the circumstances known to the Contractor about the Employer

★ inform the Employer that, because of those circumstances, the Contractor forthwith determines his own employment under the contract

★ remind the Employer that such determination is without prejudice to any other rights or remedies he may have under the contract or at Common Law.

Consequences of determination

Clause 28.2   The arrangements between the parties following upon determination by the Contractor of his own employment under the contract are set out in clause 28.2. The opening sentence of this clause makes clear two things. Firstly, the act of determination does not extinguish any rights the parties may already have established against the other (for example, the right of the Contractor to payment for some earlier loss and expense, or the right of the Employer to any liquidated and ascertained damages due to non-completion of the Works by the Contractor before the determination). Secondly, the obligation of the Contractor to idemnify the Employer against the liabilities described in clause 20 continues until the Contractor has finally completed the removal of his property from the site.

By clause 28.2.1, the Contractor '...with all reasonable despatch...' is required to remove his property from the site and is to permit his sub-contractors to do the same. The removal of property by the Contractor or any sub-contractor is to be carried out so as not to cause injury or damage that would, if the contract were continuing, have been the subject of indemnity by the Contractor under clause 20. This obviously includes ensuring that some critical item of plant or equipment is not removed so as to cause damage to the Works themselves. The property to be removed includes all unfixed materials and goods on the site that are not already the property of the Employer under clause 16.1. Where the Employer can demonstrate his ability to pay for them, presumably the Contractor would be pleased to return them, but the Conditions are silent on the point. Where the determination arises from or results in, bankruptcy of the Employer, then, presumably, the Contractor can dispose of the materials and goods in question. Again, the Conditions are silent on the point. In particular, there is no reference to an obligation of the Contractor to account for such sale.

The settlement of accounts following determination by the Contractor is dealt with in clause 28.2.2. The general principle is that the Employer is to pay the Contractor for all the work done, the cost of removal from the site and all claims for loss and expense incurred by the Contractor. The opening words of clause 28.2.2 make it clear that the contract anticipates, after taking account of monies previously paid, there will be a balance due to the Contractor, but the Conditions do not make clear who is to ascertain the amount due to the Contractor. In clause 27 Determination by Employer, it was clear that the Architect was to ascertain the costs incurred by the Employer in completing the Works and his loss and expense. In the present clause, the function of ascertaining the amount due to the Contractor is not assigned to anybody. Presumably the Contractor and the Employer must agree these matters among themselves. Somehow or other the parties have to settle a final statement of account that will comprise the following items:-

THE TOTAL OF:-

★ the value of work completed; such valuation to be made as if it were an interim valuation made under the rules set out in clause 30.1

★ the value of work begun but not completed; such valuation to be made on the basis of the Valuation rules detailed in clause 13.5

★ the direct loss and expense incurred by the Contractor and ascertained as if the rules of clause 26 were applicable; such valuation is to include loss and expense arising from 'matters' occurring both before and after determination

144

★ the cancellation costs of orders for materials and goods

★ the cost of removal of the property of the Contractor from the site

★ 'any direct loss and/or damage...' incurred by the Contractor and any Nominated Sub-Contractors and arising from the determination

LESS

★ the total amounts previously paid by the Employer.

The Conditions anticipate that the balance will be payable by the Employer to the Contractor. Where the determination is caused by, or results in, bankruptcy or liquidation of the Employer, then the claim by the Contractor for the balance due goes to the trustee in bankruptcy or liquidator, and the Contractor takes his chance along with all the other creditors. In this case, the balance due is **not** described as a debt payable one to the other, so that it could be more difficult to proceed to legal action for recovery. Clauses 27 and 28 are not the same on this detail.

By clause 28.2.3 the Employer is required to inform both the Contractor and any Nominated Sub-Contractors concerned of the amounts payable to Nominated Sub- Contractors as a consequence of the ascertainment of the various amounts included in the final statement.

Clause 28 ends at this point. Comparison of clause 28 with the similar clause in the 1963 Edition shows that the final proviso, giving the Contractor a lien on unfixed materials and goods on site pending settlement of the financial affairs, has been removed. This is due once again to the possibility, where the Employer is bankrupt or in liquidation, that such a provision would be against the rules of bankruptcy, etc. by creating a preferential creditor.

Postscript to clause 28

Finally, in regard to determination by the Contractor it should be noted that there is no reference to any timetable for the final settlement of the financial affairs between the Contractor and the Employer.

OUTBREAK OF HOSTILITIES

Clause 32

The possibility of outbreak of war is contemplated by clause 32. Where there has been a general mobilisation of the armed forces then by clause 32.1 either party may -it is not compulsory - give the other notice of determination of the employment of the Contractor. Such notice must be given by registered post or recorded delivery and may be given at any time after the expiry of twenty eight days from the mobilisation, but not later than Practical Completion of the Works unless the Works have suffered war damage, see clause 33. The requirement for twenty eight days to elapse after mobilisation being, presumably, to ensure that the outbreak of war is substantial or real and not a local skirmish. The qualification regarding damage to the Works is intended to ensure that the Contractor retains responsibility for making good defects in the Works, but not for reinstatement of war damage to the Works. That is dealt with in clause 33.

The notice of determination takes effect 'forthwith'. In clause 32.3 there is an oblique reference to clause 28.2 which details the rights and duties of the parties in the event of determination by the Contractor. Under that clause the Contractor will remove his plant, equipment, temporary buildings, etc., from the site, but presumably not before he has carried out the instructions of the Architect referred to in the next paragraph.

Clause 32.1 allows the Architect to issue instructions in regard to the execution of protective work by the Contractor before he leaves the site and enables the Architect to specify the point up to which the work is to proceed before cessation. The Architect may issue such instructions within fourteen days after the notice of determination, and the Contractor must comply with those instructions. The Conditions anticipate that the work comprised in the instructions of the Architect will not take more than three months, for after that time the Contractor may abandon the Works if he is unable to proceed.

Calculation of the amounts due for payment to the Contractor following determination under this clause is set out in clause 32.3. Any work carried out as a result of instructions of the Architect issued under clause 32.2 will be valued under the Valuation rules of clause 13.5. Otherwise the basis of final payment to the Contractor shall be computed by reference to the provisions of clause 28.2, except that the Contractor shall not be entitled to any amount for his direct loss and expense. The timing of the final payment to the Contractor is therefore, left open as was the case under clause 28.

The foregoing describes the formal arrangements laid down by the Conditions. Perhaps the most appropriate point to note is the hint given in footnote (u) - in the event of hostilities, the parties may make whatever arrangements suit themselves.

WAR DAMAGE TO THE WORKS

Clause 33 Damage to the Works caused by war damage is dealt with in clause 33. 'War damage' is defined (clause 33.4) as that sustained by the matters detailed in the War Damage Act 1943, section 2(1). That is to say:-

'(a) damage occuring (whether accidentally or not) as the direct result of action taken by the enemy, or action taken in combating the enemy or in repelling an imagined attack by the enemy;

(b) damage occuring (whether accidentally or not) as the direct result of measures taken under proper authority to avoid the spreading of, or otherwise to mitigate, the consequences of such damage as aforesaid;

(c) accidental damage occuring as the direct result −

    (i)   of any precautionary or preparatory measures taken under proper authority with a view to preventing or hindering the carrying out of any attack by the enemy, or

    (ii)   the precautionary or preparatory measures involving the doing of work on land and taken under proper authority in any way in anticipation of enemy action,

being, in either case, measures involving a substantial degree of risk to property:

Provided that the measures mentioned in paragraph (c) of this sub-section do not include the imposing of restrictions on the display of lights or measures taken for training purposes.'

It will be seen that this is a wide definition and the damage is not limited to that caused by enemy action. The concept, however, of 'accidental' war damage requires careful thought. The reference in the Conditions to the War Damage Act 1943 is solely for the purpose of identifying a definition of war damage.

The present clause is concerned with war damage occurring either before or after any determination under clause 32 and the two clauses are intertwined to the extent that war damage as contemplated here may well precipitate determination under clause 32.

By the concluding words of clause 33.1 '...notwithstanding anything expressed or implied elsewhere in this contract' it appears that in the event of the Works suffering war damage as defined, then the entire Conditions can be abandoned in favour of the matters set out in clauses 33.1.1 to 33.1.4. The Contractor is entitled to be paid for all work carried out even though it has been destroyed (clause 33.1.1), for the removal of debris and the execution of protective work (clause 33.1.2), and for reinstating the damaged work (clause 33.1.3). All to be valued as a Variation under clause 13.2 and 13.5 (clause 33.1.4).

Clause 33.2 is a rather complicated provision detailing the situation where war damage under the present clause precipitates determination under clause 32. In effect, instructions of the Architect already given under clause 33 to clear away, protect or restore damaged work are automatically deemed to have been given under clause 32 where there has been a determination as a result of that damage.

The Employer may be entitled to receive compensation from the government to the extent provided by statutory law from time to time. The present position is that a new Act of Parliament would be required for the payment of the compensation arising from war damage, since the War Damage Act 1943 only applies to claims for compensation made before 1st October 1968. Claimants under the War Damage Act 1943 were entitled to be paid '...an amount equal to the proper cost of the works executed for the making good...' of the damage.

The entitlement of the Employer to receive compensation from the government is set out in clause 33.3. By its wording, it is made clear that payment to the Contractor for work done to clear away, protect and restore damage is not dependent, either as to quantum or timing, upon receipt of such compensation by the Employer.

ANTIQUITIES

Clause 34

A more likely occurrence is dealt with in clause 34, the discovery of antiquities. Clause 34.1 provides that 'All fossils, antiquities and other objects of interest or value...', found during the execution of the Works become the property of the Employer. Most builders will have an idea of the type of thing meant by fossils, antiquities and '...other objects of...value...'. The expression '...other objects of interest...' is open to wider interpretation. In this case, the Employer and the Architect are in reality relying on the judgement of the actual labourer working in the trench. If the object does not interest him, then it will not be seen again. In practice, one would hope that the Employer and the Architect will give the Contractor some guidance in these matters prior to commencement of a project in an area where there is the possibility of antiquarian finds.

Upon the discovery of such an object, by clauses 34.1.1 and 34.1.2, the Contractor is required not to disturb it and its immediate surroundings, and must cease work in the area around the object if that is the only way to ensure that it is preserved in its precise location. The Contractor must (clause 34.1.3) forthwith advise the Architect or clerk of works of the discovery and its whereabouts. There is nothing in the present clause requiring such notice to be given in writing, reflecting, perhaps, the urgency with which action is required under this clause.

As the Contractor is only entitled to an extension of time following the issue (or non-issue) of instructions of the Architect in relation to the discovery, it is imperative that the Contractor give immediate notice to the Architect requesting the issue of his instructions

Such notice must be sent to the Architect by registered post or recorded delivery and should:-

★ refer to clause 34.1.3

★ confirm that the Architect and/or Clerk of Works has been informed (by personal contact; by telephone; by telegram) of the discovery

★ give a brief (one sentence) description of the object discovered and its location

★ confirm the action taken by the Contractor to protect and preserve the object

★ (if appropriate) state the extent to which progress of the Works is being, or is likely to be, delayed

★ request that the Architect immediately issue his instructions under clause 34.2 in regard to both the discovery itself and the carrying out of further work in the vicinity of the discovery.

The Architect is required (clause 34.2) to issue instructions to the Contractor as to his future actions both in regard to the object discovered and the Works themselves. The extent of the powers of the Architect are apparently unlimited. One could readily envisage instructions to cease work around the discovery, to change the method of working, to postpone part or all of the Works, perhaps to redesign part of the building around it. The powers of the Architect are deliberately drawn widely because of the totally unpredictable nature of the potential discovery. In particular, the Contractor must, if requested, permit an expert engaged by the Employer to enter upon the site and examine the discovery. All instructions issued under this clause would become variations required by the Architect under clause 13.2 and would be valued under clause 13.5.

Upon the issue of instructions by the Architect, the discovery at last becomes a Relevant Event for the purposes of extension of time under clause 25. Upon receipt of such instructions, the notices, particulars of the effects and estimates of delay required by clause 25 must all be submitted by the Contractor should the instructions give rise to delays in the progress or completion of the Works. The procedures detailed in the earlier discussions for securing a proper extension of time must be followed.

The Architect could instruct that some or all of the Works be postponed, but such instructions do not seem to permit determination by the Contractor of his own employment under the contract under clause 28. This apparently is irrespective of the length of such a postponement.

Only in the event that the Architect does not issue instructions in regard to any discovery does the question of determination by the Contractor of his own employment under clause 28 arise. Even so, there are several preconditions before the determination could occur:-

★ the Works must have been suspended for the period stated within the Appendix;

★ the Contractor must have requested the issue of instructions at the proper time (hence the advice to give immediate written notice upon making the discovery)

★ those instructions have not been issued by the Architect.

Clause 34.3.1 provides that any direct loss and expense incurred by the Contractor as a consequence of the discovery or because of work carried out in consequence of instructions of the Architect, is to be ascertained by the Architect or Quantity Surveyor. There are no procedural requirements laid down in connection with any claim by the Contractor for reimbursement of loss and expense. It would be in the best interests of the Contractor if he gave notice at the earliest opportunity in the manner discussed when considering these matters under clause 26. Clause 34.3.2 provides that, where necessary to ascertain the loss and expense of the Contractor, the Architect will inform him of the extent of any extension of time awarded by reason of instructions issued under clause 34.2.

Clause 34.3.3 provides that any loss and expense ascertained under clause 34.3.1 is to be added to the Contract Sum; included in interim valuations (clause 30.2.2.2);and paid in Interim Certificates. Again, it matters not whether the loss and expense incurred by the Contractor has been ascertained in full or in part, or is agreed or not.

Others engaged upon the Works

The nature of the construction industry today is such that few, if any, builders employ operatives in all the varied skills and trades that come together in the construction of a building. The Conditions recognise this, and in this Section the methods by which the Contractor is permitted or required to allow others onto the site to carry out specialised activities will be examined (clause 19 - Assignment and Sub-Contracts). In addition, the Employer is entitled to carry out work upon the site (clause 29 - Works by the Employer or by persons employed or engaged by the Employer) and the rights of the parties in this situation will be examined. The Conditions also permit appointment by the Architect of specialist suppliers (clause 36 - Nominated Suppliers) and the rules for the appointment and administration of them will be considered. For an extended treatment of Nominated Sub-Contractors, see Section Eleven commencing on page 161.

ASSIGNMENT AND SUB-LETTING

The right of the Contractor to assign the contract and his authority to sub-let any part of the Works are set out in clause 19. The clause has been substantially rewritten by comparison with the 1963 Edition.

Assignment

Clause 19.1   By clause 19.1, each party to the contract requires the written agreement of the other before he can assign the contract. To assign the contract is to transfer it to another by means of an assignment (ie the legal document). An assignment would occur, for example, where the Contractor arranged for another contractor to carry out the whole of the work on his behalf, but where the Contractor retains full responsibility for the Works. Where the Contractor elects to withdraw from the entire contract and arranges for a substitute contractor to carry out or to complete the Works, then this is a novation agreement. Such an agreement is between three parties, the Contractor, the substitute contractor, **and** the Employer, and so is not mentioned in the present clause, for the Employer is a party to the legal document creating the novation agreement.

Sub-letting

Clause 19.2   The first sentence of clause 19.2 repeats the 1963 Edition. The Contractor can only sub-let any part of the Works with the written consent of the Architect. Where the Contractor wishes to sub-let part of the Works a simple letter to the Architect would suffice. Such a letter should:-

★ refer to clause 19.2

★ identify the part of the Works that the Contractor wishes to sub-let

★ name the sub-contractor proposed to be entrusted with the specialist work and (if desired) offer a brief (one sentence) explanation of the capability and performance of the proposed sub-contractor

★ request that the Architect give his formal written consent.

It is not clear from the Conditions whether the name of a proposed sub-contractor is absolutely necessary when requesting permission to sub-let. The Architect may well wish to make his own enquiries about the proposed sub-contractor for certain important parts of the Works, and there seems to be no reason why the name should not be given so that the grant of permission to sub-let may be expedited.

Where the traditional cost fluctuation clauses 38 and 39 apply, the approval of the Architect to sub-letting is a condition precedent to recovery by the Contractor of increased costs incurred by a Domestic Sub-Contractor.

The second sentence of clause 19.2 is entirely new and contains the definition of 'Domestic Sub-Contractor', that is to say, any sub-contractor who is not a 'Nominated Sub-Contractor'.

Specified Domestic Sub-Contractors

Clause 19.3 An entirely new procedure for the selection of sub-contractors is introduced in clause 19.3. By way of introduction, the situation envisaged by this clause is that an Employer may wish to have some control over the specialist sub-contractor employed to carry out certain work but does not wish to go to the extent of nomination. The key to the control exercised by the Employer and his professional advisers is by naming in the Contract Bills not less than three specialist sub-contractors, one of whom must eventually carry out the specialist work.

The rules for this method of selection of a sub-contractor are set out in clause 19.3.1. The work concerned is to be measured, or, may be '...otherwise described...' (whatever that means - the expression does not appear in SMM 6) in the Contract Bills and must be clearly set out there for pricing by the Contractor. The Contractor may price the work how he wishes. There is no apparent obligation to obtain quotations from any particular sub-contractors, although one imagines that the Contractor will approach those named in the Contract Bills. The Contractor must note that the normal risk of those specialist sub-contractors not in fact being able to carry out the works or some reason is not relieved by any provision in the present clause or elsewhere in the Conditions. The Contractor is obliged to appoint one of the named specialist sub-contractors to carry out the specialist work.

By clause 19.3.2.1, the list of specialist sub-contractors named in the Contract Bills shall comprise not less than three. The Employer (or the Architect on his behalf) and the Contractor may agree to add further specialist sub-contractors to the list. Where the Contractor wishes to make suggestions as to the content of the list, then presumably a simple letter to the Architect would suffice. The only restraint upon making additions to the list is that no addition shall be made after the Contractor has entered into a binding sub-contract for the work concerned. This is logical, for the Contractor carries the entire risk of failure of the sub-contractor from that point on.

Clause 19.3.2.2 deals with the position where, at any time before the Contractor has entered into a binding sub-contract for the work concerned, the number of specialist sub-contractors ready, willing and able to carry out the work falls below three. The Contractor and the Employer (no mention of the Architect in this case) may, either, agree the names of other specialist sub-contractors for inclusion in the list so as to make up the minimum of three names, or, agree that the Contractor shall be permitted to carry out the work himself or have it carried out by a Domestic Sub-Contractor of his own choice. While the latter option is presumably only meant to be used in extreme circumstances, it does appear to make nonsense of the whole arrangement.

Clause 19.3 outlines the various matters dealing with the appointment of Domestic Sub-Contractors. However there are various potential problems that this clause does **not** seem to have anticipated. The following questions are relevant:-

★ What happens if the Contractor cannot obtain quotations during the tender period from at least three named specialist sub-contractors? Suppose this is only discovered a short time before the tender is due and it is impracticable to make up the numbers and have quotations produced in time. What would the Contractor put in his tender? The use of prime cost and provisional sums would seem to be inappropriate, for instructions as to the expenditure of such sums would appear to result in the appointment of Nominated Sub-Contractors and the whole point surely of the procedure detailed in clause 19.3 is to provide an alternative to the Nominated Sub-Contract arrangements

★ What happens if none of the specialist sub-contractors named in the Contract Bills are ready willing and able to carry out the sub-contract work? Presumably the arrangements detailed in clause 19.3.2.2 can be used to provide the names of further prospective specialist sub-contractors. However, the Conditions do not deal with the position of any additional costs faced by the Contractor in this situation. Perhaps the agreement of the Contractor to the additional named specialist sub-contractors could be made conditional upon the prices tendered by them, so that the Contractor was not out of pocket. The agreement by the Contractor to any further named specialist sub-contractors proposed by the Architect must not be unreasonably withheld. One imagines that a potential loss by the Contractor arising from the execution of the sub-contract works concerned would be a valid reason for withholding agreement.

Clause 19.4   In clause 19.4, it is required that the employment of Domestic Sub-Contractors shall automatically determine upon the determination of the employment of the Contractor under the main contract. The Domestic Sub-Contract issued by the NFBTE and others contains provision for the automatic determination of the employment of the sub-contractor in such a case.

Clause 19.5   Clauses 19.5.1 and 2 are new. Clause 19.5.1 reminds the parties that the provisions regarding Nominated Sub-Contractors are in clause 35. It is made clear in clause 19.5.2 that the Contractor has no responsibility to carry out work described in the Contract Bills as being reserved for Nominated Sub-Contractors, except where the tender of the Contractor for such work has been accepted.

WORK BY THE EMPLOYER

Clause 29   Clause 29 sets out the circumstances under which the Employer himself, or persons engaged by him, may enter on to the site and carry out work that is not part of the Works. The extent of such work is not limited by the text of the clause and it could, therefore, embrace quite substantial parcels of work. This clause is really only intended to cover minor items that can readily be incorporated without disturbing the programme of the Contractor. It is common, for example, for murals and other works of art to be carried out under such arrangements, for, while they are only decoration, they often have to be built into the structure.

Planned work by the Employer

Clause 29.1   Where such work has been anticipated from the conception of the project, then clause 29.1 requires that the Contract Bills detail the work concerned and set out the circumstances under which it is proposed to be carried out together with details of the anticipated programme. These requirements are in excess of those detailed in clause B.12 of SMM6.

In these circumstances the Contractor will have had the opportunity to take account in his tender of the effect on his own programme or sequence of working by the execution of this work. In this case the Contractor is given no choice in the matter, he must permit the execution of such work.

Unexpected work by the Employer

Clause 29.2
Clause 29.2 deals with the situation where work to be carried out by the Employer himself, or persons engaged by him, has arisen as an afterthought and has not been described as such in the Contract Bills. Obviously the Contractor was not aware when tendering that such work was to be carried out by the Employer, and in this case, the Contractor has to give his consent before the Employer can arrange for the work to be carried out. The Contractor must not unreasonably withhold his consent. Whether or not the Contractor gives his consent will depend on the work concerned and its relationship to the uncompleted work. For example, whether the Contractor already has people working in the area concerned when the work is to be done and whether it can be accommodated without upsetting the existing programme for completion.

In either case, the permission of the Contractor must be given before the Employer, or persons engaged by him, can enter upon the site, for by clause 23.1 the Contractor has been given exclusive possession of the site.

Insurance and indemnities

Clause 29.3
Clause 29.3 states that any person employed or engaged by the Employer is '...a person for whom the Employer is responsible and (is) not...a sub-contractor'. The importance of this is in relation to the indemnities given under clause 20. Where the Employer, or persons engaged by him, have been permitted to enter upon the site and during the execution of the direct work cause injury or death to persons or loss or damage to property, then the indemnities given to the Employer by the Contractor under clause 20 do not always apply. In the case of injury or death to persons, the Contractor will be excused where the injury or death is caused by the act or neglect of the Employer '...or of any person for whom (he) is responsible'. In the case of loss or damage to property, the Contractor is only liable where the loss or damage is caused by himself or a sub-contractor.

The time for direct work of the Employer

Finally, in respect of direct work carried out by the Employer, or persons engaged by him, delay in progress of the remainder of the Works caused by the execution of this work becomes a 'Relevant Event' (clause 25.4.8.1) giving rise to an extension of time, a 'matter' (clause 26.2.4.1) leading to a claim for loss and expense, and an 'act' (clause 28.1.3.6) giving grounds for determination of the employment of the Contractor under the contract.

NOMINATED SUPPLIERS

Clause 36 contains all the provisions of the contract in regard to Nominated Suppliers. The clause has been substantially rewritten and expanded by comparison with the 1963 Edition although the philosophy and general principles remain unchanged. A Nominated Supplier is introduced into the contractual arrangement where the Architect wishes to have absolute control over the produce incorporated into the Works, but where it is quite practicable for the Contractor to fix the materials or goods. Such a situation would normally arise where the Employer would be concerned in making the final decision in relation to the decorative requirements of the building. Common examples these days are wallpaper, ironmongery, light fittings and the like. There is no apparent restriction on the materials that could become the subject of supply by a Nominated Supplier.

Definitions

Clause 36.1   A supplier becomes a 'Nominated Supplier' when he has been nominated under one of the arrangements detailed in clause 36.1.1 that is to say:-

★ where there is a prime cost sum in the Contract Bills and the supplier is named, either in the Contract Bills, or, in a subsequent instruction of the Architect

★ where an instruction of the Architect as to the expenditure of a provisonal sum contains a prime cost sum for the supply of materials or goods, and the supplier is named in that instruction or in another instruction of the Architect

★ where an instruction of the Architect as to the expenditure of a provisional sum requires the Contractor to purchase materials from a single manufacturer or supplier

★ where an instruction of the Architect requiring a Variation requires the Contractor to purchase materials from a single manufacturer or supplier.

An instruction issued by the Architect in either of the last two cases requires special attention before acceptance by the Contractor, for it may be invalid under the Conditions. This is because the Architect may be unaware that his instruction refers to materials or goods that are only obtainable from a single manufacturer or supplier. Examination of provisional sum instructions and Variation instructions will reveal when the Contractor is obliged to purchase materials from a single supplier or manufacturer and the Contractor should request that the Architect remedy the situation. The request could be by notice to the Architect and should:-

★ identify the instruction concerned

★ inform the Architect that certain (specified) materials are only obtainable from a single supplier or manufacturer

★ request the issue of a new instruction under clause 36.2 introducing a prime cost sum for such supply and naming the supplier.

A new instruction issued in response to the above notice, containing **both** a prime cost sum **and** the name of a supplier would then satisfy the Conditions.

Suppliers named in the Contract Bills

Clause 36.1.2   In clause 36.1.2, it is made clear that where materials or goods referred to in an item in the Contract Bills, and described as being supplied and fixed by the Contractor (ie a measured item, **not** a prime cost item) are only obtainable from a single supplier or manufacturer, then that supplier or manufacturer is **not** a Nominated Supplier, even though he may be named in the Contract Bills.

It is not difficult to envisage the position where such a supplier, being the holder of a monopoly in the supply of certain materials or goods, could seek to impose terms and conditions on the Contractor that are wholly unreasonable, for example, that they must be paid for before delivery. In such a case, the Contractor must price the risk concerned in his tender. There is no obvious alternative course of action.

The instructions of the Architect

Clause 36.2   Clause 36.2 sets out the duty of the Architect to issue an instruction naming the supplier for which a prime cost sum occurs in the Contract Bills, or is created by a provisional sum or Variation instruction. It would appear that an instruction of the Architect is required even where the proposed supplier is named in the actual prime cost item in the Contract Bills. There can be no Nominated Supplier unless he is named by the Architect in an instruction.

Payment to the Contractor

Clause 36.3   The amounts to be included in the final adjusted Contract Sum in regard to Nominated Suppliers are set out in clause 36.3. The starting point is the amount properly payable by the Contractor for the materials or goods in question. That is to say, the measured quantity of the materials and goods concerned at the rates quoted by the supplier. No allowance is permitted for waste, damage or theft, for that is deemed to be included in the rates of the Contractor for fixing and profit. To the amounts properly payable are to be **added:-**

> ★ any taxes properly payable by the Contractor on the procurement of the materials or goods, but excluding
>
> > ★★ amounts recoverable under any other clause in the Conditions (eg the fluctuations clauses) and/or
> >
> > ★★ value added tax capable of being treated as input tax
> > (Note: for the type of building project contemplated by JCT 80, no value added tax would be included here even if the materials and goods formed part of a taxable supply to the Employer, for in such a case, value added tax would be charged to the Employer on an amount calculated on the basis of the cost and supply **plus** the charges made by the Contractor for fixing and profit, etc. See also the notes on clauses 15.2 and 15.3, page 126.)
>
> ★ any packing or delivery charges properly payable by the Contractor, less any credit to be allowed for the return of crates etc. where these have been charged
> (Note: the Quantity Surveyor will take the credit, whether or not the crates have been returned).
>
> ★ the effect of any price adjustment clause in the contract of sale
>
> ★ **less** any trade or cash discounts obtained other than a cash discount of 5%.

Provision is made in clause 36.3.2 for payment to the Contractor of expense not otherwise recoverable under the items listed above and which has been properly incurred in obtaining materials and goods from a Nominated Supplier.

The contract of sale

Clause 36.4   Clause 36.4 provides that, unless otherwise agreed between the Architect and the Contractor, the Architect may only nominate a supplier who will enter into a contract of sale containing the terms and conditions prescribed in clauses 36.4.1 to 36.4.9. There can be other terms and conditions but those listed must be included. In addition to the terms

155

and conditions appearing in the 1963 Edition, three new ones have been included. A brief explanation of the terms and conditions follows with particular emphasis on the new and changed items.

36.4.1 **Quality of materials.** The text now reflects more closely the general position under clause 2.1. The quality of materials and standard of workmanship in the materials and goods of the Nominated Supplier are only required to be to the satisfaction of the Architect where it is expressly stated to be so, perhaps in the Contract Bills, or in the nomination instruction of the Architect.

Otherwise, it would seem that the entire responsibility for quality of materials and standards of workmanship falls upon the Contractor.

36.4.2 **Responsibility for defects.** It is now made clear that the Nominated Supplier is responsible for defects only up to the end of the Defects Liability Period under the main contract, **not** the date of the Certificate of Completion of Making Good Defects. The obligation of the Nominated Supplier to remedy defects is qualified. For example, the Nominated Supplier is not responsible for remedying defects that could reasonably have been observed by the Contractor prior to fixing or where defects are solely caused by inadequate storage, or by maltreatment by the Contractor, the Architect, or the Employer.

The Conditions do not expressly deal with the position where the Nominated Supplier is **not** required to remedy defects in these circumstances. One may only presume, therefore, that the Contractor assumes total responsibility for such defects under his general obligations to carry out and complete the Works. ★

36.4.3 **Programme.** The materials and goods are now to be supplied according to a programme agreed between the Contractor and the Nominated Supplier.

36.4.4 **Discount.** The Nominated Supplier is obliged to allow the Contractor 5% cash discount for payment not later than the end of the month following delivery of the materials or goods.

36.4.5 **Determination.** The duty of the Nominated Supplier to deliver the materials and goods is suspended upon determination of the employment of the Contractor under the main contract unless they have been paid for in advance. Under the provisions of clause 27.4.2, the contract of sale may have been assigned from the Contractor to the Employer, and the present clause facilitates the organisation of further deliveries should the Employer so require.

36.4.6 **Payment.** The Contractor is obliged to make payment to the Nominated Supplier and the time by which payment must be made by the Contractor in order to earn the 5% cash discount is restated. Payment is not dependent on an Interim Certificate of the Architect, payment must be made whether or not any amounts in respect of Nominated Suppliers are included in an Interim Certificate or the Final Certificate of the Architect. There are no arrangements which provide for payment of a Nominated Supplier by the Employer in the event of the failure of the Contractor to make payment, except after the determination of the employment of the Contractor under the contract.

36.4.7 **Ownership of materials.** This item is entirely new and it is provided that the materials or goods become the property of the Contractor upon delivery to the site. This item will causes some aggravation and will undoubtedly be the principle reason for objection to proposed Nominated Suppliers by the Contractor. (The steps to be taken by the Contractor where a supplier has been nominated but who refuses to agree to this provison, are discussed on page 157).

★ Under Common Law, the Sale of Goods Act, 1893 and the Supply of Goods (Implied Terms) Act, 1973 the supplier must provide goods that are, inter alia, reasonably fit for the purpose, and of merchantable quality. If the supplier has completed the Warranty by the Nominated Supplier (JCT form TNS/2, see page 159) he will have given certain warranties to the Employer. The Contractor and/or the Employer may have recourse to remedies against the supplier other than those set out in the Contract of Sale to which clause 36 refers in the case of defects in materials and goods supplied by a Nominated Supplier.

36.4.8   **Arbitration.** This item is entirely new and introduces provision for arbitration under the arbitration agreement. The dispute between the Contractor and Nominated Supplier must be substantially the same as a dispute under the main contract in order to be subject to the joinder provisions of the arbitration agreement. It is difficult to imagine a situation where a dispute between the Contractor and a Nominated Supplier would not be related to a similar dispute under the contract, but, were the dispute not to be related then arbitration under the present clause would not be possible.

36.4.9   **Conflicts.** This item is entirely new and provides that no other term in the contract of sale between the Contractor and Nominated Supplier can alter the sense or purpose of the compulsory conditions detailed in clauses 36.4.1 to 36.4.9. Thus, there can be additional conditions, but they must not override the compulsory conditions.

The foregoing conditions are those that must appear in the contract of sale between the Contractor and the Nominated Supplier. The Architect must not instruct the appointment of a Nominated Supplier who will not agree to them. The Contractor may enter into a contract of sale with such a supplier, but he is not compelled to do so. Upon discovery that the Architect has named a supplier in a nomination instruction who will not accept the compulsory conditions in the contract of sale, and the Contractor does not wish to enter into a contract of sale containing those terms, then the Contractor must immediately give notice to the Architect. Such notice must:-

★ identify the instruction concerned and the name of the supplier

★ specify the compulsory conditions set out in clauses 36.4.1 to 36.4.9 that the supplier will not agree to

★ request that the Architect issue a new nomination instruction naming a supplier who will enter into a contract of sale in the specified terms

★ set out the date by which the new nomination must be received.

Where the Contractor enters into a contract of sale containing terms and conditions outside those listed in clause 36.4.1 to 36.4.9, then, naturally enough, he loses all rights to object to the nomination.

An instruction of the Architect nominating a supplier could cause delay to the progress or completion of the Works if issued late. Such a late instruction could qualify as a 'Relevant Event' under clause 25.4.5.1 (Extension of time) and a 'matter' under clause 26.2.1 (Loss and expense...).

Where the Nominated Supplier attempts to limit his liability

Clause 36.5   Clause 36.5 deals with the situation where the terms and conditions of a proposed Nominated Supplier contain additional clauses that are repugnant to the Contractor. The additional clauses complained of must be such that they would so restrict, limit or exclude the liability of the supplier that the Contractor may be unable to satisfy the requirements of the main contract. In these circumstances, clause 36.5 permits the Architect and Contractor to agree upon the terms that will be applicable in the case of any particular supplier and the liability of the Contractor to the Employer will be similarly restricted, limited or excluded.

Upon discovery that the terms and conditions of a proposed Nominated Supplier named in an instruction of the Architect do not properly protect the position of the Contractor under the Conditions because they restrict, limit or exclude the liability of the supplier to the Contractor, and the Contractor is not willing to enter into a contract of sale

157

in such terms, then the Architect must be informed by notice. Such notice should:-

★ identify the instruction concerned and the name of the supplier

★ draw attention to the additional clauses in the terms and conditions of the supplier that are repugnant to the Contractor

★ give a brief (one sentence) explanation of the objection by the Contractor

★ request that the Architect either:-

   ★ ★   name a supplier whose terms and conditions are acceptable to the Contractor, or

   ★ ★   approve in writing, on behalf of the Employer, the specified restriction limitation, or exclusion

★ set out the date by which the new nomination or approval of the terms and conditions of the supplier must be received.

Again, it could be that the renomination instruction, or approval of the restriction, limitation, or exclusion by the Architect could cause delay to the progress or completion of the Works if issued late. Such a late instruction could qualify as a 'Relevant Event' under clause 25.4.5.1 (Extension of time) and a 'matter' under clause 26.2.1 (Loss and expense...).

The necessity for the Architect to give his written approval to the restriction, limitation or exclusion identified in this situation cannot be over-emphasised. For by that approval the Architect is doing two things, firstly he approves the restriction, limitation or exclusion in the contract of sale between the Nominated Supplier and the Contractor and, secondly, perhaps more importantly, the liability of the Contractor to the Employer in regard to the materials and goods in question is similarly restricted, limited or excluded. Clause 36.5.2 restates this by making it clear that until the approval of the Architect has been given the Contractor is not required to enter into a contract of sale with the Nominated Supplier. He may do so, but he cannot be required to do so.

Finally, in regard to Nominated Suppliers, clause 36.5.3 makes it clear that any additional terms and conditions in the contract of sale of a Nominated Supplier that become the subject of representations under clause 36.5, can only be any that are additional to the compulsory terms and conditions detailed in clause 36.4. No approval by the Architect to such additional terms and conditions can change the compulsory terms and conditions detailed in clause 36.4.

THE JCT NOMINATED SUPPLIER DOCUMENTS

The Joint Contracts Tribunal has published a form of tender for use by Architects and Nominated Suppliers and a warranty agreement to be given by a Nominated Supplier to the Employer. The use of these documents is not obligatory upon the Employer, the Architect, or the Contractor, but are recommended as good practice. The use of standard documents should ensure uniformity between the main Contract Documents and the contract of sale between the Contractor and the supplier. The following notes identify the documents that have been published and give general observations on their character, the contents and their use. The documents are:-

Tender TNS/1 - the JCT Standard Form of Tender by Nominated Suppliers. This is four pages long and is probably designed to be used in triplicate. It comprises:-

★ **Form of Tender** to be completed by the tendering supplier. In addition to the actual offer by the supplier, the form of tender contains certain other matters affecting the validity of the tender. Among other things, the supplier

    ★ ★   states the period for which his tender remains open for acceptance

    ★ ★   undertakes that none of his conditions of sale will conflict with JCT 80

    ★ ★   declares that a contract of sale for the materials and goods in question is conditional upon

        (i) nomination by the Architect

        (ii) agreement of a delivery programme with the Contractor

        (iii) an order from the Contractor.

★ **Schedule 1** containing, initially, the various particulars relevant to the tender of the supplier as proposed by the Architect. In tendering, the supplier may make alternative proposals that would form the basis of his offer. Before nominating the supplier the Architect must have agreed the alternative proposals. The particulars covered by Schedule 1 include:-

    ★ ★   the description of the materials or goods (both proposed and agreed)

    ★ ★   access to the Works

    ★ ★   certain particulars of the main contract (completion date, defects liability period, amendments to clause 25, liquidated and ascertained damages)

    ★ ★   delivery programme (anticipated by the Architect; proposed by the supplier; agreed by the Contractor)

    ★ ★   fluctuation arrangements

    ★ ★   whether the contract of sale is to be under hand or under seal.

★ **Schedule 2** which comprises a reprint of clauses 36.3 to 36.5 of JCT 80.

(Note. Clause 36.4 contains the nine compulsory conditions that must appear in the contract of sale between the Contractor and the supplier. Thus the supplier is informed or reminded of these important conditions when tendering, so that there shall be no misunderstanding of the requirements of the Contractor when he issues his order).

Warranty TNS/2 (Schedule 3 to Tender NSC/1) - the Warranty by a Nominated Supplier to the Employer. This is in two pages and is probably designed to be used in duplicate. It comprises:-

★ **A recital** placing Warranty TNS/2 into the context of previous events (ie the supplier has submitted a tender; the Architect has nominated the supplier; the Contractor has placed his order with the supplier).

★ **Conditions 1.1 to 4.4** setting out the terms of the warranty. The supplier

  ★ ★ warrants that he will properly design the materials and goods

  ★ ★ undertakes that he will so

      (i) provide the Architect with design information

      (ii) provide the Contractor with construction information

      (iii) deliver the materials and goods according to the programme agreed with the Contractor

    that the Contractor does not become entitled to, either, an extension of time, or, to reimbursement of loss and/or expense under the main contract by reason of delay in progress or completion of the Works caused by the Nominated Supplier

    (Note. A breach of these undertakings by the supplier could result in the award of an extension of time to the Contractor under clause 25.4.7 and reimbursement to the Contractor of loss and/or expense under clause 26.2.1.)

  ★ ★ indemnifies the Employer against any additional costs incurred by the Employer by reason of the failure of the supplier to fulfill those undertakings

  ★ ★ acknowledges the amount of liquidated and ascertained damages entered into the Appendix of the main contract

  ★ ★ declares that nothing in his tender will limit the warranties etc given in the Warranty TNS/2.

The Employer and the supplier

  ★ ★ agree to arbitrate on the terms and conditions of the Warranty TNS/2 in the case of any dispute between them.

It will be apparent from the foregoing observations that a real attempt has been made by the Joint Contracts Tribunal to regularise the relationships between builders and Nominated Suppliers.

Nominated Sub-Contractors

In this Section the tripartite relationship Contractor - Nominated Sub-Contractor - Employer (or the Architect on his behalf) will be examined. These matters appear in the longest clause in the Conditions (Clause 35 -Nominated Sub-Contractors). The text bears no resemblance whatsoever to the provisions dealing with Nominated Sub-Contractors in the 1963 Edition and contains nearly all the matters in the Conditions that relate to Nominated Sub-Contractors. The only exception are the arrangements for the inclusion of work by Nominated Sub-Contractors in Interim Certificates and the Final Certificate which are included in the payment procedures of clause 30.

INTRODUCTION

Objectives

The principles adopted in this clause are probably no more than those that should ordinarily be adopted by Architects and Contractors as good practice. Briefly the objectives of the new arrangements are:-

★ to set down precisely the conditions under which a nomination may occur and to describe the mechanics of properly achieving that nomination

★ to provide a detailed procedure that converts a tender by a prospective Nominated Sub-Contractor (invited and received by the Architect) into a formal sub-contract agreement between a sub-contractor and the Contractor

★ to introduce proper disciplines into the procedures for settling the final account of each Nominated Sub-Contractor, including early releases of retentions and special arrangements for dealing with final payments

★ to deal more precisely with the failure of either the Contractor or the sub-contractor to carry out their respective obligations under the main contract and the sub-contract

★ to introduce a more comprehensive direct agreement between the sub-contractor and the Employer covering such matters as design, the provision of design information, guarantees after early final payment, indemnity in the case of re-nomination and direct payments by the Employer.

These objectives have probably been achieved, but the result of the cumbersome, long winded, sometimes impossible, often impracticable procedures will be to cause many to turn away from the concept of the nomination of sub-contractors. When discussing Domestic Sub-Contractors, a perfectly adequate process was set out involving measurement of the specialist work in the bills, naming three or more sub- contractors and,·letting the Contractor choose one of them. By comparison with the nomination procedures this process is by far the easier.

In this commentary, the rights and responsibilities of the Contractor under clause 35 will be considered. Where necessary reference will be made to the other JCT Nominated Sub-Contract documents, but a full study of the set of JCT Nominated Sub-Contract documents is a subject in its own right and warrants a separate treatment.

Definitions

Clause 35.1   Clause 35.1 defines a Nominated Sub-Contractor, or, more precisely, defines the situations under which a sub-contractor can become a Nominated Sub-Contractor. The Architect is permitted to nominate a sub-contractor to carry out certain parts of the Works:-

EITHER where is a prime cost sum is

★ entered in the Contract Bills

★ created by an instruction of the Architect as to the expenditure of a provisional sum

★ created by an instruction of the Architect requiring a Variation comprising additional work of a kind for which the Architect is already permitted to nominate a sub-contractor

OR where a sub-contractor is named (presumably as a prospective Nominated Sub-Contractor and with an amount in respect of the sub-contract work concerned) in

★ the Contract Bills

★ an instruction of the Architect as to the expenditure of a provisional sum

★ an instruction of the Architect requiring a Variation comprising additional work of a kind for which the Architect is already permitted to nominate a sub-contractor

OR by agreement between the Contractor and the Employer.

Two points to be stressed arise from these restrictions on the rights of the Architect to nominate a sub-contractor. Firstly, a specific nomination instruction must be issued in each case (see clauses 35.10.2 and 35.11.2). The provisional sum instruction or Variation instruction is not sufficient. Secondly, where the sub-contractor is 'named', an amount must be specified in the Contract Bills or in the instruction of the Architect in order that the accounting procedures may operate (see clause 30.6.2.1, adjustments to the Contract Sum).

Some background to the need for express agreement between the Contractor and the Employer where the Architect desires to nominate a sub-contractor to carry out work measured in the Contract Bills for execution by the Contractor has already been given in the discussion on clause 13.1.3, page 73. It is worth restating that if possible it is desirable for the Contractor and the Employer to reach agreement on further items of work to be carried out by Nominated Sub-Contractors. The alternatives are arbitration, or an impasse. In either case, the building does not get built and considerable difficulty is caused to both the Contractor and the Employer.

The final sentence of clause 35.1 recognises that the foregoing circumstances permitting nomination of sub-contractors go beyond the requirements of SMM 6, where clause B.9.1 provides that nomination can **only** arise from prime cost sums. For the purpose of this particular point **only,** clause 35.1 overrides SMM 6.

Right of Contractor to carry out prime cost sum work

Clause 35.2   Clause 35.2 recognises that the Contractor may be permitted to carry out work described in the Contract Bills as being reserved for Nominated Sub-Contractors. Clause 35.2.1 sets out the procedure where the Contractor wishes to have the opportunity to tender for such work and carry it out. The items of work concerned must be entered into the Appendix. The Architect is not obliged to invite the Contractor to tender for such work, he may do so if he wishes. If the tender of the Contractor is 'accepted', (there is no reference to an instruction of the Architect), he may only sub-let the work to a Domestic Sub-Contractor with the consent of the Architect. Where work reserved for Nominated Sub-Contractors is created by the issue of a provisional sum instruction under clause 13.3, then that parcel of work is deemed automatically to have been entered into the Appendix and the Contractor may request the opportunity to tender for it. There is no reference in the present clause to the Contractor being permitted to tender for and carry out work reserved for a Nominated Sub-Contractor that is created by a variation instruction. Presumably, this is because the varied nominated work is expected to be carried out by the Nominated Sub-Contractor already appointed to carry out the original prime cost sum work.

The content of clause 35.2.2 has already been referred to in the discussion on the Valuation of Variations under clause 13. Where there are Variations in prime cost sum work carried out by the Contractor for which his tender has been accepted under clause 35.2.1, then those Variations are to be **valued** under the Variation rules of clause 13, but **measured** against the tender document for the prime cost sum work concerned — not the main Contract Drawings and Contract Bills. The intention is presumably to ensure that the amount paid to the Contractor for the varied work is similar to the amount that would be paid to an independent Nominated Sub-Contractor for the same work. Thus the Contractor would not secure any advantage over an independent Nominated Sub-Contractor by way of mesurement of variations and the Employer would not expect to pay any more for the same variation. The position in regard to claims for reimbursement of loss and expense by the Contractor and by an independent Nominated Sub-Contractor may not be quite the same.

It is made clear in clause 35.2.3 that only clause 35.2 governs any prime cost sum work carried out by the Contractor for which his tender has been accepted under clause 35.2. The remainder of clause 35 does **not** apply to such work.

THE JCT NOMINATED SUB-CONTRACT DOCUMENTS

Clause 35.3   Clause 35.3 comprises a schedule of the JCT documents applicable to Nominated Sub-Contractors. JCT 80 contains two entirely separate procedures for the nomination of sub-contractors, and for the appointment of those sub-contractors by the Contractor. Firstly, the full procedure known as the 'Basic method' and, secondly, a less formal or shortened procedure known as the 'Alternative method'. Naturally enough, in each case the documents used to administer the two procedures are different. The following notes identify the documents associated with each method and give general observations on their character, the contents and their use.

The Documents — Basic Method

Tender NSC/1 - the JCT Standard Form of Sub-Contract Tender and Agreement.
This is twelve pages long and is used in triplicate. It comprises:-

★ **Form of Tender** to be completed by the tendering sub-contractor. To be 'approved' by the Architect prior to the issue of a preliminary nomination instruction (see clause 35.7.1) and 'accepted' by the Contractor before the issue of the final nomination instruction (see clause 35.10.2).

★ **Stipulations** (for conditions of tender) detailing various matters affecting the validity of the tender. In particular the tendering sub-contractor is to enter the period for which his tender remains open for acceptance.

★ **Schedule 1** containing the particulars of the main contract, the main contract Appendix entries, the order of the Works, access, the obligations of the Employer, etc.

(Notes. 1. These particulars are to be entered by the Architect. They must be CHECKED AND DOUBLE CHECKED by the Contractor, for under the provisions of clause 2.2 of Sub-Contract NSC/4 or NSC/4a dealing with conflicts in the Sub-Contract Documents, it is stated that the details entered in Schedule 1 of Tender NSC/1 shall prevail over the actual main contract details EVEN WHERE THEY ARE WRONG. Many things could go wrong if Schedule 1 is not completed correctly and it must be checked thoroughly before the contents are agreed with the sub-contractor and Architect.

2. Where prospective Nominated Sub-Contractors have been invited to tender early in the design process, the particulars of the terms of the main contract may not have been finally settled by the Employer and his professional advisers and this will encourage the entry of incorrect details in Tender NSC/1.)

★ **Appendices A or B to Schedule 1** detailing the fluctuation arrangements to apply to the sub-contract. The relevant Appendix is to be completed by the Architect and/or the sub-contractor as appropriate.

★ **Schedule 2** containing, initially, the particular conditions applicable to the sub-contract proposed by the tendering sub-contractor and forming the basis of his offer. Later these same matters, perhaps amended, become the agreed Particular Conditions applicable to the sub-contract between the Contractor and the sub-contractor. The Particular Conditions covered by Schedule 2 include:

★★ programme (both proposed and agreed) including the completion date for the sub-contract works

★★ the order of the Works

★★ 'special attendances' (both proposed and agreed)

★★ insurances

★★ special conditions for the employment of labour (both proposed and agreed)

★★ adjudicator, etc

★★ the status of the parties under the Construction Industry Tax Deduction Scheme

★★ method of accounting for Value Added Tax

★ ★ 'Any other matters...' (both proposed and agreed) including, perhaps, any limitation on working hours.

Provision is also made for the insertion of any item already agreed between the Architect and the proposed sub-contractor but the Conditions do not anticipate that such an item is not acceptable to the Contractor, so that there is no mention of a procedure to resolve a difference on one of these points. The parties will agree whether the sub-contract is to be executed under hand or under seal.

In fact, Schedule 2 includes all the matters that one expects to find in the Appendix to a form of sub-contract.

(Notes. 1. Reference is made in Part 2 of Schedule 2 to the 'Order of Works...' and examination of the footnote and Schedule 1 show that the particulars to be entered are to comprise any requirements of the Employer as to the order of the main contract Works. The Conditions do not anticipate a situation where the Contractor requires, perhaps because of the extent or nature of the following trades, that the sub-contractor complete the sub-contract works in a different order to that of the Works required by the Employer.

2. In regard to insurances by the sub-contractor (Part 4 of Schedule 2) the Contractor must enter the precise detailed insurances required to be effected by the sub-contractor. These particulars must include the actual risks to be covered by the insurance and the limit of indemnity to be provided under 'Third Party' or 'Public Liability' insurance policies. It is important that this item be properly completed, for under clause 7.1 of Sub-Contract NSC/4 or NSC/4a, the only contractually compulsory insurance is employers liability which is in any case a statutory requirement. **All** other insurances to be effected by the sub-contractor **must** be entered in Schedule 2.

3. The facility granted to both the sub-contractor and the Contractor to include in Part 9 of Schedule 2 'Any other matters...' is interesting. The way is, therefore, open for the Contractor to include within the sub-contract his own 'House Rules' regarding works by sub-contractors on the site. Such matters could include detailed arrangements for the administration of the safety policies of the Contractor and the sub-contractor, arrangements for shared welfare facilities, rules for the character, content and timing of applications for payment, etc. The only items that seem to be prohibited would be any that conflict with the Sub-Contract Conditions.)

After agreement of all these matters between the Contractor and the Sub-Contractor, the parties sign all three copies of the completed Tender NSC/1 (in two places) and the Contractor returns it to the Architect.

Agreement NSC/2 - the JCT Standard Form of Employer/Nominated Sub-Contractor Agreement. This is four pages long and is used in duplicate. It comprises:-

★ **Articles of Agreement**

★ **Four Recitals** placing Agreement NSC/2 into the context of previous events (ie the Sub-Contractor has submitted a tender; the Architect has approved that tender) and relating it with future events (ie the Architect intends to nominate the Sub-Contractor).

★ **Conditions 1 to 10** setting out the rights and duties of the parties. The Sub-Contractor:-

★ ★ agrees that he will attempt to settle the Particular Conditions of Schedule 2 of Tender NSC/1 with the Contractor

★★ warrants that he will properly design the sub-contract works

★★ undertakes that he will

(i) provide the architect with design information, drawings, etc so as not to delay the main contract works

(ii) not cause the Architect to instruct determination of the employment of the sub-contractor by reason of default by the sub-contractor

(iii) so carry out the sub-contract works that the Contractor does not become entitled to an extension of time by reason of delay to the Works caused by the Nominated Sub-Contractor

★★ indemnifies the Employer against

(i) additional costs incurred by reason of the nomination of a substitute Nominated Sub-Contractor, following the failure of the sub-contractor to complete the sub-contract works

(ii) costs of remedial work required after the Contractor has made final payment.

The Employer agrees that he will

★★ pay for design work carried out and materials ordered prior to issue of the final nomination instruction by the Architect
(Note. See clause 2.2.4 where the sub-contractor seemingly only has to order the materials in order to qualify for payment. They do not have to have been delivered to the site, nor do they have to have been paid for. There is no requirement for an indemnity as in clause 30.3 of the main contract.)

★★ operate the direct payment provision of the main contract in the event of the failure of the Contractor to make payment.

The Employer and the sub-contractor both agree to arbitrate on the terms and conditions of the Employer/Sub-Contractor Agreement in the case of any dispute between them.

Nomination NSC/3 - the JCT Standard Form for Nomination of a Sub-Contractor where Tender NSC/1 has been used. This is a single sheet and is used in sextuplicate. It comprises a simple pro-forma instruction where the Contract, Contractor and Sub-Contractor are named.

Sub-Contract NSC/4 - the JCT Standard Form of Sub-Contract for sub-contractors who have tendered on Tender NSC/1 and executed Agreement NSC/2 and been nominated by Nomination NSC/3 under the Standard Form of Building Contract. This is 42 pages long and is used in duplicate. It comprises:-

★ **Articles of Agreement** consisting of a statement of the names and addressses of the parties, seven Recitals, three Articles (including the arbitration agreement) and space for attestation of the Agreement by the parties

★ **the thirty-four Sub-Contract Conditions.**

There is no Appendix, for it is intended that the completed Tender NSC/1 (including the Particular Conditions detailed in Schedule 2) should be appended to the Sub-Contract

NSC/4. It will be seen therefore that proper agreement of the Particular Conditions set out in Schedule 2 of the Tender NSC/1 is critical, for that document becomes, in effect, the Appendix to the Form of Sub-Contract.

The Documents - Alternative Method

Agreement NSC/2a - the Agreement NSC/2 adapted for use where tender NSC/1 has not been used. This is an optional agreement, four pages long and is used in duplicate. It comprises:-

★ **Articles of Agreement**

★ **Six Recitals** placing Agreement SC/2 into the context of previous events (ie the sub-contractor has submitted a tender; the Architect has approved that tender) and relating it with future events (ie the Architect intends to nominate sub-contractor)

★ **Conditions 1 to 8** setting out the rights and duties of the parties. The Sub-Contractor

★ ★ warrants that he will properly design the sub-contract works

★ ★ undertakes that he will

(i) provide the Architect with design information, drawings etc so as not to delay the main contract works

(ii) not cause the Architect to instruct determination of the employment of the sub-contractor by reason of default of the sub-contractor

(iii) so carry out the sub-contract works that the Contractor does not become entitled to an extension of time by reason of delay to the Works caused by the Nominated Sub-Contractor

★ ★ indemnifies the Employer against

(i) additional costs incurred by reason of the nomination of a substitute Nominated Sub-Contractor following the failure of the sub-contractor to complete the sub-contract works

(ii) costs of remedial work required after the Contractor has made final payment.

The Employer agrees that he will

★ ★ pay for design work carried out and materials ordered prior to issue of the final nomination instruction by the Architect
(Note. See clause 1.2.4 where the sub-contractor seemingly only has to order the materials in order to qualify for payment. They do not have to have been delivered to the site, nor do they have to have been paid for. There is no requirement for an indemnity as clause 30.3 of the main contract.)

★ ★ operate the direct payment provision of the main contract in the event of the failure of the Contractor to make payment.

The Employer and the sub-contractor both agree to arbitrate on the terms and conditions of the Employer/Sub-Contractor Agreement in the case of any dispute between them.

(NOTE. The differences between Agreement NSC/2 and NSC/2a are concerned solely with the differences between the documentation used in the basic and alternative methods. For example, there are ten conditions in Agreement NSC/2 and only eight in Agreement NSC/2a. The omitted conditions concern the obligation of the sub-contractor to settle the Particular Conditions of Tender NSC/1 and remove the provision dealing with any conflict between the Tender NSC/1 and Agreement NSC/2, neither of which apply since Tender NSC/1 is not used in the alternative method).

Sub-Contract NSC/4a - the Sub-Contract NSC/4 adapted for use where Tender NSC/1 has not been used. This is some sixty pages long and is used in duplicate. It comprises:

★ **Articles of Agreement** consisting of a statement of the names and addresses of the parties, seven Recitals, three Articles (including the arbitration agreement) and space for attestation of the Agreement by the parties.

★ **the thirty-four Sub-Contract Conditions.**

★ **the Appendix** in thirteen parts and containing provision for entry of the following details:-

★★ a description of the sub-contract works and the identity of the numbered documents (ie the documents expressly incorporated into the sub-contract agreement)

★★ particulars of the main contract and the main contract Works, the main contract Appendix entries, the obligations of the Employer, the order of the Works, and access

★★ insurances, the programme for the sub-contract works but not, in this case, the completion date for the sub-contract works, daywork rates, the Retention percentage, the Adjudicator and Trustee/Stakeholder, attendances, particulars of the operative fluctuation clause and the necessary entries applicable to the chosen method, the status of the parties under the Construction Industry Tax Deduction Scheme, and 'Any other matters...' including, perhaps, special conditions on the employment of labour or limitations on working hours.

(Notes.1 Reference is made in part 2, Section C of the Appendix to the 'Order of Works...' and the text makes it clear that the particulars to be entered are to comprise any requirements of the Employer as to the order of the main contract Works. The Conditions do not anticipate a situation where the Contractor requires, perhaps because of the extent or nature of the following trades, the sub-contractor to complete the sub-contract works in a different order to that of the main contract Works required by the Employer.

2. In regard to insurances by the sub-contractor (Part 3 of the Appendix), the Contractor must enter the precise detailed insurances required to be effected by the sub-contractor. These particulars must include the actual risks to be covered by the insurance and the limit of indemnity to be provided under 'Third Party' or 'Public Liability' insurance policies. It is important that this item be properly completed, for under clause 7.1 of Sub-Contract NSC/4a, the only contractually compulsory insurance is employers liability which is in any case a statutory requirement. **All** other insurances to be effected by the sub-contractor **must** be entered in part 3.

3. The facility granted to both the sub-contractor and the Contractor to include in part 13 of the Appendix 'Any other matters...' is interesting. The way is therefore open for the Contractor to include within the sub-contract his own 'House Rules' regarding works by sub-contractors on the site. Such matters could include detailed arrangements for the administration of the safety policies of the Contractor and the sub-contractor, arrangements for shared welfare facilities, rules for the character, content and timing of applications for payment, etc. The only items that seem to be prohibited would be any that conflict with the Sub-Contract Conditions.

4. There is no reference in this Appendix to the choice of the alternative provision to be used for the administration of Value Added Tax. This must be dealt with in the execution of the sub-contract by deletion of the appropriate clause from the body of the text.)

The differences between Sub-Contract NSC/4 and NSC/4a are concerned solely with the differences between the documentation used in the basic and alternative methods. In Sub-Contract NSC/4a the Appendices obviously replace the Schedules 1 and 2 of Tender NSC/1. Otherwise the texts of Sub-Contract NSC/4 and NSC/4a seem to be identical apart from the references to the Appendices or Tender Schedules as the case may be.

PROCEDURES FOR NOMINATION

The procedures for the nomination of a sub-contractor using the JCT documents referred to in the preceding notes are set out in clauses 35.4 to 35.12.

Objection by the Contractor

Clause 35.4   Clause 35.4.1 provides that the Contractor may make reasonable objection to the proposed nomination of any person as a Nominated Sub-Contractor. Where the 'basic' method of nomination is used, clause 35.4.2 requires that notice of objection shall be made not later than the date by which the Contractor would otherwise return the fully completed Tender NSC/1 to the Architect. That is to say, within ten working days of receipt by the Contractor of the preliminary notice of nomination of the Architect. Where the 'alternative' method of nomination is used, clause 35.4.3 requires that notice of objection shall be made not later than seven days after receipt by the Contractor of the nomination instruction of the Architect.

What is a reasonable objection? There seem to be three principal reasons for objection by the Contractor to the proposed nomination of a sub-contractor.

★ The sub-contractor may not be capable of carrying out the value of work involved. For example, the sub-contract works may involve work to the value of £100,000 per annum, whereas the entire turnover of the sub-contractor is only £50,000 per annum.

★ The Contractor may be able to demonstrate to the Architect that his previous experiences lead him to doubt the ability of the sub-contractor to, say, carry out the class of work required, or, carry out the work to a demanding programme.

★ Where the 'alternative' method of nomination is used the sub-contractor may decline to enter into a sub-contract in the terms of Sub-Contract NSC/4a. This cannot occur where the 'basic' method of nomination is used, for in completing Tender NSC/1 the sub-contractor is agreeing to enter into a sub-contract in the terms of Sub-Contract NSC/4 subject only to agreement of Schedule 2 of Tender NSC/1.

Where the Contractor wishes to make objection to a proposed Nominated Sub- Contractor, notice must be given to the Architect and sent recorded delivery or registered post. In drafting the notice, the Contractor must take especial care to ensure that the reasons given for his objection are valid, genuine and justifiable, for it would be quite easy to include in the notice remarks which defame the character of the sub-contractor.

Such notice should:-

★ identify the preliminary notice of nomination (the basic method), **OR** the nomination instruction (the alternative method) as the case may be

★ state that the Contractor makes a formal objection to the named sub-contractor

★ set out the reasons (one sentence each) for which the objection is being made

★ request that the Architect issue his instructions to resolve the difficulty

★ offer to discuss with the Architect the acceptability of another sub-contractor

★ (if appropriate) inform the Architect of the date by which an acceptable Nominated Sub-Contractor must be appointed in order to avoid an effect on the regular progress of the Works or delay in the completion of the Works.

The instruction of the Architect issued in response to such a notice could be concerned with minor or technical matters, such as an instruction to change the fluctuation arrangements, or to amend the price to include cash discount, etc. and there would not normally be any difficulty in resolving these points. The instructions of the Architect could also involve the naming of a new prospective Nominated Sub- Contractor and there may be more difficulty here. Suppose the Contractor was objecting to a sub-contractor who has designed and was to construct a fundamental part of the building. Where the Architect does not sustain the objection of the Contractor and declines to name an alternative sub-contractor, then the only recourse open to the Contractor is to proceed to arbitration and have the 'reasonableness' of the objection heard by an arbitrator. It is believed that the matter would be subject to immediate arbitration '...on the question whether...the issue of an instruction is empowered by the Conditions' - Article 5.2.2.

The last point in the notice is necessary in order to introduce the general question of delay and extension of time. The late issue of a nomination instruction could become a 'Relevant Event' under clause 25 leading to extension of time and a 'matter' under clause 26 giving rise to a claim for reimbursement of loss and expense. The notice referred to in the preceding paragraph should not be regarded as the only notice with which to raise the question of a late nomination instruction. The sensible rules of contract management and the more formal notice requirements under clauses 25 and 26 must always be applied.

The method to be adopted

Clause 35.5　Clause 35.5.1 informs the Contractor how he will know whether it is intended that the 'basic' or 'alternative' method of nomination is to be used. Clause 35.5.1.2 provides that the Contract Bills, or a variation instruction creating a prime cost sum for Nominated Sub-Contract work, or a provisional sum instruction creating a prime cost sum for Nominated Sub-Contract work, will state when the 'alternative' method will be used (that is to say, the Tender NSC/1 and the Agreement NSC/2 will **not** be used). In addition, where the 'alternative' method is to be used, the Contract Bills, the Variation instruction, or the provisional sum instruction must also inform the Contractor whether or not the optional Agreement NSC/2a will be used.

If there is no statement that the 'alternative' method is to apply, then clause 35.5.1 provides that the 'basic' method will apply.

The Architect is permitted (clause 35.5.2) to issue an instruction changing the method of nomination in all cases, or in any particular case, from the 'basic' to the 'alternative', or vice versa. Such an instruction becomes a 'Variation' under clause 13.2 to be valued under the valuation rules of clause 13.5. A change from the 'basic' to the 'alternative' method of nomination and the non-use of Agreement NSC/2a could result in the Contractor assuming a greater risk in regard to the choice of materials for use in the Nominated Sub-Contract works. This provision would enable the additional risk to the Contractor to be valued and paid to him.

Naturally, the Architect may not issue such an instruction after he has issued a preliminary notice of nomination (the basic method, clause 35.7.1), or the nomination instruction (the alternative method, clause 35.11), except where a substitute sub-contractor is required to be nominated (see comments on clauses 35.23 and 35.24, page 186).

The Basic Method – procedure

A flow chart of the 'basic' method of nomination showing the progressive stages of the procedure and the distribution of the various multiple copy forms appears on pages 172 and 173.

Clause 35.6　Where the 'basic' method applies, clause 35.6 prohits the nomination of a sub-contractor who has not completed Tender NSC/1 and executed Agreement NSC/2.

Clause 35.7　Clause 35.7.1 provides that the Architect issue to the Contractor a 'preliminary notice of nomination', the completed Tender NSC/1 and a copy of Agreement NSC/2. The preliminary notice of nomination is to instruct the Contractor to settle the Particular Conditions of Schedule 2 of Tender NSC/1 (clause 35.7.2). The Conditions do not prescribe any particular document for this purpose. Any document signed by the Architect and using clear words to instruct the Contractor to reach agreement with the proposed sub-contractor would suffice.

Under the Conditions, the information sent to the Contractor at this stage is somewhat sparse, there being no express reference to the drawings, specification, bills, or schedules of rates against which the sub-contractor has tendered. The Contractor must request that the Architect pass these documents to him before having to settle the matters detailed in Schedule 2 of NSC/1.

Clause 35.8　The Contractor is given (clause 35.8) ten working days during which he is to settle all the outstanding matters in Schedule 2 of NSC/1 that remain to be agreed. It will probably prove to be impracticable to settle all these matters in the time scale given. Perhaps, as has already been mentioned, the Contractor has not been given sufficient information

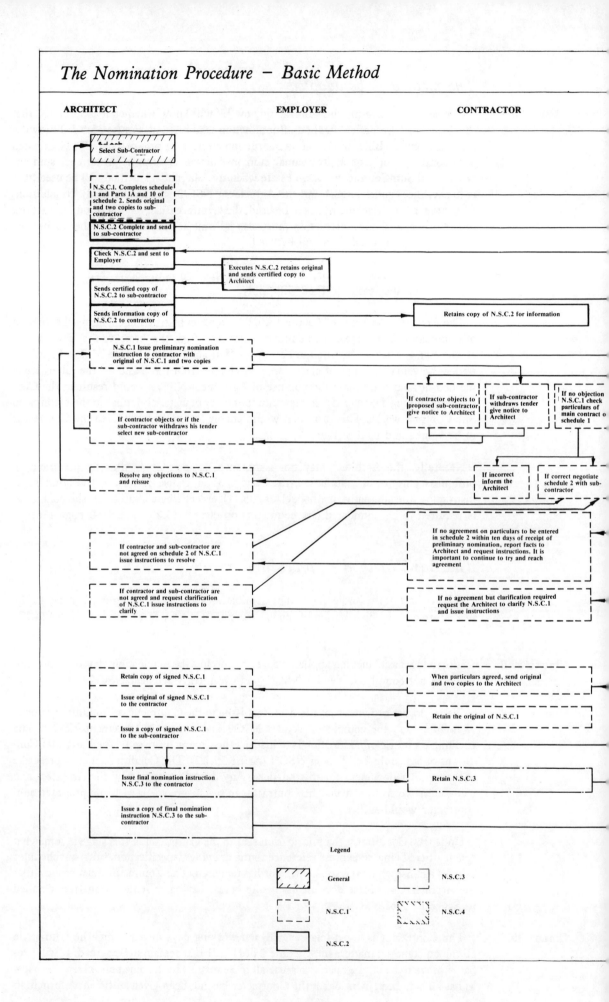

The Nomination Procedure – Basic Method

ARCHITECT **EMPLOYER** **CONTRACTOR**

Select Sub-Contractor

N.S.C.1. Completes schedule 1 and Parts 1A and 10 of schedule 2. Sends original and two copies to sub-contractor

N.S.C.2 Complete and send to sub-contractor

Check N.S.C.2 and sent to Employer

Executes N.S.C.2 retains original and sends certified copy to Architect

Sends certified copy of N.S.C.2 to sub-contractor

Sends information copy of N.S.C.2 to contractor

Retains copy of N.S.C.2 for information

N.S.C.1 Issue preliminary nomination instruction to contractor with original of N.S.C.1 and two copies

If contractor objects to proposed sub-contractor give notice to Architect

If sub-contractor withdraws tender give notice to Architect

If no objection N.S.C.1 check particulars of main contract o schedule 1

If contractor objects or if the sub-contractor withdraws his tender select new sub-contractor

If incorrect inform the Architect

If correct negotiate schedule 2 with sub-contractor

Resolve any objections to N.S.C.1 and reissue

If no agreement on particulars to be entered in schedule 2 within ten days of receipt of preliminary nomination, report facts to Architect and request instructions. It is important to continue to try and reach agreement

If contractor and sub-contractor are not agreed on schedule 2 of N.S.C.1 issue instructions to resolve

If contractor and sub-contractor are not agreed and request clarification of N.S.C.1 issue instructions to clarify

If no agreement but clarification required request the Architect to clarify N.S.C.1 and issue instructions

Retain copy of signed N.S.C.1

When particulars agreed, send original and two copies to the Architect

Issue original of signed N.S.C.1 to the contractor

Retain the original of N.S.C.1

Issue a copy of signed N.S.C.1 to the sub-contractor

Issue final nomination instruction N.S.C.3 to the contractor

Retain N.S.C.3

Issue a copy of final nomination instruction N.S.C.3 to the sub-contractor

Legend

General		N.S.C.3	
N.S.C.1		N.S.C.4	
N.S.C.2			

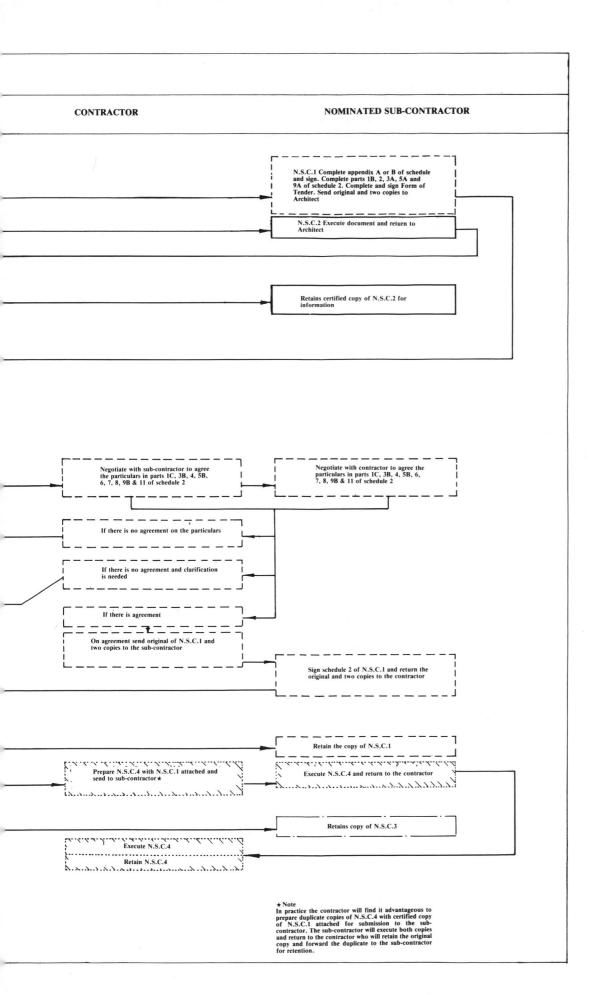

CONTRACTOR

NOMINATED SUB-CONTRACTOR

N.S.C.1 Complete appendix A or B of schedule and sign. Complete parts 1B, 2, 3A, 5A and 9A of schedule 2. Complete and sign Form of Tender. Send original and two copies to Architect

N.S.C.2 Execute document and return to Architect

Retains certified copy of N.S.C.2 for information

Negotiate with sub-contractor to agree the particulars in parts 1C, 3B, 4, 5B, 6, 7, 8, 9B & 11 of schedule 2

Negotiate with contractor to agree the particulars in parts 1C, 3B, 4, 5B, 6, 7, 8, 9B & 11 of schedule 2

If there is no agreement on the particulars

If there is no agreement and clarification is needed

If there is agreement

On agreement send original of N.S.C.1 and two copies to the sub-contractor

Sign schedule 2 of N.S.C.1 and return the original and two copies to the contractor

Retain the copy of N.S.C.1

Prepare N.S.C.4 with N.S.C.1 attached and send to sub-contractor★

Execute N.S.C.4 and return to the contractor

Retains copy of N.S.C.3

Execute N.S.C.4

Retain N.S.C.4

★ Note
In practice the contractor will find it advantageous to prepare duplicate copies of N.S.C.4 with certified copy of N.S.C.1 attached for submission to the sub-contractor. The sub-contractor will execute both copies and return to the contractor who will retain the original copy and forward the duplicate to the sub-contractor for retention.

about the Nominated Sub-Contract works to enable him to reach agreement. More likely that the Contractor and sub-contractor are not able to agree to a programme, for the programme requirements to be agreed seem to be more comprehensive than anything anticipated under the nominated form of sub-contract applicable to the 1963 Edition.

Where the Contractor is unable to reach agreement with the sub-contractor within the · required time scale, then the Contractor is required to give notice in writing to the Architect. Such notice should:-

★ identify the preliminary notice of nomination and the prospective Nominated Sub-Contractor concerned

★ inform the Architect that agreement on the outstanding items in Schedule 2 of Tender NSC/1 has not been (or perhaps, will not be) achieved within in ten working days required by the Conditions

★ set out the reasons (one sentence each) for which agreement cannot be reached

★ request that the Architect issue his instructions to resolve the difficulty

★ confirm that the Contractor will continue to discuss the outstanding matters for which agreement remains to be achieved

★ (if appropriate) inform the Architect of the date by which the formal nomination instruction must be received in order to avoid an effect on the regular progress of the Works or delay in the completion of the Works.

The instructions of the Architect could again involve the naming of a completely new prospective Nominated Sub-Contractor, or could concern the issue of supplementary information not previously given, or most likely, would involve an extension of time allowed for the purpose of reaching agreement with the sub-contractor.

The last item in the notice is necessary in order to remind the Architect of the need to properly settle the outstanding matters with the Nominated Sub-Contractor. The late issue of the formal nomination instruction could become a 'Relevant Event' under clause 25 leading to extension of time and a 'matter' under clause 26 giving rise to a claim for reimbursement of loss and expense. The notice referred to above must only be considered as a precursor to the more formal notice requirements under clauses 25 and 26.

Clause 35.9   If in response to the enquiries made by the Contractor following receipt of the preliminary notice of nomination, the sub-contractor withdraws his tender then clause 35.9 requires that the Contractor immediately inform the Architect of that fact. The Contractor is then to take no further action until instructions are given by the Architect.

Clause 35.10   When the outstanding matters in Schedule 2 of Tender NSC/1 are agreed to the satisfaction of both the Contractor and the sub-contractor and both parties have confirmed that agreement by signing Tender NSC/1, clause 35.10.1 requires that the Contractor send all three copies to the Architect.

Clause 35.10.2 provides that the Architect shall (not 'may') issue the formal Nomination NSC/3.

There is again no mention of the issue to the Contractor of any other documents relative to the Nominated Sub-Contract Works. Where the Contractor receives only the Nomination NSC/3, he must protest immediately and demand to be given all the documentation relative to the tender of the sub-contractor. Considering the complexity of these arrangements, it is unfortunate that these matters are not clearly defined in the Conditions.

The Alternative Method - procedure

Where the 'alternative' method applies, there is no prescribed tender document and this immediately leads to the first area of difficulty. The sub-contractor will presumably have submitted a tender of some sort, and will perhaps have been told that the form of sub-contract applicable will be Sub-Contract NSC/4a, but there is nothing in the Conditions that prohibits the introduction by the sub-contractor of other terms and conditions into his offer.

Clause 35.11   It is made clear in clause 35.11.1 that the Agreement NSC/2a is optional and that the choice is that of the Employer.

The Architect is required by clause 35.11.2 to issue an instruction naming the proposed Nominated Sub-Contractor. The Conditions do not prescribe any particular document for this purpose. Any document signed by the Architect and using clear words to instruct the Contractor to enter into a sub-contract agreement with the named sub-contractor for the specified prime cost sum work would suffice. Again, there is no express requirement for the Architect to issue to the Contractor any of the documents that may have formed the basis of the invitation to tender, or even the tender itself. The Contractor must demand that the drawings, specification, bills of quantities, schedules of rates, design details and other relevant documents are passed to him before being required to enter into a Nominated Sub-Contract agreement.

Clause 35.12   The Contractor is given (clause 35.12) fourteen days in which to 'conclude' the sub-contract in the terms of Sub-Contract NSC/4a. It is believed that the word 'conclude' means a completed, binding sub-contract agreement. This is an onerous task. The Appendices alone are in thirteen parts spread over six or seven pages, and entering all the data required takes considerable time. There is then the imponderable question of the time taken for postage of the documents to and from the sub- contractor.

It may well prove impracticable to conclude the sub-contract agreement in the time scale given. Perhaps the Contractor has not been given sufficient information to enable him to reach agreement, more likely that the Contractor and sub- contractor are not able to agree to the programme requirements or the attendances, for both these items are more comprehensive than anything anticipated under the nominated form of sub-contract applicable to the 1963 Edition. The Conditions do not appear to contemplate the position where the Contractor is unable to conclude the sub-contract agreement within the time scale given. Where the matters not capable of resolution are serious, and are identified soon enough, then the Contractor will make objection to the nomination of the sub-contractor by a notice to the Architect in the terms outlined in the discussion on clauses 35.4.1 to 35.4.3 (page 169).

A difficulty here is that the notice of objection under the 'alternative' method must be given within seven days of receipt of the nomination instruction of the Architect. If the Contractor discovers on the eighth day that he cannot conclude the sub-contract agreement and therefore wishes to make objection then the Contractor must give notice to the Architect in the terms previously outlined, and give special emphasis to the late discovery of the particular reason that has come to light. It is certain that the Contractor cannot be compelled to enter into a sub-contract with a nominated sub-contractor where terms can be shown to be unreasonable, merely because the notice of objection is, say, one or two days late. Of course, if the Contractor does nothing for a month after receiving the nomination instruction of the Architect, and then objects, then the position is clearly different and the Contractor may no longer be entitled to object.

The preceding two paragraphs have presumed that the matters not resolved are serious. Where the unresolved points are anticipated to be resolvable by further discussion between the Contractor and sub-contractor but beyond the fourteen day time scale given by the Conditions, then the Contractor should give notice to the Architect. Such notice should:-

★ identify the nomination instruction and the prospective Nominated Sub-Contractor concerned

★ inform the Architect that it has not been (or, perhaps, will not be) possible to conclude a sub-contract agreement within the fourteen days required by the Conditions

★ set out the reasons (one sentence each) for which the sub-contract agreement cannot be concluded

★ (if necessary) request that the Architect issue instructions that could resolve the difficulty

★ confirm that the Contractor will continue to discuss the outstanding matters for which agreement remains to be achieved

★ request that the Architect approve an extension of the time specified in clause 35.12 for the conclusion of the sub-contract agreement.

It is necessary to raise the last matter in the notice so as to be sure that, where the Contractor does not properly 'conclude' the sub-contract agreement until after the expiry of the fourteen days required by clause 35.12, the Contractor cannot be penalised for any resulting delay in the execution of the Works.

Where the 'alternative' method is used there is no requirement for the Contractor to inform the Architect in writing of the withdrawal of the Tender of a proposed Nominated Sub-Contractor. In view of the consequences developing from this the Contractor is recommended to give the facts in writing to the Architect at the earliest opportunity.

The late issue of further instructions could become a 'Relevant Event' under clause 25 leading to extension of time and a 'matter' under clause 26 giving rise to a claim for reimbursement of loss and expense.

Postscript to clauses 35.11 and 35.12

The arrangements detailed in clause 35.11 and 35.12 dealing with the appointment of Nominated Sub-Contractors under the 'alternative' method are wholly inadequate, incomplete and open ended. Where the 'alternative' method is to apply, the Contractor really must take great care in the administration of these matters, for it will be easy to fail to meet the time scales specified in these clauses.

INTERIM PAYMENT ARRANGEMENTS

Generally

Clause 21.2.1 and 21.3.1.1 of Sub-Contract NSC/4 or NSC/4a make it clear that the Architect is required, as part of his duties under the main contract, to include in Interim Certificates monies due to Nominated Sub-Contractors. Consequently, there is no obligation under the main contract or the sub-contract for the sub- contractor to make an application for payment. However, clause 21.2.2 of Sub- Contract NSC/4 or NSC/4a permits the sub-contractor to make written 'representations' to the Contractor as to the amount to be included in an Interim Certificate. If the sub-contractor does make 'representations', the Contractor is obliged to pass them on to the Architect. It would be possible for the sub-contract documents to be amended to include a requirement that the sub-contractor must make an application for payment each month. However, the presentation of such an application for payment cannot be made a condition precedent to the carrying out of a valuation or the issue of an Interim Certificate, for such a requirement would be of no effect by the provisions of clause 2.2 of the Sub-Contract NSC/4 and NSC/4a dealing with conflicts within the sub-contract documents.

The duty of the Architect to certify

Clause 35.13　　The duty of the Architect in regard to payments to Nominated Sub-Contractors is set out in clause 35.13.1. He is required (clause 35.13.1.1) to issue to the Contractor with each Interim Certificate a direction as to the amounts due to each Nominated Sub-Contractor. The amounts so directed must have been included in the Interim Certificate issued to the Contractor. The Architect is also required (clause 35.13.1.2) to issue to each Nominated Sub-Contractor a note of any amounts so included in an Interim Certificate on their behalf. This sum is to be computed by reference to the rules for ascertainment of the gross valuation of the sub-contract works set out in clauses 21.4.1 (work subject to Retention), 21.4.2 (work **not** subject to Retention) and 21.4.3 (deductions) of Sub-Contract NSC/4 or NSC/4a. Briefly, these are:-

Clause 21.4.1 (ie subject to Retention)

★ the value of:-

　　★ ★　work properly executed (including sub sub-contractors and work carried out as a result of instructions as to the expenditure of provisional sums)

　　★ ★　variations (ascertained by reference to the sub-contract valuation rules, ie including daywork, lump sum adjustments, preliminaries, etc)

　　★ ★　formula fluctuation additions

　　★ ★　materials on site (properly, not prematurely, and protected)

　　★ ★　materials off site (for which the sub-contractor has obtained indemnities and other documents and passed them to the Contractor).

Clause 21.4.2 (ie not subject to Retention)

★ the amount of costs actually incurred by the sub-contractor by reason of:-

　　★ ★　fees or charges payable to local authorities or statutory undertakers (clause 6.2 of the main contract)

★★ instructions of the Architect amending errors in setting out (clause 7 of the main contract)

★★ defects and the like rectified at the cost of the Employer (clause 14.4 of Sub-Contract NSC/4 or NSC/4a).

★ any loss and expense ascertained and caused by disruption, etc. (clause 13.1 of the Sub-Contract NSC/4 or NSC/4a)

★ the amount of any increased costs due under the cost fluctuation clause (clause 35 or 36 of the Sub-Contract NSC/4 or NSC/4a)

★ an amount representing one thirty-ninth of the total of the amounts not subject to Retention (to allow discount to the Contractor on those items).

Clause 21.4.3 (ie deductions)

★ any amount allowable by the sub-contractor under the cost fluctuation clause (clauses 35 and 36 of the Sub-Contract NSC/4 or NSC/4a).

★ an amount representing one thirty-ninth of any amount allowable by the sub-contractor under the cost fluctuation clause (to allow discount to the Contractor on those allowances).

The obligation of the Contractor to pay the sub-contractor

The Contractor is required (clause 35.13.2) to 'discharge' the amounts so included in Interim Certificates issued to the Contractor. The word 'discharge' is important, for by its use it is made clear that the Contractor may have legitimate reasons for not paying the full amount directed by the Architect. A footnote to clause 21.3 of Sub- Contract NSC/4 or NSC/4a draws attention to the 'set-off' rights of the Contractor (clause 23 of Sub-Contract NSC/4 or NSC/4a) and to the possibility of a deduction of tax by the Contractor under the Construction Industry Tax Deduction Scheme (clause 20A or 20B of Sub-Contract NSC/4 or NSC/4a). Several other legitimate deductions are permitted by the Sub-Contract Conditions:-

★ the cost to the Contractor of the failure of the sub-contractor to comply with directions of the Contractor (clause 4.5 of Sub-Contract NSC/4 or NSC/4a) (Note. It is presumed that this includes any failure of the sub-contractor to comply with instructions of the Architect, but the Sub-Contract Conditions do not seem to say this clearly.)

★ the cost to the Contractor of insurance following failure of the sub-contractor to insure (clause 9.2 of Sub-Contract NSC/4 or NSC/4a)

★ any loss or damage incurred by the Contractor and caused by failure of the sub-contractor to complete the sub-contract works by the due time (clause 12.2 of Sub-Contract NSC/4 or NSC/4a)

★ any loss or expense incurred by the Contractor as a result of disruption to the regular progress of the main contract Works caused by the sub-contractor (clause 13.3 of Sub-Contract NSC/4 or NSC/4a)

★ any deduction made by the Employer from amounts due to the Contractor in an Interim Certificate or the Final Certificate under the main contract provided the deduction is the result of some act, default or omission of the sub-contractor (clause 21.3.1.2 of Sub-Contract NSC/4 or NSC/4a)

★ the direct loss and/or damage incurred by the Contractor **OR** by the Employer as a result of the determination of the employment of the sub-contractor under the sub-contract.

The honouring period for payments to Nominated Sub-Contractors is seventeen days from the issue of any Interim Certificate (including the special, penultimate, Interim Certificate containing the final payments to all Nominated Sub-Contractors referred to in clause 35.17, see page 183). Since the honouring period for payment to the Contractor by the Employer is fourteen days, it would appear to be the intention that the payment of the Contractor is to be received by the Sub-Contractor within the seventeen day period. It is no good posting the payment cheque on the seventeenth day.

Proof of payment

Clause 35.13.3 requires the Contractor to obtain proof that amounts directed for payment to Nominated Sub-Contractors have been discharged and that proof is to be produced to the Architect before the issue of the next Interim Certificate.

The Contractor will have to consider carefully how he is to procure the 'reasonable proof' required by the Conditions. In many cases, the problem is already solved since the sub-contractor will be operating the Authenticated Receipt procedure for the administration of Value Added Tax and a copy of such an Authenticated Receipt would clearly suffice. Another document automatically providing reasonable proof is the returned cheque. It could be that the next application for payment by the sub-contractor will show (or can be arranged to show) cash received by the sub-contractor. It is made clear in clause 35.13.4 that the Contractor shall be deemed to have produced the required proof where the Architect is reasonably satisfied that the Contractor has paid the sub-contractor and that the proof has not been obtained solely due to the failure of the sub-contractor to produce the required document.

Where the Contractor does not produce the proof required, and has been unable to satisfy the Architect, then the Conditions presume that the Contractor has not paid the sub-contractor. Clause 35.13.5 details a procedure for direct payment to the sub-contractor by the Employer in the light of presumed default by the Contractor of his obligations to make payment. Direct payment by the Employer is subject to several contractual restraints and financial restrictions.

The contractual restraint is that direct payment is only obligatory where the Employer and the sub-contractor have entered into Agreement NSC/2 or NSC/2a (clause 35.13.5.1). The Architect must be satisfied that the absence of the required proof is due to default by the Contractor and has to issue a certificate to that effect to the Employer including details of the amount(s) alleged to be unpaid (clause 35.13.5.2). The Employer may then (clause 35.13.5.3) reduce the amount due to the Contractor in an Interim Certificate by the amount(s) not discharged to Nominated Sub-Contractors from any earlier Interim Certificate, and to pay those sums direct to the Nominated Sub-Contractors concerned.

The financial restrictions on the Employer are:-

★ that the Employer may first reduce the amount of any payment to the Contractor by any sum due to him from the Contractor (clause 35.13.5.3)

★ that the Employer is not obliged to pay amounts to Nominated Sub-Contractors in excess of the amount then due to the Contractor (clause 35.13.5.3)

179

★ that the direct payment is to be made to the Nominated Sub-Contractor when the amount would otherwise be paid to the Contractor (clause 35.13.5.4.1)

★ that where the amount of the Interim Certificate includes payment of Retention, the reduction made by the Employer for the purpose of direct payment to Nominated Sub-Contractors shall not exceed the 'Contractor's Retention' within that Interim Certificate (clause 35.13.5.4.2).

This, in effect, prevents the Employer from using retention monies held by him for one Nominated Sub-Contractor to make direct payment to another, ie the retention of each Nominated Sub-Contractor is inviolate. Finally, where, after giving effect to the preceding restrictions, the Employer does not have enough money to make the direct payments to two or more Nominated Sub-Contractors in full, then he is permitted to apportion at his discretion the amounts of the direct payments he will make.

Irrespective of the contractual restraint and financial restrictions referred to in the two preceding paragraphs, the Employer is not required to make direct payment to a Nominated Sub-Contractor if, at the date payment would be made, a petition for the compulsory winding up of the Contractor has been presented to the Courts, or if a resolution for the winding up of the Contractor has been passed by the shareholders. Where the Contractor is not a limited company, a footnote to clause 35.13.5.4.4 draws attention to the need to amend the text of that clause so as to refer to the law on bankruptcy.

It is believed that the reason for this ultimate restriction on direct payment by the Employer is related to the law on liquidations and bankruptcies which requires the payment of monies due to the Contractor to be made in full to the liquidator or trustee in bankruptcy and does not recognise payment to a third party. Thus the Employer would not be required to make double payment. Where Agreement NSC/2 or NSC/2a is used, the sub-contractor is required (clause 7.2 of Agreement NSC/2 or clause 6.2 of Agreement NSC/2a) to refund to the Employer any direct payment if the Employer can subsequently show that the direct payment should not have been made because of the status of the Contractor at the time of the payment.

EXTENSION OF TIME

The period for the completion of the Nominated Sub-Contract Works will have been incorporated into the formal sub-contract agreement as one of the items settled as the Particular Conditions of Schedule 2 to Tender NSC/1 (Sub-Contract NSC/4) or by the agreement recorded in part 4 of the Appendix to Sub-Contract NSC/4a.

Clause 35.14   Clause 35.14 sets out the rules for the award of extension of time to the sub-contractor for the completion of the Sub-Contract Works. The Contractor is prohibited by clause 35.14.1 from granting an extension of time to the sub-contractor for any reason, except in conformity with the provisions of Sub-Contract NSC/4 or NSC/4a. Any award of extension of time must be subject to the written consent of the Architect.

The obligations of the sub-contractor

The detailed provisions for extension of the periods for completion of the sub-contract works will be found in clause 11.2 of Sub-Contract NSC/4 or NSC/4a. The obligations of the sub-contractor are almost identical to the obligations of the Contractor under clause 25 of the main contract. That is to say, the sub-contractor has to give written notice, followed by particulars of effects and then estimates of delay in respect of all matters that are delaying (or will delay) the completion of the sub-contract works. Extensions of time may be awarded to the sub-contractor by reason of delay caused by any '...act omission or default...' of the Contractor or caused by the sub-contract Relevant Events.

The Relevant Events in Sub-Contract NSC/4 or NSC/4a are not **exactly** the same as those in the main contract. In addition to the obvious and necessary changes brought about by the transposition from main contract to sub-contract, an additional sub-contract Relevant Event is delay caused by suspension of the execution of the sub-contract works by reason of the failure of the Contractor to make payment according to the Sub-Contract Conditions.

The duty of the Contractor

The written notices, particulars of effects and estimates of delay are to be forwarded to the Architect by the Contractor. The Contractor and the sub-contractor both have to request the Architect to consent to the award of an extension of time (clause 11.2.1.3 of Sub-Contract NSC/4 and NSC/4a). Where the cause of the delay is the default of the Contractor (for example, by being in delay himself and thus preventing commencement of the sub-contract works by the sub-contractor) then the same procedure applies. In such a case the Contractor will have to take care to ensure that the pleas of the sub-contractor are fairly and properly presented to the Architect.

The duty of the Architect

The Architect is required (clause 35.14.2) to consider the notices, particulars and estimates and to consent to the awards of extention of time to be given by the Contractor to the sub-contractor. The Contractor is required to award any extension of time within twelve weeks after receipt of the Sub-Contractors notices, etc.

FAILURE TO COMPLETE

The date of the expiry of the period for the completion of the Nominated Sub-Contract Works can be ascertained from the entry made in the Particular Conditions of Schedule 2 to Tender NSC/1 (Sub-Contract NSC/4) or from the entry recorded in part 4 of the Appendix to Sub-Contract NSC/4a.

Clause 35.15   Clause 35.15 sets out the procedure to be adopted by the Contractor where the Nominated Sub-Contractor fails to complete the Nominated Sub-Contract Works within the period or periods incorporated into the Sub-Contract or within any extended time awarded by the Contractor.

The obligation of the Contractor

Upon the failure of the Nominated Sub-Contractor to complete the sub-contract works within the period or periods incorporated into the sub-contract, the Contractor is required to give notice to the Architect (clause 35.15.1). The notice is to be sent registered post or recorded delivery, with a copy to the Nominated Sub-Contractor concerned. Such notice should:-

★ identify the Nominated Sub-Contractor concerned

★ inform the Architect that the Nominated Sub-Contractor has failed to complete the (specified) sub-contract works within the time (or by the date) agreed within the sub-contract agreement

★ name the date by which the Nominated Sub-Contractor should have completed

★ (if applicable) confirm that all notices, particulars and estimates received from the Nominated Sub-Contractor have properly been passed to the Architect

★ confirm that the Contractor has taken all practicable steps to avoid or reduce delay by the Nominated Sub-Contractor

★ request that the Architect issue a certificate under clause 35.15.1 certifying that the nominated sub-contractor has failed to complete the sub-contract works by the date agreed within the sub-contract agreement.

There seems to be no requirement in the Conditions setting out any limitation of the timing of the notice by the Contractor. It is in the best interest of the Contractor for the notice to be given immediately upon expiry of the completion period for the sub-contract works.

The duty of the Architect

The Architect will need to be satisfied, both as to the facts contained in the notice by the Contractor and that all notices, particulars and estimates given by the sub- contractor have been properly considered and the appropriate awards of extension of time have been granted before he will issue the certificate requested by the Contractor. A copy of any such certificate issued to the Contractor is to be sent to the sub-contractor concerned. The certificate of non-completion of the sub-contract works must be issued by the Architect within two months of the notice of the Contractor to the Architect, clause 35.15.2.

The certificate of non-completion issued by the Architect under clause 35.15.1 is a condition precedent to any claim by the Contractor against the sub-contractor for loss or damage caused by the failure of the sub-contractor to complete the sub- contract works in due time (clause 12.2 of Sub-Contract NSC/4 or NSC/4a).

PRACTICAL COMPLETION

The right of the sub-contractor

Under clause 14.1 of Sub-Contract NSC/4 or NSC/4a, the sub-contractor is permitted to give written notification to the Contractor when the sub-contractor is of the opinion that the Nominated Sub-Contract works have reached practical completion. The Contractor is required to pass such written notifications to the Architect and may add his own observations; perhaps pointing out items or areas of work that are **not** complete.

The certificate of the Architect

Clause 35.16 The Architect is required by clause 35.16 to decide when the Nominated Sub- Contract Works have reached practical completion and to issue a certificate of practical completion of the sub-contract works. Copies of that certificate are to be sent to the Contractor and the Nominated Sub-Contractor.

The effect of the certificate

The issue of the certificate of practical completion of the Nominated Sub- Contract works by the Architect has the effect of releasing further payment to the sub-contractor in the next Interim Certificate, as the value of work certified to be practically complete will only be subject to half Retention. In addition, the issue of such certificate determines the commencement of the defects liability period for the sub-contractor and facilitates the early final payment procedures.

EARLY FINAL PAYMENT

The obligations of the sub-contractor

Clause 35.17 Clause 35.17 sets out the circumstances under which a Nominated Sub-Contractor is able to secure early final payment. There are a number of conditions precedent to the issue of an Interim Certificate by the Architect directing early final payment to the sub-contractor:-

★ the Employer and the sub-contractor must have entered into Agreement NSC/2 or NSC/2a and clause 5 of NSC/2 or clause 4 of NSC/2a remain unamended. (Note. These clauses contain an indemnity to the Employer in regard to defects in the Nominated Sub-Contract Works appearing after an early final payment.)

★ the defects liability period for the Nominated Sub-Contract Works must have expired.
(Note. The defects liability period would normally be equal to that under the main contract. It can be different, but cannot apparently exceed twelve months. If it is to be different, the details must have been agreed in Tender NSC/1.)

★ the sub-contractor shall have made good defects appearing within that time. (Note. There is no reference here or in Sub-Contract NSC/4 or NSC/4a to a certificate of completion of making good defects such as appears in the main contract. In view of the important changes in responsibilities resulting from that event, this appears to be a serious omission from the Conditions.)

★ the sub-contractor shall have passed the sub-contract final account documentation to the Architect or Quantity Surveyor.
(Note. The sub-contractor only has to have sent the documentation; no mention here of agreement of the Ascertained Final Sub-Contract Sum.)

The duty of the Architect

When these conditions have been satisfied, the Architect may issue an Interim Certificate that includes the '...Ascertained Final Sub-Contract Sum as finally adjusted or ascertained...'. It is not stated that this means agreed. The final payment to the sub-contractor will thus be released, for Retention is expressly not held on amounts included in an Interim Certificate that have arisen by the operation of the early final payment provision of clause 35.17, see clause 30.4.1.3.

Defects after early final payment

Clause 35.18 The position in the event of '...any (further) defect, shrinkage or other fault...' in the sub-contract works resulting from defects in workmanship, materials or goods appearing after final payment to the sub-contractor, but before the issue of the Final Certificate under the main contract, is dealt with in clause 35.18. The Conditions do not contain a requirement for an instruction to be issued by the Architect requiring such further defects be remedied. However, some sort of instruction or other communication will be necessary from the Architect to the Contractor and thence to the sub-contractor requiring the remedying of these further defects or else the provisions of clause 35.18 will not work.

If the sub-contractor fails to remedy these further defects, then the Architect is empowered (clause 35.18.1.1) to nominate a substitute sub-contractor solely for the purpose of making good these further defects. It is made clear that the whole of clause 35 applies to such a substitute nominated sub-contractor. This means that monies will be certified and paid to the Contractor and thence to the substitute nominated sub-contractor, all as previously described.

THIS PROCEDURE WILL COST THE CONTRACTOR MONEY!!

Under clause 5.2 of Agreement NSC/2 or clause 4.2 of Agreement NSC/2a, the sub-contractor has undertaken to '...rectify...any omission, fault or defect in the Sub-Contract Works...' (note the difference in the text quoted here and that of clause 35.18 - why?) or, in the event of his failure so to rectify, to be responsible for the costs incurred by the Employer in having the rectification work done by others. Clause 35.18.1.2 provides that if, after taking reasonable steps to recover such costs, the Employer has not been able to recover them in full, then any shortfall (which could include the whole cost of the substitute nominated sub-contractor) will be paid or allowed by the Contractor to the Employer. The position therefore is that the sub-contractor has received his final payment; the Employer is indemnified against any consequential costs; and the Contractor is left to make up any shortfall.

This arrangement is iniquitous. Why should the Contractor be required to carry the burden of this additional risk as he receives no benefit and cannot allow for the item in his tender? Consider the position where the cost of remedying such defects results in liquidation or bankruptcy of the sub-contractor. In such a case the Contractor will be expected to meet the bill for the entire cost of the remedial work.

The final sentence of clause 35.18.1.2 allows the Contractor to agree the prices to be charged by the substitute sub-contractor.

It is made clear in clause 35.19 that an early final payment to a Nominated Sub-Contractor does not reduce the responsibility of the Contractor to protect and insure the entire, main contract Works.

RELATIONSHIP OF EMPLOYER TO NOMINATED SUB-CONTRACTOR

Clause 35.20   It is made clear in clause 35.20 that the only relationship between the Employer and any Nominated Sub-Contractor is through Agreement NSC/2 or NSC/2a.

DESIGN BY NOMINATED SUB-CONTRACTOR

Clause 2.1 of Agreement NSC/2 or clause 1.1 of Agreement NSC/2a set out certain warranties given by the sub-contractor to the Employer in regard to the design, etc. of the Nominated Sub-Contract Works. The warranties given by the sub-contractor are that, in so far as the sub-contractor has a responsibility for such matters, he has exercised reasonable skill and care in:-
    ★the design of the sub-contract works

184

★ the selection of materials and goods for the sub-contract works

★ the satisfaction of any performance specification incorporated into the Sub-Contract Documents.

Clause 35.21   Clause 35.21 makes it clear that for these three matters the Contractor is not responsible to the Employer. The intention is that the Employer and the sub- contractor enter into Agreement NSC/2 or NSC/2a, so that the sub-contractor can give direct warranties to the Employer for the same three matters. In the event that there was some failure of design, etc., then the Employer would have a direct right of action against the sub-contractor concerned. If the Employer and the sub- contractor do **not** enter into Agreement NSC/2 or NSC/2a, the position of the Contractor is unchanged. To the extent of the three matters previously referred to, the Contractor still has no responsibility to the Employer. Presumably the Employer carries the risk of failure in the design, etc. of those particular works carried out by the Nominated Sub-Contractor. In some situations the Employer may have a right of action at Common Law for negligence against the Nominated Sub-Contractor.

The last sentence of clause 35.21 provides that, for the avoidance of all doubt, the Contractor remains entirely responsible for the execution of any Nominated Sub-Contract Works. That is to say, the Contractor is entirely responsible for ensuring that the workmanship, materials and goods provided by the Nominated Sub- Contractor for the purpose of carrying out the Nominated Sub-Contract Works are acccording to the drawings, bills of quantities, specification, and other documents contained in the sub-contract agreement.

SUPPLIERS AND SUB SUB-CONTRACTOR TO THE NOMINATED SUB-CONTRACTOR

Clause 2.3 of Sub-Contract NSC/4 or NSC/4a provides that where the sub-contractor is required by the Sub-Contract Documents to enter into a sub sub- contract or a supply contract that contains restrictions or limitations, then the sub- contractor shall inform the Contractor of the said restriction or limitation. Any such information received by the Contractor is to be passed on to the Architect. The Architect and the Contractor may both approve the restriction or limitation, in which case the liability of the sub-contractor to the Contractor is restricted or limited to the extent that the restriction or limitation has been approved by the Architect and the Contractor.

Clause 35.22   Clause 35.22 provides that where the liability of the sub-contractor to the Contractor is limited as described in the preceding paragraph, then the responsibility of the Contractor to the Employer is similarly limited.

These arrangements might apply where perhaps a mechanical services sub-contractor is required by the mechancial services specification to provide a proprietary material. The supplier may only trade on the basis that his entire liability in the event that he supplies faulty materials is that they be replaced. There may be no mention of costs of removal and refixing or any cost to the Employer while such work is carried out. In this situation it is clear that the terms of trading of the supplier do indeed contain a restriction or limitation that would prevent the sub-contractor and the Contractor from taking the full responsibility required of them under both the sub-contract and the main contract for the quality of materials installed.

This clause only comes into operation where the sub-contractor is required by the Sub-Contract Documents to enter into a sub sub-contract or supply contract with a particular manufacturer or supplier. Where the choice of sub sub-contractor or supplier is open, then this clause cannot be operated.

PROPOSED NOMINATION NOT FINALISED

Clause 35.23   Where a proposed nomination does not result in a formal sub-contract agreement bet-ween the Contractor and a proposed Nominated Sub-Contractor by reason of:-

★ an objection by the Contractor being sustained by the Architect

★ (the basic method) the sub-contractor fails within a reasonable time to settle the Particular Conditions of Schedule 2 of Tender NSC/1

★ (the alternative method) the sub-contractor fails within a reasonable time to enter into Sub-Contract NSC/4a

then the Architect is required to issue further instructions. Only two types of instruction are contemplated in this case, either to omit the prime cost sum work or to nominate an alternative prospective Nominated Sub-Contractor.

Several observations spring to mind after considering this clause.

★ In the case of failure of the sub-contractor to settle the particular conditions or to enter into a sub-contract, the timetables within which the Contractor is required to operate (ten working days – clause 35.8, fourteen days – clause 35.12) are not repeated.

★ The sub-contractor is given the benevolent 'within a reasonable time' period in which to agree. The present clause makes no reference to notice by the Contractor (or sub-contractor) to the Architect reporting failure to reach agreement. Without any time specified the Architect cannot know when to act. The Contractor who follows the advice given earlier in this paper will already have given notice, see pages 171 (the Basic Method) and 175 (the Alternative Method).

★ The Architect is not authorised to instruct the Contractor to carry out the work himself or by a Domestic Sub-Contractor of his own choice. This would seem to be a beneficial alternative to the Employer.

RE-NOMINATION OF SUB-CONTRACTORS

Clause 35.24   Clause 35.24 provides for the naming of a new Nominated Sub-Contractor to carry out and/or to continue to carry out and/or to complete the Nominated Sub-Contract Works where the employment of the original Nominated Sub-Contractor has been determined under Sub-Contract NSC/4 or NSC/4a. Clause 35.24 sets out the procedures between the Contractor and the Architect leading to the actual determination of the employment of the sub-contractor. Where the sub-contractor is in default, the Contractor is prohibited from determining the employment of the Nominated Sub-Contractor without an instruc-tion of the Architect requiring him to do so. There is no parallel requirement for the sub-contractor to obtain instructions from the Architect prior to determination of his own employment under the sub-contract where the Contractor is in default. Clause 35.24 also sets out the obligation of the Architect to nominate a new sub-contractor and deals with some of the financial consequences of the determination and re-nomination.

There are three broad groups of circumstances that may lead to determination of the employment of the sub-contractor:-

★ default by the sub-contractor

★ bankruptcy or liquidation of the sub-contractor

★ default by the Contractor.

Since the procedural requirements are different for each of the groups of circumstances, these are considered together. Thus, the clause numbers referred to in the next few pages will be out of sequence.

Default by the sub-contractor

Subject to compliance with the specified procedures, clause 29.1 of Sub-Contract NSC/4 or NSC/4a provides that the Contractor may determine the employment of the sub-contractor if the sub-contractor is in default by reason of:-

★ wholly suspending the sub-contract works without reasonable cause (clause 29.1.1 of Sub-Contract NSC/4 or NSC/4a)

★ failing to proceed with the sub-contract works in accordance with the programme details agreed either in Schedule 3 of Tender NSC/1 or in Appendix part 4 of Sub-Contract NSC/4a without reasonable cause (clause 29.1.2 of Sub-Contract NSC/4 or NSC/4a)

★ refusing to remove defective work after proper notice, or, refusing to rectify defects, shrinkages or other faults in the sub-contract works (clause 29.1.3 of Sub-Contract NSC/4 or NSC/4a)

★ assigning or sub-letting without the consent of the Contractor and the Architect, or, failing to comply with the requirements of the sub-contract dealing with fair wages (clause 29.1.4 of Sub-Contract NSC/4 or NSC/4a).

Where the Contractor is of the opinion that the sub-contractor is in default by reason of one of these matters, the Contractor must (clause 35.24.1) 'inform' the Architect of his opinion, and must send to the Architect any written comments by the sub-contractor in regard to the alleged default. There is no obligation to actually seek out comments by the sub-contractor; if he has made any, the Contractor must pass them on. Neither the main contract nor Sub-Contract NSC/4 or NSC/4a specify any timetable for action by the Contractor in these circumstances. It is clearly in the best interests of the Contractor to give notice to the Architect as soon as it becomes apparent that the sub-contractor is or is likely to be in default. Nothing is to be gained by postponing the notice to the Architect, just in case the sub- contractor improves his performance. Indeed, the reverse may be true; the action of highlighting to both the Architect and the sub-contractor the apparent default may be just sufficient to encourage the sub-contractor to remedy the situation.

It is recommended that the Contractor 'inform' the Architect of the alleged default of the sub-contractor by notice in writing sent registered post or recorded delivery. (It would be prudent to send a copy to the sub-contractor concerned, but this does not seem to be a contractual requirement). Such notice should:-

★ identify the Nominated Sub-Contractor concerned

★ inform the Architect that in the opinion of the Contractor, the sub-contractor is in default of the Sub-Contract

★ specify the reasons (one sentence each) for the alleged default

★ (if applicable) enclose any written observations of the sub-contractor that are relative to the alleged default

★ request that the Architect instruct the Contractor to give notice to the sub-contractor specifying the default.

The Conditions do not contemplate the situation where the Architect does not agree that the sub-contractor is in default and the Architect does not seem to have to tell the Contractor that he will not issue the instruction requested.

Where the Architect does agree ('...is reasonably of the opinion...' - clause 35.24.1) that the sub-contractor is in default, then he must (clause 35.24.4.1) issue an instruction requiring the Contractor to give a preliminary notice to the sub- contractor specifying the default ('the first notice'). The Architect may, in his instruction regarding the first notice, require that the Contractor obtain a further instruction of the Architect before permitting the Contractor to give the actual notice of determination ('the second notice'). Otherwise it would appear that the second notice can be given without further reference to the Architect.

Following the issue of the instruction of the Architect under clause 35.24.4.1, the Contractor must issue the first notice to the sub-contractor specifying the default. The notice must be sent registered post or recorded delivery (copy by registered post or recorded delivery to the Architect). Such notice need only:-

★ inform the sub-contractor that in the opinion of the Contractor the sub-contractor is in default

★ specify (one sentence) the default

★ remind the sub-contractor that if the default continues for fourteen days, or if the default is repeated, then the Contractor may determine the employment of the sub-contractor

★ confirm that the notice has been given in consequence of an instruction of the Architect.

Where the default of the sub-contractor continues for fourteen days after receipt of the first notice of the Contractor, then the Contractor may within a further ten days give the second notice determining the employment of the sub-contractor under the sub-contract. If so required by the Architect in his instruction authorising the first notice, the Contractor must request the Architect to issue an instruction authorising the second notice. Such a request should be considered to be a notice to the Architect and sent registered post or recorded delivery. (Again, it would be prudent to send a copy to the sub-contractor concerned, but this is not a requirement of either the main contract or the sub-contract). Such notice should:-

★ identify the Nominated Sub-Contractor concerned

★ refer to the earlier instruction of the Architect authorising the issue of the first notice to the (specified) sub-contractor

★ confirm that in the opinion of the Contractor, the sub-contractor continues to be in default of the sub-contract

★ (if applicable) enclose any further written observations of the sub-contractor relative to the alleged default

★ request that the Architect instruct the Contractor to determine the employment of the sub-contractor

★ specify the date by which the Contractor must give the second notice determining the employment of the sub-contractor (ie a date within ten days after the expiry of fourteen days after **receipt** by the sub-contractor of the first notice of default).

It is necessary to raise the last matter in the notice so as to be sure that the Contractor does not, by default - perhaps of the Architect - miss the last date by which the second notice can be given.

The second notice determining the employment of the sub-contractor must be sent registered post or recorded delivery. Such notice should:-

★ inform the sub-contractor that the default specified in the first notice of the Contractor has continued for a period of fourteen days

★ determine forthwith the employment of the sub-contractor under the sub-contract

★ confirm that such determination is in consequence of an instruction of the Architect.

At this point a potential problem must be clarified. Under clause 29.1 of Sub- Contract NSC/4 or NSC/4a, the Contractor has an automatic right to determine the employment of the sub-contractor where an earlier default by the sub-contractor (that is to say, a default for which a first notice specifying the default has been issued to the sub-contractor) is repeated. However the main contract does not refer to this right. It would appear that the Contractor can determine the employment of a sub- contractor without further reference to the Architect upon repetition of an earlier default except, of course, where the Architect has chosen to require the Contractor to obtain a second instruction before issuing the second notice determining the employment of the sub-contractor. A difficulty here is that the Contractor has only ten days after the alleged repetition in which to issue the second notice determining the sub-contractor's employment. In that time it may not be possible for the Contractor to ask for and receive instructions of the Architect.

Clause 35.24.4.2 requires the Contractor to inform the Architect when the employment of the sub-contractor has been determined. It is recommended that this important point be dealt with by giving notice to the Architect. Such notice need only:-

★ identify the Nominated Sub-Contractor concerned

★ inform the Architect that in accordance with his instructions, the employment of the sub-contractor has been determined

★ send to the Architect a copy of the second notice of determination of employment of the sub-contractor

★ request that the Architect nominate another sub-contractor to carry out and/or to continue to carry out and/or to complete the Nominated Sub-Contract Works

★ inform the Architect of the date by which the preliminary notice of nomination (the basic method) or the nomination instruction (the alternative method) must be received in order to avoid an effect on the regular progress of the Works or delay in the completion of the Works.

Under clause 35.24.4.3 the Architect is then required to name a substitute nominated sub-contractor to carry out and/or to continue to carry out and/or to complete the Nominated Sub-Contract Works. It is made clear in clause 35.24.7 that the amounts due to the substitute nominated sub-contractor are to be included in Interim Certificates and the final adjusted Contract Sum, thus providing the proper machinery for accounting and payment purposes. The Conditions do not appear to set out any timetable within which the Architect is required to act upon the request by the Contractor and to issue a preliminary notice of nomination (the basic method) or a nomination instruction (the alternative method).

The last point in the clause 35.24.4.2 notice referred to above is necessary in order again to introduce the general question of delay and extension of time. The late issue of a (re)-nomination instruction could become a 'Relevant Event' under clause 25 leading to an extension of time or a 'matter' under clause 26 giving rise to a claim for reimbursement of loss and expense. The notice referred to should not be regarded as the only notice with which to raise with the Architect the question of a late re- nomination instruction. The sensible rules of contract management and the more particular notice requirements under clauses 25 and 26 must always be applied.

ANY RE-NOMINATION COULD COST THE CONTRACTOR MONEY!!

Where the determination arises from default by the sub-contractor by reason of the failure of the sub-contractor to remove defective work or improper materials or goods, or failure to rectify defects, shrinkages, or other faults in the sub-contract works, then by clause 35.24.4.3 the Contractor is to be given the opportunity to 'agree' the rates and prices of the new sub-contractor. Reference is made in clause 35.24.4.3 to clause 35.18.1 and the **implication** is that there are some costs that have to be met by the Contractor. It has already been seen that this occurs where the Contractor has made the final payment to the sub-contractor and further defects are discovered, see comments on clause 35.18.1 (page 183).

Clause 35.24 deals with the determination of the employment of a Nominated Sub-Contractor for a much wider range of matters than are referred to in clause 35.18.1 and there is little connection. There are no express words in clause 35.24 saying that the Contractor **is** responsible for any costs, and clause 35.24.7 states clearly that the amounts due to a substitute nominated sub-contractor are to be included in Interim Certificates and added to the Contract Sum. Unless the reference to clause 35.18.1 is intended to deal with the situation, there is no machinery for any recovery by the Employer of any sums that may be due to him under the present clause.

Insolvency of the sub-contractor

Clause 29.2 of Sub-Contract NSC/4 or NSC/4a provides that the employment of the sub-contractor shall automatically be determined where:-

★ (if an individual or partnership) the sub-contractor becomes bankrupt

★ (if a limited company) the sub-contractor is voluntarily or compulsory wound up

★ a provisional liquidator, or a receiver or manager is appointed to run the affairs of a limited company
(Note. A 'provisional liquidator' is normally the official reciever and is appointed immediately a Court has made a winding up order. He may become the permanent liquidator or the creditors may request the Court to appoint a liquidator.)

★ possession is taken of the property of the company by debenture holders.

There is no requirement in this case for the Architect to issue instructions in regard to the termination of the employment of the sub-contractor, it is automatic. The sub-contractor is not required to inform the Contractor of the happening of any of these events, presumably the trustee in bankruptcy, liquidator, receiver, or manager is expected to inform the Contractor. In the meantime, of course, work on the site will often have ceased completely. While the Contractor does not seem to have to inform the Architect of the happening of one of these events, the Architect obviously must be told at the earliest opportunity, for he is required to nominate a substitute sub-contractor.

It is recommended therefore that, upon receipt of authoritative information regarding one of these events, the Contractor acquaint the Architect with the known facts by notice, sent registered post or recorded delivery. A wide variety of situations will arise and the content of the notice from the Contractor to the Architect will also vary. The most common situations to be covered in the notice by the Contractor are:-

Where the sub-contractor is insolvent:-

★ identify the Nominated Sub-Contractor concerned

★ inform the Architect that the sub-contractor is bankrupt, or is in liquidation

★ (if possible) enclose any documentary evidence received from the trustee in bankruptcy or liquidator

★ request that the Architect nominate another sub-contractor to carry out and/ or continue to carry out and/or to complete the Nominated Sub-Contract Works

★ inform the Architect of the date by which the preliminary notice of nomination (the basic method) or the nomination instruction (the alternative method) must be received in order to avoid an effect upon the regular progress of the Works or delay in the completion of the Works.

Where a receiver or manager has been appointed who proposes to complete the sub- contract works and his proposals are acceptable:-

★ identify the Nominated Sub-Contractor concerned

★ inform the Architect that a receiver or manager has been appointed to run the business of the sub-contractor

★ (if possible) enclose any documentary evidence received from the receiver or manager

★ inform the Architect that the receiver or manager has submitted proposals to continue to carry out or to complete the sub-contract works and enclose the proposals received and discussed with the receiver or manager

★ confirm to the Architect that the proposals of the receiver or manager for continuation or completion of the sub-contract works are acceptable to the Contractor, his Domestic Sub-Contractors, and the other Nominated Sub-Contractors

★ request that the Architect confirm that the proposals of the receiver or manager are acceptable to the Architect and the Employer.

Where a receiver or manager has been appointed and his proposals to complete the sub-contract works are unacceptable:-

★ identify the Nominated Sub-Contractor concerned

★ inform the Architect that a receiver or manager has been appointed to run the business of the sub-contractor

★ (if possible) enclose any documentary evidence received from the receiver or manager

★ inform the Architect that the receiver or manager has presented proposals to continue to carry out or to complete the sub-contract works and enclose such proposals

★ inform the Architect that the proposals of the receiver or manager for continuance or completion of the work are not acceptable since they will prejudice the position of the Contractor and/or his Domestic Sub-Contractors and/or other Nominated Sub-Contractors

★ give reasons (one sentence each) for the unacceptability of the proposals of the receiver or manager

★ request that the Architect nominate another sub-contractor to carry out and/ or to continue to carry out and/or to complete the sub-contract works

★ inform the Architect of the date by which the preliminary notice of nomination (the basic method) or nomination instruction (the alternative method) must be received in order to avoid an effect on the regular progress of the Works or delay in the completion of the Works.

Where a receiver or manager has been appointed and he is unable to complete the sub-contract works:-

★ identify the Nominated Sub-Contractor concerned

★ inform the Architect that a receiver or manager has been appointed to run the business of the sub-contractor

★ (if possible) enclose any documentary evidence received from the receiver or manager

★ inform the Architect that the receiver or manager is unable to carry out and/or to continue to carry out and/or to complete the sub-contract works

★ request that the Architect nominate another sub-contractor to carry out and/or to continue to carry out and/or to complete the sub-contract works

★ inform the Architect of the date by which the preliminary notice of nomination (the basic method) or the nomination instruction (the alternative method) must be received in order to avoid an effect on the regular progress of the Works or delay in the completion of the Works.

Except where the proposals of the receiver or manager of the business of a Nominated Sub-Contractor have been accepted by the Contractor and approved by the Architect and the Employer, the Architect is required under clause 35.24.5 to nominate a substitute sub-contractor to carry out and/or to continue to carry out and/or complete the Nominated Sub-Contract Works. It is made clear in clause 35.24.7 that the amounts due to a substitute nominated sub-contractor are to be included in Interim Certificates and in the final adjusted Contract Sum, thus providing the proper machinery for payment and accounting purposes. Again the Conditions do not appear to set out any timetable within which the Architect must issue his preliminary notice of nomination (the basic method) or his nomination instruction (the alternative method).

Where the Contractor requires a new nomination, the aforementioned notices again introduce the question of delay and extension of time. The late issue of a (re)-nomination instruction could become a 'Relevant Event' under clause 25 leading to an extension of time and a 'matter' giving rise to a claim for reimbursement of loss and expense under clause 26. The notice referred to should not be regarded as the only notice with which to raise with the Architect the question of late re-nomination instructions. The sensible rules of contract management and the more particular notice requirements under clauses 25 and 26 must always be applied.

Default by the Contractor

Subject to compliance with the specified procedures, clause 30 of Sub-Contract NSC/4 or NSC/4a provides that the sub-contractor may determine his own employment under the sub-contract if the Contractor is in default by reason of:-

★ wholly suspending the main contract works without reasonable cause (clause 30.1.1.1 of Sub-Contract NSC/4 or NSC/4a)

★ failing to proceed with the main contract works so that the progress of the Nominated Sub-Contract Works is '...seriously affected'.
(Note: there is no mention here of non-payment by the Contractor, for that is dealt with under clause 21.8 of Sub-Contract NSC/4 or NSC/4a by giving the sub-contractor the right to suspend the execution of the sub-contract works; and under Agreement NSC/2 or NSC/2a where the Employer will make direct payments to the sub-contractor).

The procedural requirements in Sub-Contract NSC/4 or NSC/4a are quite simple. A preliminary notice from the sub-contractor specifying the default is to be sent by registered post or recorded delivery to the Contractor (with a copy to the Architect). If the default continues for fourteen days after receipt by the Contractor of the preliminary notice of the sub-contractor, or, if the previously specified default is repeated, then the sub-contractor may '...thereupon...' issue the actual notice determining his own employment under the sub-contract. The use of the word 'thereupon' here - meaning directly after the expiry of fourteen days after the preliminary notice, or directly after the repetition of the default - is important, for it imposes a timetable on the sub-contractor for the issue of the actual determination notice. To send the actual determination notice one month, say, after the expiry of fourteen days after the preliminary notice would seem to be too late. It is odd that the position of the sub-contractor here is not the same as the position of the Contractor under clause 29 of Sub-Contract NSC/4 or NSC/4a, where ten days are allowed before the actual notice of determination must have been issued.

The Conditions do not require a copy of the actual determination notice to be sent to the Architect, nor is the sub-contractor required to obtain an instruction of the Architect prior to determining his own employment under the sub-contract. Neither the Contractor nor the sub-contractor seem to have to tell the Architect that the sub-contractor has determined his own employment under the sub-contract. But the Architect must obviously be told at the earliest opportunity, for he is required to name a substitute nominated sub-contractor.

Therefore, upon such a determination it is recommended that the Contractor aquaint the Architect with the known facts by notice, sent registered post or recorded delivery. Such notice should:-

★ identify the Nominated Sub-Contractor concerned

★ inform the Architect that the sub-contractor has determined his own employment under the sub-contract

★ (if applicable) inform the Architect that the determination has not been accepted and is to be disputed under the sub-contract arbitration agreement and specify (one sentence) the reasons for such dispute

★ request that the Architect nominate another sub-contractor to carry out and/or to continue to carry out and/or to complete the sub-contract works

★ inform the Architect of the date by which his preliminary notice of nomination (the basic method) or the nomination instruction (the alternative method) must be received in order to avoid an effect on the regular progress of the works or delay in the completion of the Works.

Irrespective of any notice by the Contractor or the sub-contractor, by clause 35.24.6 the Architect is required to name a substitute nominated sub-contractor to carry out and/or to continue to carry out and/or to complete the sub-contract works. Again, the Conditions do not appear to set out any timetable within which the Architect must issue his preliminary notice of nomination (the basic method) or his nomination instruction (the alternative method). The aforementioned notice to the Architect again introduces the question of delay and extension of time. The late issue of a (re)-nomination instruction could become a 'Relevant Event' under clause 25 leading to an extension of time and a 'matter' giving rise to a claim for reimbursement of loss and expense under clause 26. The notice referred to should not be regarded as the only notice with which to raise with the Architect the question of a late re-nomination instruction. The sensible rules of contract management and the more particular notice requirements of clauses 25 and 26 must always be applied.

RE-NOMINATION WILL COST THE CONTRACTOR MONEY!!

Because the determination arises from default by the Contractor by reason of the matters set out in clause 30 of Sub-Contract NSC/4 or NSC/4a, then under clause 35.24.6 the Contractor may be required to assume responsibility for the additional cost of the substitute nominated sub-contractor. The only significant qualification in clause 35.24.6 to the liability of the Contractor for these additional costs is that the original Nominated Sub-Contractor must have 'validly' determined his own employment under the sub-contract. It is for this reason that reference must be made in the notice to the Architect informing him of the determination by the sub- contractor to the possibility of disputing the determination by the sub-contractor through the arbitration agreement. Should an arbitrator find that the sub-contractor was not properly entitled to determine his sub-contract, then the Contractor could not be responsible for the additional costs of a substitute nominated sub-contractor.

The responsibility for these additional costs would then fall upon the sub-contractor for he would not have 'validly' determined his own employment under the sub- contract and therefore becomes liable under the indemnity given by the sub- contractor under Agreement NSC/2 or NSC/2a.

The means of ascertaining any additional costs to the Employer by reason of the employment of the substitute sub-contractor nominated under this clause are not described, neither is there any mention of who is to make the ascertainment. More importantly, the Contractor is not, in this case, given the opportunity to agree the price to be paid to the substitute sub-contractor. Perhaps the latter point is an oversight in the drafting, but it is unfortunate that these matters are not dealt with in the Conditions.

It is made clear in clause 35.24.6 that, irrespective of how the additional cost is ascertained and who is to ascertain it, the amount of the additional cost may be deducted by the Employer from any amount otherwise due to the Contractor under Interim Certificates, and that is to be regarded as recoverable by the legal procedures available to the Employer.

In both preceding cases of re-nomination under clause 35.24, it has been possible to say that clause 35.24.7 provides for the amounts due to the substitute nominated sub-contractor to be included in Interim Certificates and in the final adjusted Contract Sum, thus providing machinery for payment and accounting purposes. It is not possible to say that in this case because clause 35.24.7 only makes reference to such amounts arising from re-nomination under clauses 35.24.4.3 (after default by the sub-contractor) and 35.24.5 (after bankruptcy or liquidation of the sub-contractor). There is no mention of any such amounts arising from re-nomination under clause 35.24.6 (after default by the Contractor). One must presume that this is an oversight in the drafting of clause 35.24.7 that will soon be corrected. Even though the additional costs may have to be paid by the Contractor, there would seem to be no difficulties in having the amounts due to a substitute nominated sub-contractor appointed under clause 35.24.6 included in Interim Certificates and the final adjusted Contract Sum. Clause 35.24.6 also includes an express right entitling the Employer to deduct that additional cost from amounts due to the Contractor, thus the Employer would recover the additional costs by exercising the rights given to him under clause 30.1.1.2.

Postscript to clause 35.24

The appointment of a substitute Nominated Sub-Contractor is a long winded, sometimes clumsy procedure. In certain circumstances, a substitute Nominated Sub-Contractor can be imposed upon the Contractor without settlement of the Contractor's ultimate financial liability. The extent of any additional costs that may have to be met by the Contractor depends upon the terms of a separate contract (the warranty agreement between the Employer and the original Nominated Sub-Contractor) and the skill of the Employer in pursuing the claim against the original sub-contractor. There is no particular incentive for the Employer to proceed with his claim expeditiously or effectively for under the Conditions the Employer is effectively indemnified by the Contractor.

Except where the determination occurs as a result of default by the Contractor, the principle that the Contractor should be liable for some or all of the additional costs incurred by the Employer as the direct result of the determination of the employment of a Nominated Sub-Contractor is questionable. In effect, the Contractor is being asked to take the risk of default by sub-contractors chosen by the Architect or the Employer. This is a risk that the Contractor must somehow assess and price in his tender.

The best advice to the Contractor is that he must, before accepting or appointing a sub-contractor nominated by the Architect, make more thorough enquiries into the financial resources and abilities of that proposed Nominated Sub-Contractor than previously. The Contractor must also be prepared to take a more positive line with the Architect in the matter of objecting to prospective Nominated Sub-Contractors, and to demand, if necessary, that the sub-contractor produce a Performance Bond to protect the Contractor against failure to complete the sub-contract.

DETERMINATION OF NOMINATED SUB- CONTRACT

In the preceding notes dealing with re-nomination of sub-contractors by the Architect under clause 35.24, the starting point has been the determination of the employment of the original sub-contractor under the sub-contract. It has **not** been the determination of the sub-contract itself; only the employment of the sub- contractor, for Sub-Contract NSC/4 or NSC/4a, besides dealing with determination of employment, also sets out the various contractual and financial rights and liabilities arising from that determination. The sub-contract itself remains in existence to deal with these matters.

Clause 35.25 However, clause 35.25 introduces the alternative concept of determination of the sub-contract itself and makes it clear that an instruction of the Architect is required before the Contractor can determine the sub-contract. The Conditions contemplate the Contractor wishing to determine the sub-contract '...by virtue of any right to which he may be...entitled...', and this is presumably a reference to the opening words of clause 29.1 of Sub-Contract NSC/4 or NSC/4a 'Without prejudice to any other rights or remedies which the Contractor may possess... (the Contractor may determine the employment of the sub-contractor)...'.

The range of matters that could be embraced by this clause is extensive and may include:-

★ repudiation by the sub-contractor

★ frustration

★ mistake

★ impossibility.

Each of these expressions are exact legal terms and reference must be made to any of the standard legal textbooks on the law of contract for an explanation of them and the circumstances under which they may occur.

Since the Contractor cannot act without an instruction of the Architect, the Contractor has the opportunity to take proper advice on the legal procedures to be followed before being required to determine a sub-contract under this clause.

No explanation of the purpose of this clause is given. It has probably been included for the benefit of the Employer, perhaps enabling him to change his mind about the nature or character of the work to be carried out by a sub-contractor. There seems to be little or no advantage to the Contractor, who would probably prefer to determine the employment of the sub-contractor in accordance with the procedures of clause 35.24 and NSC/4 or NSC/4a, for then he would have the benefit of the rules laid down there for dealing with the situation. In the present clause, the practical and financial effects of such a determination are not dealt with and no guidance is given as to how the parties should proceed.

As regards the time for the work, the position of the Contractor after the determination of a sub-contract under this clause is that, if the sub-contract works are still required to be carried out, then a new sub-contractor must be named by the Architect. The late issue of a (re)-nomination instruction could become a 'Relevant Event' under clause 25 leading to an extension of time or a 'matter' under clause 26 giving rise to a claim for reimbursement of loss and expense. The sensible rules of contract management apply here and the particular notice requirements of clauses 25 and 26 must be applied.

DIRECTIONS OF THE ARCHITECT AFTER DETERMINATION

Clause 35.26   It is made clear in clause 35.26 that where the employment of a Nominated Sub-Contractor is determined under clause 29 of Sub-Contract NSC/4 or NSC/4a (that is to say by reason of the default of the sub-contractor, or the insolvency of the sub-contractor) then the Architect remains responsible for directing the Contractor as to the amounts to be paid to the sub-contractor. Reference is made in the present clause to clause 29.4 of Sub-Contract NSC/4 or NSC/4a and, after examining that clause the purpose of clause 35.26 of the main contract becomes clear. Clause 29.4 of Sub-Contract NSC/4 or NSC/4a provides:-

★ that the Architect is to include in an Interim Certificate the balance (if any) due to the sub-contractor after completion of the sub-contract works by a substitute sub-contractor

★ that the Architect is to ascertain the expenses incurred by and the loss and/or damage caused to the Employer by reason of the determination of the employment of the sub-contractor

★ that the Employer shall be entitled to deduct from the amount included in that Interim Certificate the amount of his own expenses and loss and/or damage.

Thus clause 35.26 is a device for incorporating into the Conditions this further right of the Employer to deduct monies from amounts due to the Contractor in Interim Certificates, for the inclusion of these rights in Sub-Contract NSC/4 or NSC/4a alone does not satisfy the requirements of the main contract clause 30.1.1.2 '...the Employer is entitled to exercise any right **under this Contract** of deduction from monies due...to the Contractor against any amount...due under an Interim Certificate...'.

Postscript to clause 35

In the introduction to this Section, there were set down the objectives of the new Nominated Sub-Contract arrangements. It will have been seen from the preceding discussion that the objectives have probably been achieved. Whether the resulting morass of documentation and procedures will prove to be better than previous methods used by the industry remains to be seen.

The one indisputable merit of the Nominated Sub-Contract documents is that they are clearly an integrated set of documents where the principles and procedures of the main contract and the sub-contract dovetail together. No longer will builders find themselves caught between the conflicting provisions of the 1963 Edition and the old 'green' form of sub-contract.

There can be little doubt that, despite its length, clause 35 of JCT 80 does not provide a **complete** 'code of behaviour' for the management of Nominated Sub-Contracts. The JCT must itself reconsider certain parts of the documents:-

★ more realistic timetable must be given for the operation of both the 'basic' and 'alternative' methods of nomination

★ the apparent anomolies must be corrected

★ the inconclusiveness of certain of the clauses must be tidied up.

Finally, the construction industry as a whole must give serious consideration to the extent to which the Contractor is to assume liability for the failure of sub-contractors nominated by the Architect under JCT 80. The procedures that have been set out appear to leave the Contractor with a contractual risk that is undefinable and therefore unpriceable at the time of preparing his tender and this is unreasonable to both the Contractor and Client. The Client is likely to receive higher tender prices if the Contractor realistically prices the risk involved.

APPENDICES

SUPPLEMENTAL AGREEMENT FOR MATERIALS OFF-SITE - FORM A

(Guidance Notes. 1. This supplemental agreement is used in all cases where payment is to be requested for materials off-site.

2. If the materials, goods or manufactured articles have been ordered from a supplier by the Contractor or have been manufactured or assembled by a sub-contractor, then the supplemental agreement should be completed by the supplier or the sub-contractor.

3. If the materials, goods or manufactured articles have been ordered from a supplier by a sub-contractor or have been manufactured or assembled by a sub sub-contractor to a sub-contractor, then the supplemental agreement should be completed by the sub-contractor.

4. This supplemental agreement may be used as the documentary evidence to demonstrate that property in the materials, goods or manufactured articles has vested in the Contractor, see clause 30.3.8 of the Main Contract.)

THIS SUPPLEMENTAL AGREEMENT is made the........day of........19

BETWEEN ....

of (or whose registered office is situated at)

....

(hereinafter called 'the Contractor') of the one part

AND ....

of (or whose registered office is situated at)

....

(hereinafter called 'the Supplier/Sub-Contractor ★') of the other part.

WHEREAS

First   by an Agreement (hereinafter called 'the Main Contract')
made the........................day of........................19 between
....
(hereinafter called 'the Employer') of the one part and the Contractor of the other part the Contractor agreed to carry out certain works described therein (hereinafter called 'the Main Contract Works') on the terms and conditions contained therein;

Second
   ★(A)   by an Agreement (hereinafter called 'the Contract of Sale')
made the........................day of........................19 between
the Contractor of the one part and the Supplier of the other part the Supplier agreed to supply certain materials, goods or manufactured articles described therein on the terms and conditions contained therein;

OR   ★(B)   by an Agreement (hereinafter called 'the Sub-Contract')
              made the.......................day of.......................19 between
              the Contractor of the one part and the Sub-Contractor of the other part the Sub-Contractor
              agreed to carry out certain works described therein on the terms and conditions contained
              therein;

Third   this Agreement is supplemental to the Main Contract and the Contract of Sale/Sub-
              Contract★;

Fourth   under the provisions of clause 30.3 the Main Contract the Supplier/Sub-Contractor★
              desires payment for certain materials, goods or manufactured articles (hereinafter called
              'the materials') before delivery to or adjacent to the Main Contract Works.

              NOW IT IS HEREBY AGREED AS FOLLOWS

              1   Upon payment by the Supplier/Sub-Contractor★ of the sum of one pound (£1.00)
              to the Contractor the Contractor will request the Architect named in the Main Contract
              to exercise the discretion granted to him and to include in the next Interim Certificate
              issued under the Main Contract the sum of £........ in respect of the materials described
              and listed in the attached Schedule.

              2   In respect of the materials the Supplier/Sub-Contractor★ warrants that the date
              hereof:

              2.1   the materials are intended for incorporation in the Main Contract Works;

              2.2   nothing remains to be done to the materials to complete the same up to
                     the point of their incorporation in the Main Contract Works;

              2.3   the materials are in every respect in accordance with the Main Contract
                     and the Contract of Sale/the Sub-Contract★;

              2.4   the materials have been set apart and stored at the premises named
                     in the attached Schedule, and have been clearly and visibly marked
                     thus:
                     'SOLD, the property of..
                     (insert the name of the Contractor or the Sub-Contractor)
                     for use at

                     ....
                     (insert the name of the Main Contract Works).'

              2.5   the materials are insured for their full reinstatement value under a
                     policy of 'Contractor's All Risks' insurance protecting the interests
                     of the Employer and the Contractor against loss or damage
                     howsoever arising (and including the contingencies known as Clause
                     22 Perils in the Main Contract) until such time as they are delivered
                     to or adjacent to the site of the Main Contract Works and docu-
                     mentary evidence of the said insurance policy is attached hereto;

              2.6   property in the materials (including, but not limited to, components,
                     raw materials, goods or manufactured articles received by the
                     Supplier/Sub-Contractor★ for incorporation in the materials) is
                     vested absolutely in the Supplier/Sub-Contractor★ and the materials
                     are free from all encumbrance and documentary evidence to this
                     effect is attached hereto;

       ★ Delete where not applicable

200

2.7 the property in the materials has passed unconditionally to the Contractor. Provided that property in the materials shall revest in the Supplier/Sub-Contractor ★ if the next Interim Certificate issued under the Main Contract does not contain any amount in respect of the materials.

3 The Supplier/Sub-Contractor ★ undertakes:

3.1 not to remove or cause or permit the materials to be moved or removed from the premises named in the attached Schedule except for delivery or to use upon the site of the Main Contract Works;

3.2 to retain full responsibility without charge to the Contractor for the cost of storage, warehousing, security, maintenance, insurance handling and delivery of the materials.

4 The Supplier/Sub-Contractor ★ agrees:

4.1 the materials can be inspected at any time upon reasonable notice by the Employer, the Architect, or the Contractor;

4.2 neither execution of this Supplemental Agreement by the Contractor, nor payment by the Contractor of any amount resulting from presentation of this Supplemental Agreement to the Architect shall constitute or imply approval by the Architect or the Contractor of any part of the materials or the workmanship therein.

5 Within seventeen days of receipt by the Contractor of the duplicate copy of an Interim Certificate under the Main Contract the Contractor shall pay to the Supplier/Sub-Contractor ★ the value certified therein in respect of the materials, less

5.1 retention money at the rate specified in the Sub-Contract;

5.2 discount at the rate specified in the Contract of Sale/Sub-Contract ★.

6 The Supplier/Sub-Contractor ★ indemnifies the Contractor against any costs, claims, demands, expenses, losses (including consequential losses) arising from any breach or non-observance of the warranties or undertakings herein contained.

SIGNED by or on behalf

of the Contractor ....

in the presence of ....

★Delete where not applicable

★A   SIGNED by or on behalf

of the Supplier . . . .

in the presence of . . . .

★B   SIGNED by or on behalf

of the Sub-Contractor . . . .

in the presence of . . . .

To be signed by a Director or other person authorised to sign sub-contracts.

★Delete where not applicable

202

SUPPLEMENTAL AGREEMENT FOR MATERIALS OFF-SITE - FORM B

(Guidance Notes. 1. This supplemental agreement is used in conjunction with the Supplemental Agreement for Materials Off-Site - Form A.

2. If the materials, goods or manufactured articles have been ordered from a supplier by a sub-contractor or have been manufactured or assembled by a sub sub-contractor to a sub-contractor, then the supplemental agreement should be completed by the supplier or the sub sub-contractor.

3. This supplemental agreement may be used as the documentary evidence to demonstrate that property in the materials, goods or manufactured articles has vested in the sub-contractor, see clause 2.6 of the Supplemental Agreement for Materials Off-Site - Form A.)

THIS SUPPLEMENTAL AGREEMENT is made the........day of........19

BETWEEN ....

of (or whose registered offices is situated at)

....

(hereinafter called 'the Sub-Contractor') of the one part

AND ....

of (or whose registered office is situated at)

....

(hereinafter called 'the Supplier/Sub-Contractor'★) of the other part.

WHEREAS

First   by an agreement (hereinafter called 'the Main Contract')
made the...................... day of......................19   between

....

(hereinafter called 'the Employer') of the one part

AND ....

(hereinafter called 'the Contractor') of the other part the Contractor agreed to carry out certain works described therein (hereinafter called 'the Main Contract Works') on the terms and conditions contained therein;

Second   by an Agreement (hereinafter called 'the Sub-Contract')

made the......................day of......................19   between

the Contractor on the one part and the Sub-Contractor of the other part the Sub-Contractor agreed to carry out certain works described therein on the terms and conditions contained therein;

★Delete where not applicable.

203

Third ★(A)   by an Agreement (hereinafter called the 'Contract of Sale')

made the.............................day of...........................19
between the Sub-Contractor of the one part and the Supplier of the other part the Supplier agreed to supply certain materials, goods or manufactured articles described therein on the terms and conditions contained therein;

OR ★(B)   by an Agreement (hereinafter called 'the Sub Sub-Contract')
made the.........................day of...........................19
between the Sub-Contractor of the one part and the Sub Sub-Contractor of the other part the Sub Sub-Contractor agreed to carry out certain works described therein on the terms and conditions contained therein;

Fourth   this Agreement is supplemental to the Main Contract, the Sub-Contract, and the Contract of Sale/Sub Sub-Contract ★;

Fifth   under the provisions of clause 30.3 of the Main Contract the Supplier/Sub Sub-Contractor desires payment for certain materials, goods or manufactured articles (hereinafter called 'the materials') before delivery to the Sub-Contractor or to or adjacent to the Main Contract Works.

NOW IT IS HEREBY AGREED AS FOLLOWS

1   Upon payment by the Supplier/Sub Sub-Contractor ★ of the sum of one pound (£1.00) to the Sub-Contractor the Sub-Contractor will request the Contractor to request the Architect named in the Main Contract to exercise the discretion granted to him and to include in the next Interim Certificate issued under the Main Contract the sum of £......in respect of the materials described and listed in the attached schedule.

2   In respect of the materials, the Supplier/Sub Sub-Contractor ★ warrants that at the date hereof:

2.1   the materials are intended for incorporation in the Sub-Contract Works;

2.2   nothing remains to be done to the materials to complete the same up to point of their incorporation in the Sub-Contract Works;

2.3   the materials are in every respect in accordance with the Sub-Contract and the Contract of Sale/the Sub Sub-Contract ★;

2.4   the materials have been set apart and stored at the premises named in the attached Schedule, and have been clearly and visibly marked thus:

'SOLD, the property of..
(insert the name of the Sub-Contractor) for use at

....
(insert the name of the Main Contract Works)'.

★ Delete where not applicable

204

2.5 the materials are insured for their full reinstatement value under a policy of 'Contractor's All Risks' insurance protecting the interests of the Employer, the Contractor and the Sub-Contractor against loss or damage howsoever arising (and including the contingencies known as Clause 22 Perils in the Main Contract) until such time as they are delivered to or adjacent to the site of the Main Contract Works or to or adjacent to premises of the Sub-Contractor and documentary evidence of the said insurance policy is attached hereto;

2.6 property in the materials (including, but not limited to components, raw materials, goods or manufactured articles received by the Supplier/Sub-Contractor ★ for incorporation in the materials) is vested absolutely in the Supplier/Sub Sub-Contractor ★ and the materials are free from all encumbrance and documentary evidence to this effect is attached hereto;

2.7 the absolute property in the materials has passed unconditionally to the Sub-Contractor.

3 The Supplier/Sub Sub-Contractor ★ undertakes:

3.1 not to remove or cause or permit the materials to be moved or removed from the premises named in the attached Schedule except for delivery to or adjacent to the site of the Main Contract Works or to or adjacent to the premises of the Sub-Contractor;

3.2 to retain full responsibility without charge to the Sub-Contractor for the cost of storage, warehousing, security, maintenance, insurance, handling and delivery of the materials.

4 The Supplier/Sub Sub-Contractor ★ agrees:

4.1 the materials can be inspected at any time upon reasonable notice by the Employer, the Architect, or the Contractor;

4.2 neither execution of this Supplemental Agreement by the Sub-Contractor, nor payment by the Sub-Contractor of any amount resulting from this Supplemental Agreement shall constitute or imply approval by the Architect, the Contractor or the Sub-Contractor of any part of the materials or the workmanship therein.

5 Within seventeen days of receipt by the Sub-Contractor of any payment from the Contractor the Sub-Contractor shall pay to the Supplier/Sub Sub-Contractor ★ the value certified therein in respect of the materials, less

5.1 retention money at the rate specified in the Sub Sub-Contract;

5.2 discount at the rate specified in the Contract of Sale/Sub Sub-Contract ★

6 The Supplier/Sub Sub-Contractor ★ indemnifies the Sub-Contractor and the Contractor against any costs, claims, demands, expenses, losses (including consequential losses) arising from any breach of non-observance of any of the warranties or undertakings herein contained.

★ Delete where not applicable

SIGNED by or on behalf

of the Sub-Contractor ....

in the presence of ....

★A   SIGNED by or on behalf

of the Supplier ....

in the presence of ....

★B   SIGNED by or on behalf

of the Sub Sub-Contractor ....

in the presence of ....

★Delete where not applicable

SCHEDULE TO SUPPLEMENTAL AGREEMENT FOR MATERIALS OFF-SITE - 'FORM C'

(**Guidance Note.** 1. This Schedule is to be completed by the person holding the materials, goods or manufactured articles.)

_____

The following materials, goods or manufactured articles are held

by...

at ....

and are marked

'SOLD, the property of ....

for use at..'

Quantity   Description   Value

Signed ....

for and on behalf of...

Date..

List of Tables

Notices and letters to be provided by the Contractor

(continued overleaf)